The Cordillera Volume 5

The 2013 Tour Divide Race

Peter Kraft Jr. On Richmond Peak

Editors: Christopher R. Bennett and Lis Pedersen

Volume 5, November 2013

ISBN 978-1-304-60767-6

ISBN 978-1-304-60767-6

Acknowledgements

Cover Photo and Layout: Scott Thigpen
Title Page Photo: Peter Kraft Sr.
Finishing Photos (L-R): Mike, Jesse, Thomas, Andrew and Hal, Ian, Scott, Michael, Peter, Jeff, Arran, Fred, Mike, James, Peter Jr. and Peter Sr., Chris

Other Photos: Christopher R. Bennett, Arran Pearson, the individual authors.

Thanks to:

- My wife Lis Pedersen for her help as co-editor.
- Scott Thigpen for the cover layout.
- Eric Bruntjen, Founding Editor for the concept of the Cordillera
- All those who completed the gear survey.
- Ollie Whalley (Tour Divide 2012) for taking my bike to the beach in Tarawa, Kiribati leaving me with nothing to do but to sit in the one star hotel and finish editing the Cordillera. At least I got the Forward out of him in return.
- Mike Kerley (Tour Divide 2012) for helping with the proofing of the hard copy.
- Above all, the Tour Dividers who put up with my harassing e-mails and contributed. I hope you all enjoy the final product.

Christopher R. Bennett

November, 2013

Contributors

Alex Harris
Billy Rice
Christopher Bennett
Dennis Carlsson
Erick Armentrout
Greg Andre-Barrett
Greg Thompson
Hamish McKee
Ian MacNab
James Gilles
Jean Louis Doridot
Jesse Carlsson
Kathy Schoendoerfer
Markley Anderson
Michael Grünert
Mike Komp
Nick Legan
Pat Olsen
Peter Maindonald
Scott Thigpen
Thomas Borst

Arran Pearson
Chris Culos
Cjell Money
Eric Foster
Fred Arden
Greg Strauser
Hal Russell
Hugh Harvey
J.D. Pauls
James Olsen
Jeff Mullen
Joseph Holway
Marion Esfandiari
Michael Arenberg
Mike Hall
Mirko Haecker
Oliver Whalley
Peter D Kraft Sr.
Ruth Olsen
Tammy Pal

All proceeds from the sale of this edition of the Cordillera go toward the education of Linnaea Blumenthal, daughter of fallen Tour Divide Racer Dave Blumenthal.

This image donated by Trevor Browne

www.eatdrinkpaperink.com

Contents

Forward

Oliver Whalley

Watching the race unfold from Australia brought back memories, many as vivid as their genesis in my hunger and fatigue addled brain back in 2012. Even while asleep my dreams returned to the Tour Divide, pedalling the desolate roads, legs twitching with phantom cramps. Like nothing else, the Tour Divide is as thrilling a race to watch as it is to participate in.

The 2013 race was an extraordinary spectacle of bikepacking as our dot watching contributors all attest. With a snowless north, the course was lightning fast. Then the return of the infamous peanut butter mud stopped many wheels with a sludgy paste. Forest fires were another of nature's whims, another sign that the Tour Divide is a harsh mistress who would never let racers have an easy run to Antelope Wells.

I watched in awe as Craig and Mike crushed the course to Rawlins, their tit for tat aggression worlds apart from the truce Craig and I formed in 2012. Craig's heart breaking call in at Kremmling after he scratched left me reeling. Truly, there is honour in fighting a battle that tough.

One reflection I have made reading the tales from this year's racers is the common threads that tie each racers journey with others of the same year, and indeed across years. It is the people who make the race, the genuine, salt of the earth high country folk who support the race with unflinching loyalty.

The tales within this Cordillera will only serve to bolster the already weighty Tour Divide lore. The trials and tribulations of Kraft Junior and Senior, who overcame tremendous adversity so close to the finish; Jesse's lightning strike is another example, the high voltage encounter imparting time bending pace akin to Marty McFly in Back to the Future; Micheal Arenberg's misadventure with bear spray had me in hysterics, reflecting on the dim witted things we all get up to when in a fatigued state.

The Cordillera V5

Each year as the Tour Divide plays out, the experiences it brings participants and observers alike are profound. I'm certain that this year's edition of the Cordillera will serve as inspiration for others to saddle up and make the fabled Canada to Mexico journey a goal. The words within, like the feats of all racers, are truly inspirational.

First place finisher 2012 Tour Divide

Racing

An Interview with Mike Hall

TC: Tell us about yourself.

I'm Mike, 32 originally from North Yorkshire, England. I now reside in Cardiff, South Wales. I started mountain biking in my early teens with some friends from school and rode just for fun up until 2009 when I started taking things a little more seriously and racing 24 hour solos. The Tour Divide in 2011 was my first introduction to bikepacking and multiple day endurance races, and I have learnt a lot since.

TC: How did you first hear about the Tour Divide and what made you want to race?

I first heard about the race from Aidan Harding's 2010 ride. That kind of planted the seed and I researched the race. I was still riding 24s then and improving a lot. I'll admit though that it was hearing about two celebrity 'adventurers' from the UK who said they were going to race in 2011 for a TV show and break the record that got me more fired up to race, probably for the wrong reasons. With them not being bike racers it seemed quite presumptuous to be so confident about coming to a sport they knew little about and set new records on the Tour Divide. I was kind of curious to see how it would all go down first hand and also feeling like I was ready to get involved and make them race for it. Their project didn't happen for unfortunate reasons, but by that time I was hooked anyway and ready to race for the right reasons.

TC: What experience did you have of long distance racing before the Tour Divide?

For the 2011 Tour Divide, only 24 hour races and a weekend bikepacking test trip: the Tour Divide was my introduction to bikepacking. This time around I'd had plenty of time to get my kit sorted and miles in my legs on the world cycle race. It also gave me great form but ruined my head. I was unsure if I would ever be able to race hard and complete such a race when I came to Banff in 2013. It was kind of make or break.

How did you train for the race?

I built up the miles through the winter as a cycle courier in Cardiff, did my first 200 mile road ride in March; then did a couple of Audaxes through the spring— 400 km and 300 km. Then I got my 'Pivot' race bike about a month before the Tour Divide and took it on a charity ride across Vietnam as a singlespeed with slicks on it and a nice hard gear. I had trained for the World Cycle Race on a fixed gear and it was the best type of training I've done for many reasons. Vietnam was experiencing a heat wave at the time and it was hotter than hot! It reached 55° C one day as we were climbing long 10% climbs in the mountains in the North West. We were getting ice water thrown on us every ten minutes to keep us cool, without it your muscles would just overheat and become dead weight. It was harsh but I came home lighter and more powerful and when I got to New Mexico the heat didn't bother me one bit.

TC: Tell us about your rig and gear.

Pivot Les 29er with Kenesis IX carbon fork, Reynolds carbon 29er rims, custom drilled 32H onto Exposure dynamo front hub and Kenesis rear. XTR 1 x 10 groupset. Continental Race King tyres. WTB Laser Saddle from my WCR bike. Exposure Revo light on the front, Garmin 705 GPS charged through a Supernova Plug II. The bags were Revelate seat pack and gas tank and a modified side pouch from a British Army Bergen on the bars which held a Rab Ridge Raider Bivi bag and Infinity SL sleeping bag and a Nemo Zor sleeping mat. For tools I had minimalist trail tool, patch kit and pump from Lezyne.

TC: Tell us about the highlights of your ride.

Racing with Craig: going too fast and not knowing how long we could keep it up, that was risky and exciting and it really felt like racing. When I finally worked out what was affecting my breathing and took the Loretadine (Claritin) which started to work on the way out of Helena; I've never been so happy just to be able to breathe normally and I suddenly felt like I had unlimited power.

Others were: encountering grizzlies in the Flathead Valley, reaching the border in less than 24 hours, covering ground quickly across the Basin and realising I'd done a 300 mile day.

TC: How did you handle the nutritional and hydration challenges on the ride?

The quicker you go, the less these are issues. When your range is 200 miles in a day you can hit a least two decent resupplies daily. Even the day we did the Basin we hit Pinedale for a late breakfast and Atlantic City for an early dinner. I reached Rawlins at breakfast time and still had 1.5 litres of water on board. I was actually overstocked for most of the ride but I wasn't too worried about the extra weight. I missed Wise River and got pretty dry looking for the Fire Base on the Gila re-route as the cues were unproven. Those hurt quite a bit.

TC: Did you have any mechanical problems during the race and how did you deal with them?

Not really. I replaced my chain frequently and kept on top of things. The rear tyre leaked a bit, inevitable since it wasn't a dedicated tubeless tyre. I was a little concerned about the front at first as it was its second outing on the Tour Divide but it was fine. I dropped the chain a few times but not much. Really should have been using a chain keeper or guide. The clutch mechanism is so good though that I got away without.

TC: All riders hit rock bottom eventually, a new low during their race, can you tell us about your darkest hour?

The first divide crossing out of Lincoln was harsh. I had lost control of my breathing again on Huckleberry pass and could barely breathe. I took an Aleve anti-inflammatory and that helped a bit by the top. I hit the store in Lincoln about 6 p.m. and stocked up on food and meds. I had decongestant, lozenges and some Loretadine. As I rode out of Lincoln I took the decongestant first, with the lozenges, as there were a lot of things coming up when I coughed. It cleared the mucus okay, but I was drowsy and bloated. The dust was playing hell with my lungs too. I took a caffeine shot but was still so drowsy I could hardly ride in a straight line. I lay down at the side of the road to try and get a short nap, but I just laid there for a while. The caffeine was keeping me from actually sleeping and the mosquitoes were feasting on me. I was kind of delirious by now and I didn't want to add any more meds into the mix.

I lost my breathing again and could only walk up the climb to keep it under control. I stopped near the top with a stomach 'event' and seriously considered rolling back down the hill into Lincoln and calling it a day. I literally stood there for two minutes looking either way. In the end it had taken me until nearly 11 p.m. to get to the top of that climb—about 15 miles from Lincoln. I talked myself into camping on the ridge and choosing which way to descend in the morning. I spent a good hour looking up at the stars and coughing up what looked like bits of lung before drifting off, no alarm set.

Procrastinating at the re-route in Abiquiu and eventually accepting that I had to leave the main route was pretty depressing too, but that was mainly apathy.

TC: What advice would you give to future Tour Dividers?

Get out there and do it. You learn so much more so quickly being there and seeing it than you ever will sitting at home and planning it. Do your homework for sure, but get the main stuff sorted and then just go. Be aware of how to overcome strain injuries—particularly Achilles—and don't obsess about weight too much. Sure it takes more energy over the ride to carry the weight further and up and down the hills, but if you have a good engine you can just put extra fuel in. Make things as light as you reasonably can. Know that you can't make things too much lighter, and then don't think about it too much. What matters is how hard and for how long you can press the gas pedal and that's all in your head.

TC: Will we see you on the Tour Divide again or are you going after other challenge?

It gets its hooks into you. I don't think the Tour Divide is done with me just yet.

2013 Result: 1st Place - 14:11:55

An Interview with Jesse Carlsson

TC: Tell us a little about yourself

I live in Melbourne, Australia and I'm 35 years old. Once upon a time I raced BMX bikes which took me to a number of countries around the world. When I was 20 years old a major ankle injury made me less competitive and I decided to call it quits. After this I focused on my studies for a PhD in theoretical physics and, following that, commenced wage-slavery, all the time doing nothing physical. About five years ago a few old friends dragged me out on a cross-country mountain bike ride. I must've had fun because I've been riding mountain bikes ever since.

TC: How did you first hear about the Tour Divide and what made you want to race?

I thought the 24 hour format was as hard as it got in mountain bike racing. The concept of racing for 24 hours seemed ridiculous. I was drawn to it, probably just to see if I could do it. While researching training tips and nutrition for 24 hour racing, I came across the blogs of a few Tour Divide riders. At that stage the Tour Divide seemed way out of reach; I'd never really camped or spent much time in the outdoors, but the idea was appealing. From what I could tell the Tour Divide was the toughest bike race I'd ever be able to take part in. I was interested to see if I could actually pull it off.

Watching the 'Ride the Divide' movie sealed the deal for me, particularly a quote from Matthew Lee that went something like, "life's too short not to take these adventures." By that stage I had been drawn to longer and longer rides, and racing was less appealing. I was having fun buying maps and heading out into the bush exploring. Each year, with increasing enthusiasm, I was a blue dot junkie and forum-lurker during the Tour Divide. I'd stay up late following the dots and marvel at how they were still moving when I woke the next morning. Always moving!

Eventually I realised that I needed to get the Tour Divide out of my system. It's like a virus. If I didn't do it in 2013, I'd have to agonise over it for another year. So I booked a plane ticket, started getting organised and exerted extreme pressure on a couple of mates in an attempt to get them to sign up.

TC: What experience did you have with long distance racing before the Tour Divide?

I've done quite a bit of endurance mountain bike racing in teams and as a solo competitor in 6, 12 and 24 hour events. I've built up to longer events since I started riding mountain bikes in 2008. Prior to the Tour Divide I'd entered only one bike-packing event, but I'd been having fun on short adventures with a bit of camping for over a year.

TC: How did you train for the race?

I just tried to ride as much as possible; as often as I could get away with. My work-life can get pretty busy, and I'm far from a professional athlete. I seemed to be doing a lot of riding early in 2013 when work was quiet, sometimes as much as 1,000 km in a week. When work got busy in April and May I struggled to get out for a ride more than once or twice a week.

I didn't do much racing at all in the lead up to the Tour Divide. With limited time, I felt that getting out for an overnight ride was much better value. The riding fitness almost came for free while I was testing various items of gear. Building confidence in my gear and bike was the most important part of preparation; fitness was secondary.

A final, and maybe funny, aspect of preparing for the race was learning how to eat chicken again. Previously I would eat seafood occasionally but no other meat. Eating chicken and turkey made life a lot easier during the tour but I was surprised how long it took to get used to it again. It took about three weeks of effort before I left Australia before I could stomach these unfamiliar foods without feeling ill.

TC: Tell us a bit about your rig and gear

Bike: Scott Scale 29er mountain bike (hard-tail), rigid Niner carbon forks, Deda Parabolica Uno aerobars (modified to raise the elbow pads and move them back for a more comfortable position), Shimano 2 x 10 XT drive train, Shimano XT hydraulic brakes (metallic pads), tubeless tyres—WTB Nanos 2.1" to start with and towards the end Continental ProTection Race King 2.2" (rear) and X-King 2.4" (front)), carbon rims (Curve Cycling), DT Swiss 240s rear hub, WTB Rocket V Team Saddle, Ritchey WCS Flat Aluminium Bar, Ergon Grips with carbon bar ends. Mount Skidmore bottle cage adapters allowed me to shift my bottle cage mounting points to fit two bidons in around my frame bag.

Electronics: Dynamo front hub (Shutter Precision PD-8), two Exposure Diablo lights, Garmin eTrex 30 (with Canadian and US 100k topographic maps on SD cards), iPhone 4s (no SIM, used with WIFI only), Spot device, rechargeable iPhone speaker (loud music let the wildlife know I was coming), rechargeable AA batteries (for eTrex), AA battery charger, SteriPEN Freedom, one Fibre Flare rear light and a basic battery powered rear flashing light, and a few spare batteries.

Luggage: Revelate Viscacha saddle bag, two Revelate Mountain Feedbags, Revelate Pocket (zip tied to bars), small Revelate Tangle Bag (carrying a 3L Camelbak bladder) and custom-made extra-large gas tank bag (Boulder Bike Packing Gear), 2 x 600mL bidons.

Sleeping: Mountain Laurel Designs Soul bivy, Cumulus Xlite 200 sleeping bag, Inertia X Frame mat and Exped inflatable pillow.

Clothing: One jersey (Rapha Trade Team merino blend – light coloured for hot weather), one set of knickers (Rapha Classic bib shorts), thin merino vest (Icebreaker undershirt), merino arm and knee warmers (Rapha – merino), Gore Bikewear waterproof gear (jacket, gloves and socks), Rab Drillium waterproof pants, Rapha wind proof vest, thin riding beanie and buff

Tools: Small multi-tool (with chain-breaker), separate 4mm Allen key (for rear hub) and Leatherman Juice S2.

Emergency gear: one spoke of each length with nipples attached, disaster kit (various spare nuts and bolts, fishing line, tyre boots, patches, aluminium shims, a thick needle, safety pins, FiberFix spoke, Steiner Tool (for removal of rear cassette), puncture repair kit, jockey wheel, spare chain links, chain quick-links, one bottom bracket cup due to weird sizing, spare brake pads (two sets), two tubes, Lezyne hand pump wrapped with tape (cloth, electrical and duct tape), athletic strapping tape and a very basic first aid kit.

Other essentials: Hand sanitizer, pills (caffeine, Ibuprofen, Naproxen tablets, multi-vitamin, ginseng + vitamin B, and iron), antibiotic cream, chamois cream, tooth brush & paste, sun screen, lip balm, chain lube (Tri-Flow), water proof pouches (for credit cards, bank notes and passport), various dry bags (for storing things that just can't get wet as well as extra food), ziplock bags, small scissors, headphones, bear spray, bear bell and a wall charger with two USB ports.

TC: Tell us about some of the highlights of your ride

While the mountain and high-plain vistas were stunning, the real highlight was bringing all the suffering to an end when rolling into Antelope Wells. It was only at this point that I realised that I'd pulled it off!

I loved riding at night. One of my favourite times on the ride was starting early (around 1:30 a.m.) and whizzing through the Colorado darkness on the way up yet another big climb. I remember cresting Lynx Pass at dawn on a perfectly clear morning with a frozen Camelbak hose and ice slurry in my bottles. When the sun climbed high enough, I stopped for a breakfast of ice cold Subway and enjoyed being cold before the heat of the day set in. Life was good!

The memories I have of the ride are dominated by encounters with people along the trail. Living in Australia, I don't get to experience 'trail magic'. You're more likely to get a can of drink thrown at you from a passing car than offered to you when riding in Australia in similarly remote country. Reflecting on my tour reminds me that Americans, for the most part, are wonderful people who have retained a genuine sense of community, generosity, and eagerness to help one another. From my brief travels and limited experience around the traps, it seems that these great human qualities are lost in many parts of the world.

TC: Can you tell us a bit about the lightning strike?

I've really got no memory of what happened—there's a blank spot in my memory of about an hour. I remember cresting Boreas Pass happy to have avoided a nearby electrical storm. The next memory I have is of being in a room in the Como Depot with David (who runs the place), British ITT rider Kerrin Walker, and David's enormous white dog (which looked remarkably like the giant flying dog from 'The Never Ending Story', Falcor). I thought I was dead, and felt a little disappointed that the afterlife resembled a scene from a 1980's movie.

Kerrin had descended from Boreas Pass about 20 minutes before I did and reported another electrical storm near an exposed section of road on the way into Como. I suspect there was a lightning strike very close to me on this section of road which probably blew me off my bike. I had a few scratches on my knee and a sore wrist but otherwise seemed to be okay. I spent the evening regrouping and trying to refocus my mind on the task at hand. I was very lucky to have two cool-headed guys at Como to bring me back to my senses—thankfully they didn't rush me off to a doctor, or it would have been the end of my race!

Over the next couple of days I realised that several of my rechargeable AA batteries had been fried, and my AA charger no longer worked. One of my lights had also changed modes. Other than that all my other electronic devices continued to work fine, which was lucky.

Out of the experience I got to ride with Kerrin for a couple of days. It helped me settle back into the ride. Although I think I might have tested his patience by constantly asking him if he could hear thunder, a compulsion brought about from my new, and intense, fear of electrical storms. Kerrin is a remarkable individual and did spectacularly well riding in his first ever endurance event. While I was trying to ride fast because it was a race, Kerrin matched my sense of urgency because he had a plane to catch!

TC: How did you handle the nutrition and hydration challenges on the ride?

I tried to eat calorie-dense foods that were easy enough to consume in large quantities. When I found diners I would drink milkshakes and eat cheesy omelettes with sides of hash browns, French toast and pancakes. If I came across a Subway store I'd make sure I had extra cheese and plenty of mayonnaise. I'd always add plenty of salt to my meals for sodium, while the large quantities of potato chips and orange juice kept my potassium levels in check.

It was very important to take food on the road as well. I'd carry plenty of muesli bars (nutty ones for more calories), something very sweet (lollies of some sort) and something very salty (often crushed potato chips). I'd also try to carry an additional 'meal'–this could be a few grilled cheese sandwiches or a foot-long Subway. This was a good back-up plan for when resupply options fell through, something I didn't learn until Lima.

Different foods worked at different times. Your body usually tells you what it needs. As long as you have enough variety in what you carry you can satisfy the different cravings that arise from time to time.

It really felt like I didn't know what I was doing for most of my time out there. I was always worried about running out of water, so I was riding in 'conservation mode' more than necessary. I think this trains your body to be more efficient in its use of both food and water. I was drinking far less towards the end of the race than at the beginning, despite the heat. I drank water while on

the road and filled up on soft-drink, Gatorade and orange juice when passing through towns. I only treated water once or twice, and even then it was probably an over-the-top precaution.

TC: Did you have any major mechanical problems during the race and, if you did, how did you deal with them?

Somewhere near Salida, Colorado, a ruined rear tyre left me with a critical decision: hike close to 20 km to Salida or ride the rough and rocky descent on the rear rim. The hike was going to take too long, so I chose to ride the descent on the rim, protected only by a flat rear tyre. I was expecting the rim to be sacrificed but I was hoping that a new wheel could be built quickly in Salida.

As it turned out the carbon rim survived the descent – there is no way an aluminium rim of similar weight would have made it to the floor of the valley hitting the descent like I did. Surprisingly the wheel was still true and round. From the constant rock impact there were some areas of delamination on the bead hook, and so to be safe, I had another wheel laced up.

TC: All riders eventually hit a rock bottom, a new low during their race. Could you tell us about your darkest hour during the race?

The head winds in southern Montana were tough to deal with. The winds combined with my lack of experience made this a tough stretch of the race.

I made the mistake of thinking that the 100 mile stretch from Polaris to Lima would be relatively easy. As it turned out the headwinds were amazingly strong, it was hot, and there was nowhere to hide on the open plains. When climbing, the higher ground ahead offered some protection from the wind, but when cresting the hill and commencing a short descent the full force of the wind would be felt. I remember getting off and walking my bike on one of these descents—I wasn't strong enough to keep the pedals turning and was going slow enough that balancing was difficult. It felt like I was track-standing into the wind. This all meant that the supposedly easy 100 mile stretch became tough.

I was out of food and water by the time I reached Lima late at night. With better preparation and some knowledge of Lima, I would have had some additional food with me. As it turned out I had to refuel on cans of soft-drink and wait until the diner opened at 7 a.m. to get more fuel for the next section. By the time I left the busy diner in Lima it was close to 8 a.m. and the winds had picked up again.

TC: What advice would you give to future Tour Dividers?

Be pragmatic and build up to the Tour Divide. Test your gear thoroughly and see if you really do enjoy being alone in the wilderness. There is a lot of 'romance' about this event and plenty of jaw-dropping photos, but the reality is often very different.

TC: Will we see you again on the Tour Divide or are you going after other challenges?

Most of the time I was out riding I had no idea what I was doing. I finished the race thinking, "Right! NOW, I'm ready to race the Tour Divide!"

By riding the course you gain some very specific and valuable experience that can't be gleaned from simple desk-based research. Which sections are tough? Which are easy? Which ones do you need to load up with food and water, and which ones can be attacked with minimal supplies?

The knowledge of how your body responds to such a huge effort is also valuable. When should you push hard and how hard should you push? How much should I sleep?

It would be great to come back and use this experience to race the event again, but there are so many adventures to be tackled that I can't see it happening in the next couple of years. I hope I'm wrong though!

2013 Result: 2nd Place - 15:12:08

Jesse is a 35 year old who lives in Melbourne, Australia. He has a 'bike riding problem', which is possibly better than some other addiction options. The Tour Divide was his silliest adventure so far and he's hoping it helps him gain 'management approval' for similar adventures in the future.

Coming Soon

Alex Harris

There's a movie that plays over and over in my head. Snippets mostly. Bits and pieces of a trail or a high pass. Long, flat roads and trees. Many trees; and the odd face. I'm the leading character but there are others. They come in and out like strangers in the night. I can't tell if its fiction or a reality show. But there are always bikes. Well, always my bike.

At different times of the day the movie plays out in different ways. With a slightly different theme or angle. As I drift off with the coaxing night, it's a relentless thriller. Hell bent through some forgotten forest I'm being chased by someone. The antagonist surely? But who is he? How far back is he? I move with a greased purpose. Undistracted by the spectators, unperturbed by the night. I seem to flow on a tide outside of time. But there are nights I could swear I'm doing the chasing. I'm the hunter and the villain is a figment in some distant cloud. I'm breathless but focused. On and on the movie plays out, but it just can't seem to get to the end. No denouement. No credits to bring to an end this breathless chase.

In the day it's a highlights package. Glimpses of trails, numbers, distances. What was open, what was not. Where did I sleep? Where should I have slept? And more numbers. The numbers never stop. Number crunching over and over in a mind gone numb. Anaesthetized by the what ifs? And the should haves?

143 actors signed up but most are extras. Resigned to play a small part in a trailer that goes on for too long, somewhere behind. Somewhere back. No doubt focusing on their own movie. Sometimes I wake and stare up at the faint moonlight pushing through the curtains. I lie transfixed. It's a hill but which way must I go? It seems impossibly steep. Where is my bike? A horror fills my sleepy mind. A realization that I need to get to the end but I don't have my bike. It's an awful thought but it's just for an instant. Then I realize I am back home. The Tour Divide is in the past. It doesn't matter where my bike is. I

don't have to get on it and that's all that counts. A deep peace washes over me at this thought and I slip back into my pillow, back into the night. Lost in a slippery tide.

It has been two months now and the dream persists. This movie that rolls inexorably towards the same conclusion. It's like my bike and I were somehow metaphysically bonded during the race. We share the same DNA. The mind and the machine. Joined at the groin with a single purpose. Head south as fast as you can. Day and night. Hour after hour. Moon to the midday we are never more than five meters apart. For seventeen days we ground, we geared, we grovelled.

I feel as though I am caught between two worlds. One is the here and now. The familiarity of a life grown normal. But there is a tug. A reminder. In the numbness in my hands and a distant calling. It's that damn movie again. There it goes. A quiet sky and hunger from another world. Its starts up slowly then its racing. Flowing trails. Days and states. Night time and the nerves. How might this end? Will it end? But I know it does. The passes are endless. They climb forever into a lonely sky. Just me and the hollowed out night. Searching for a 7-11 or motel. Respite. Somewhere to hide and escape the madness. Bury my head into a pillow and try and slip into a toxic sleep. Food. More food. Never enough food.

What kind of movie is this that the dream is also a nightmare? Sometimes I want in, sometimes I want out. I order a coffee and I think. I'm lucid so I can discern and divide. Yes, it's James. Damn him. Damn you James. Back off will you! I need to sleep. Time and again I'm looking over my shoulder. Where are you? In front, behind? Sleeping, eating? The day pulls us apart but in the night we seem to coalesce. Like two vapours coming together for a few ghostly swirls only to be pulled apart again by the day. But your scent is on the high pass, your face in my mind. I know your way, your motive and your mad manner of sneaking up on me.

I press on. I pretend not to care but of course I do. I race myself and this place. I race the high passes and flat lands. Badlands and burnt out valleys. I race a memory, somehow a mix of where I've been and what's to come. And yes James, I race you. I race all these things and more. I want more, crave more. But hate every moment of that slow, miserable grovelling. When the gravel seems to suck the life out of my legs and turn my wheels to sludge. I tread on a seesaw, sometimes a trailer, sometimes a tipping point. I want out but I'm in. I'm in but my body shouts out. I drift and dangle in the conscious, and then I slip away.

At last it's just a scent. A faint trickle of a distant past. Was I ever there? It seems so long ago. An age really. The movie is finally nearing the end. I feel hollow, empty, hungry. I left so much out there. Out on the unknown trail. You know where you are. I need it back, but I know I can leave more. And there it is. That conundrum. That thing we dare not speak of. Damn it. I know what I need to do. I need to go back. Ride it again. Ride it harder. Leave everything out there. Maybe then I can finally sever this bond that holds me captive.

Mist. A new moon and the thrill of an early morning. A long, lonely trail. The lush. Aahh. There it is. Peace. I can't wait.

Alex Harris is an athlete whose interests are varied and unique. He has been climbing mountains for two decades and has led more than 20 expeditions to some of the furthest corners of the planet. In 1996 Alex resigned from a career in sales and followed his passion for exploration. With the year he led his first expedition to Mount Everest. He has climbed the 'Seven Summits', the highest mountains on all seven continents, and led expeditions to both the North and South side of Everest. In 2008, Alex became the first African to walk unsupported to the South Pole, a journey that took 65 days and covered almost 1,200 km. More recently, Alex made history by making the first unsupported crossing of the Arabian Desert, or 'Empty Quarter' as it is commonly known. Alex still has all his toes!

2103 Result: 3rd Place - 17:05:28

A Singlespeeder's Tale

Arran Pearson

Why?

I got back into mountain biking after a long absence about ten years ago. I was very overweight, desperately unfit, and it seemed like a good way to lose some kilos and have some fun all at the same time.

I hadn't been riding that long when I read a copy of Mountain Biking Australia lurking at some roadside café while I was on a 4wd trip. It had a great story of this thing called the 'Mont 24 hr Race'. Wow—I was hooked! Before long I had corralled/conned a group of mates and, despite never having been anywhere near something that looked like a bike race, we found ourselves on the start line ready to go.

Anyway, after one too many arguments over whose turn it was to get up at 3 a.m. I decided to give 24 hr solo racing a try. Again, an eye opening experience—the ability of the mind to get the body to do stupid things is nothing short of amazing. So far I've done about half a dozen solo 24 hrs and for the most part, really enjoy this style of racing.

But lately, I had begun to find that the challenge just wasn't there in a 24 hr race – again I wasn't winning (my best is a 7th at a Scott 24 hr) but I know I can ride for 24 hours now… so what's the next challenge?

I'd done a couple of stage races but one of my favourite events was something called the Mawson Marathon—a 360 km non-stop point to point race along the Mawson trail in South Australia. This had all the mental toughness and endurance aspects I love about 24 hr racing combined with a healthy amount of planning and best of all—no riding in circles!

After the first year I was all set to line up for the second running of the event only to have it cancelled less than two weeks out. Anyone who gets into training for an event knows just how frustrating this can be. All that effort and all that form going to waste! As an alternative I decided that I'd try a little multi-day ride in the mountains (okay, hills for the non-Australians!).

This was one of those 'ah-ha' moments. Whilst the actual quality of the trails certainly isn't the groomed singletrack you get used to at an XC endurance event, the sheer variety of the terrain as well as a chance to be part of the landscape is almost indescribable. That was in June 2011 and is when I mark the beginning of preparing for this adventure.

Since then I've often pondered about that 'why' – after all, ultra-racing is dangerous (as I've discovered a couple of times)... you're continually looking for that balance point between too much weight and too little gear and if you get it wrong then, well... there are consequences! I could say that it's just a natural extension of endurance racing—after all if you're bored with riding around a track then doing an ultra has a similar amount of fitness required without the repetitive nature of track based racing.

Of course that's not really it either.

Ultimately I think ultra racing and events like the Tour Divide have a spiritual dimension that offers something different to the standard mountain biking experience—or perhaps more similar to where it all began? Sure it's physically hard and the planning is almost as demanding as the training but even for those trying to set race records it is as much about the experience as it is about how fast you can complete the course.

Finally, and I think this is important; each ultra race is an Adventure. A chance to get out and connect with something that's a little more primal than sitting in an office working through the latest iteration of that PowerPoint deck. Not saying that going out and doing an ultra should be on everyone's list but in our (over) connected society it is all too easy to stay well within our comfort zone and surely a chance to explore the edges can't be a bad thing?

The Race!

I'd decided to get to Banff about six days before the ride to give myself some time to just chill out and get my head into the right space. This turned out to be one of the best decisions of the whole experience. My early arrival meant that I was one of the first racers there, and I had plenty of time to just relax. It also meant I got to see people as they arrived and participate in a bit of pre-race banter. However, I quickly worked out that sitting with a bunch of guys obsessing about the same thing just wasn't helpful to my mental state, so I tended to avoid most of the other racers!

With a few pre-race rides around Banff and Canmore under my belt, it actually became a serious effort to stick around for the Grand Depart and not just take off on and ride it as an Individual Time Trial! The feeling of waiting for the start is hard to put into words but it is a mix of anticipation, fear and doubt. I was simultaneously looking forward to the adventure whilst at the same time dreading the test I was about to go through.

What if I failed?

The race start itself would be instantly familiar to anyone who's shown up to any mountain bike Marathon or endurance race: a mix of nervous banter, fast guys trying to get their bikes as near to the start point as possible, groups of friends quietly talking and geeing each other up and of course some, like me, gazing off into the distance just trying to mentally prepare for what is to come. Finally the moment comes and you're off and can just lose yourself in the initial concentration of fighting for a place on the trail—in other words much more like the start of a 100 km race and not a 4,500 km one!

I deliberately hadn't really worked out much of a race strategy as such—pretty much my goal going in was to finish. I knew I had some good distance in my legs but my 'plan'—if you could call it that—was to just ride to how I felt and not get hung up on just how far I was riding. This meant that I was pretty hazy on where I'd stop but I knew I wanted to make  the US border by the end of the second day (about 400 km) which meant I was aiming for somewhere around the 200 km mark or so on that first day.

Unsurprisingly, the field spaced out pretty quickly and I just settled into a rhythm and got on with it—just like one of the many rides I'd done in training. Eleven singlespeeders started the race, and I was keeping a look out as I caught people to see if they were fellow nutters (not as easy as you'd think given the popularity of Rohloffs and other internally geared hubs at this race!). I was pretty pleased to get to the first resupply point (a shop in a caravan park at about the 110 km mark) having passed about four of them.

I eventually made it to Elkford (175 km) after about ten hours of riding—I was thinking that this might be a decent place to stop for the night. The rain had started to come down and I was getting pretty cold (US/Canada high country summer is usually colder than Sydney winter!) But after a pizza, followed by another pizza, at a gas (service) station I decided to see if I could make the 60 km ride or so to the next town. Yeah—the race makes you think funny, after a 175 km ride, doing another 60 after dinner seems a logical thing!

At this point I discovered a part of this race that no-one really prepares you for—the intense friendships that you form with other riders. I had ridden most of that last section on my own but then a couple of kiwis on geared bikes (Nathan Mawkes and Chris Bennett) caught up with me and we rode the last 20 or so together—just a bunch of blokes out on their bikes chatting and chewing the breeze just like pretty much any trail ride. It still amazes me weeks after the event just how close I still feel with some of these guys even though you spend very little actual time together and its one of things I really cherish about the experience.

The rest of the first week is pretty much a blur—I spent the first few days just getting used to the riding and was managing to stick to around the 200 km a day mark. The initial parts of the ride are stunningly beautiful as you climb into the Montana high country. Only problem is that it seemed that most of the roads go straight up—this translated into much singlespeed walking action! On the positive side it seemed that most of the other singlespeeders must have been walking more than I was!

I caught up with fellow singlespeeder Scott McConnell I think on about the third day and we ended up sticking within about 30 miles of each other for pretty much the rest of the race. The good news was that by the end of the first week we'd made a clear break on the remaining singlespeed field, the bad news was that we were riding with our main competition and, on singlespeeds running pretty similar gearing, the only way to get a lead was to ride longer than the other guy. This made for quite a few long days!

By day five, I was pretty much in agony—my knees were shot, my forearms were killing me and my neck was really stiff! But then, as if by magic, the fabled Tour Divide legs kicked in. It's pretty amazing—you go to sleep feeling stiff and sore but then wake up feeling refreshed and (most) of the aching body parts seem to have settled down. It's not like a whole new burst of energy or anything but at least the pain has gone.

Of course pain is replaced by a constant feeling of exhaustion but even that gets manageable after a while.

The stats say that if you can get through Montana then you're likely to go on to finish the race. It doesn't sound logical given than you still have about 2/3 of the distance to cover (which seemed unimaginably far at the time), but I remember getting to the 1,000 mile mark (roughly where Mike Dion pulls the pin in the film) and thinking to myself "You know? I can finish this thing!" This is a scary thought as you also realise that if you fail to finish then it's mental and not physical. Although everyone I spoke to post race admits to having a moment where they were wishing for some sort of serious-ish accident that would give them a reason to stop.

After the half way point I started to get a lot more serious about winning the singlespeed race which meant that as much as I was enjoying riding with Scott, I needed to make a serious effort to get away.

My first effort was in Wyoming—I managed to get a gap on the climb over Union Pass and then kept up a pretty good pace to make it through to Atlantic City—about 280 km or so. However, the next day I was to face 'The Basin'—a section of 100 miles or so with almost no water on corrugated gravel roads and to top it all off into a 40 mph headwind for most of it.

I finally made it through to Rawlins at about 9:30 p.m. or so and then made a mistake. After eating the menu at a McDonalds I was feeling a bit high on fat and sugar and, concerned that Scott would also push to Rawlins, (and I'd thus lose my lead) I decided to push on. I eventually bivied in some bushes 20 km or so out of town. Not smart given the effort of the day before. Note to self, two 18+ hour days in a row was not sustainable.

The next day I had nothing. Zip. Nada. I just seemed to be bonking all day and it didn't matter what I ate. I was so tired that I fell asleep on an 80 km/h descent. Not good (I was awakened from a dream about how to stay awake on a bike by the ripple strips on the edge of the road—that's how out of it I was!). I eventually staggered into the awesomeness that is Brush Mountain Lodge in northern Colorado to be treated to a feast by the owner, Kirsten, who'd been watching me struggle up the valley on Trackleaders. Despite it being only about 4 p.m. and having done less than 140 km for the day I decided that I needed the rest and sat back and relaxed.

Of course the downside is that when you rest, you get caught. Sure enough, Scott arrived at about 7 p.m. Sigh. Escape attempt failed! On the upside, I really enjoyed riding with him (bit of a singlespeed bromance there!) so it was all good.

Most riders needed bikes attended to in Steamboat Springs the next day but I made the decision to just push on—the Sheep was riding well and although my rear tyre was looking a little second hand I figured it probably had enough in it to get me through to Salida. This was a pretty decisive move as from then on I pretty much was on my own—well at least until the reroute from hell (more on that later).

Although there is a lot of climbing in the first half of the route, it's in Colorado where you hit altitude with several passes over 10,000 ft (3000 m) and a couple of 20+ mile climbs. On the positive side, most of the Continental Divide trail at this point is on old rail trail so most of the grades are do-able (about 4-5%) even on a singlespeed. Of course it does mean that you climb fairly constantly for most of the day.

I was very relieved to finally arrive in New Mexico—most of the major climbs were now behind me as were the hours I spent in lightning storms crossing the Colorado prairie—being the tallest thing for more than ten square miles on top of a ridge on a metal framed bicycle as lightening cracks close enough for you to feel the static would be one of the scariest experiences of my life. However, despite its reputation as being flat and boring, New Mexico had a couple of stings in its tail.

What New Mexico lacked in climbs it made up for in energy sapping peanut butter mud. This stuff clung to the wheels, frame, shoes… you name it. Given my complete fail at an Australian event earlier this year in almost the exact same conditions this was my nightmare scenario with less than 600 km to go and unable to keep going.

The massive fires this year meant that a couple of significant re-routes were in place. The disadvantage of an underground race which lacks any 'official' organisation means that finding out what they are is a little haphazard (and to tell the truth—puts back a little of the self reliance navigational aspect of the race that has been lost with the ability to simply follow a line on a GPS).

Myself and a few others were in the unfortunate position of not quite being fast enough to hit barricaded roads like the race leaders. However, we were fast enough to be in Wi-Fi and mobile dead spots so didn't get any e-mails etc. letting us know which way the leaders had gone. Following the principle of trying to ride as much of the trail as possible (see Tour Divide Rule 5), I ended up riding about 60 miles further than the route most of the other racers had taken, and got caught in a massive thunderstorm which turned the road into energy sapping mud.

This section was a nightmare—the road was impossible to ride and the nature of the mud meant that I was stopping every 50 meters or so to dig enough mud out of the frame so the bike would roll. I eventually bivied at about midnight utterly spent. I then got caught in a major thunderstorm. Any hope of the strong winds drying the roads overnight was gone as the heavens opened.

I gave up trying to sleep at about 5 a.m. and got back on the road. It took more than two hours to get 7.5 km, but I finally got more or less on track. Of course by now I'd worked out that there was a shorter route than the one I was on. The sense of moral superiority about riding more of the route is not comforting when you realise that you're behind.

The fire meant that most of the route to the finish was now on paved roads. I hit the highway at about lunchtime and after a litre of chocolate milk, a litre of Gatorade and a bottle of Coke I was on my way trying to catch up to Scott and his group. Just as an aside, the combination I drank is not good and not something I'd recommend you do before heading out into a 140 km road ride in 35°C temperatures.

I pulled into Silver City tired and sore (my Brooks Saddle had collapsed and I'd been riding on the seat rails). To my surprise, I ran into Scott and his group. With 20/20 hindsight I should have just grabbed some more chocolate milk and Gatorade and kept going, but I was pretty stuffed—I'd only had about two hours sleep in the last 24 hours and at that point had been riding/pushing for more than 14 hours. So I stopped, had something to eat and then got on with the chase.

The last 200 km were mostly fun—a significant climb out of Silver City but then downhill for most of it and for a change I even had a tailwind. Fast and fun—I love riding in the dark! The road to the Antelope Wells itself is a long lonely stretch into the desert and I was glad to be riding it at night. It was so flat and dark that when a couple of cars passed me (on the way to pick up Scott and co.) I was able to see their taillights for a good 45 minutes or so.

I was completely demotivated at this point—the road was flat and boring, I was exhausted from riding more than 28 hours and had lost the lead on the road after holding it for nearly a week. I just wanted to sit and cry... at just about my lowest point (with about ten miles to go) a car pulled over and to my surprise Scott and another guy (Brett) I'd ridden with earlier in the race got out and started cheering—this made me smile and I worked out that if I kept up my pace I'd be in line for a sub 21 day finish... just. Also they were yelling at me something about look under the sign which had me intrigued.

That last ten miles was agonising—this was the culmination of more than two years of planning, I should have been elated but instead I just felt empty and drained. I finally crossed the line in 21 days, 23 hours and 26 minutes.

Antelope Wells is probably the loneliest place to ever finish a race. It is a collection of border control buildings in the absolute middle of no-where and when I arrived it was still dawn and the border was closed. I had finished the most physically and mentally demanding thing I'd ever done and there was no-one around. It was a very empty, hollow feeling. On the positive side, under the border sign I did find a care package from Scott—a bag full of ice containing some water (nice), a Gatorade (ugh) and a beer!

As I sat waiting for my lift back to civilisation to arrive three more members of the Brush Mountain Lodge crew rolled in—this was pretty awesome as there was now someone there to share the moment with and best of all it was with guys that I'd ridden with on and off for the better part of two weeks.

And with that my Tour Divide was over. Whilst not finishing the race would have been crushing, it turns out that finishing has some mixed feelings as well.

I'm pretty stoked about my ride but given that this goal has been part of my life for a couple of years now, not having it feels a little weird. One piece of good news is that in conversations with Matt Lee afterwards it looks like that the few of us who missed the re-route details are going to get some time relief so seems like I'll share the singlespeed win with Scott.

So the great adventure has ended and with it maybe some answers to the questions that undertaking this sort of journey poses. To call the Tour Divide race a tour understates the very real competitive feeling that exists amongst all the riders out on course—whether you're aiming to beat the record or simply finish. To call the Tour Divide a race understates the inward journey that it takes you on—several weeks of being completely self reliant with no safety net forces a degree of introspection that at times is a little... uncomfortable.

After completing it I can really only say two things, firstly that the ride will change you and secondly that despite the pain, the discomfort, the fear and the loneliness I really miss it.

2013 Result: 18th Place; Co-1st Place Single Speed: 20:23:32

Bridging the Divide: Why

Billy Rice

Why

The question of why will be answered with a series of random stories, so enjoy.

I don't think it's all that challenging to answer. The challenge is to answer it in a manner that makes sense to someone living an otherwise 'normal' existence. Most people don't require something as ridiculous as a three week self supported race to move their life forward. Apparently, no one requires a six week race except me, so we will see how that goes. But the answer to 'why' must come from each racer before or, more typically, during the race if they are to be successful.

The quest for 'why' begins long before the race. When a racer decides he is in, the logistics set in. The logistics for a race this big is beyond most peoples' imagination. Even bike shops and any mechanic of lesser skill than Allen, Scot, or 'Fixie' Dave can't really grasp what the racer is trying to accomplish and are of only limited assistance during the planning phase. So the aspect of self-supported starts early. Everything must be planned for. Every part carefully chosen, not based on what the magazines say, or what wins the World Cup, but based on what will work. What will work in rain, sun, snow, and mud. Each and every time. A mechanical in the middle of the Wyoming Basin would be a serious problem, so nothing can be overlooked.

Standing at the starting line taking pictures I hear an odd 'pop'. I know something untoward has occurred but like most racing the divide I am a better rider than mechanic so I take a quick glance, not unlike a driver taking a look at his broken car engine under the hood as if he's going to solve some mechanical issue. But, alas, it strikes me and my heart sinks as I notice that a spoke is now broken. I have less than 12 hours before starting the northbound portion of my race and it's not going well.

I reluctantly finish the last few pictures and limp the bike over to the rented motor home to see what I can do. I have plenty of spare parts but a spoke broken at the nipple requires a complete replacement which means losing my tubeless set up before the race started. Mountain bikes nowadays run what we call tubeless. Like a car tire there is no tube. In 2012 I did the entire divide without a flat. It can be a bit cumbersome at times, but with the right finesse, the system is brilliant so this is definitely a blow.

Here's the deal though... this is what racing the divide is about. And if it is what the divide is about, then why not start off with a broken bike? I spend an hour or so fixing the wheel and attempting to save my tubeless set up to no avail, so I throw a tube in and get it reset and ready to go.

To 'go', or race the divide, one must make some choices. I must digress for a moment and explain the hierarchy of 'crazy' on the divide. During most discussions I have with people about divide racing the term 'crazy' or 'masochist' typically comes up. But you have no idea the 'crazies' who are out there so I must explain because there is a whole divide culture that many are unaware of.

At the bottom of the crazy list is the 'tourist'. A tourist, or touring cyclist, stereotypically has a lot of stuff. Camping gear, stoves and cooking equipment, spare tires, bike pumps, and almost every imaginable tool, strapped to their bikes in big bags called panniers, and some even have trailers. Tourists can come in pretty handy to a stranded racer without the proper equipment. Tourists have almost no time restraint and are usually in it for the beauty and enjoyment of nature which they find at a much slower pace. Your touring cyclist typically rides 40-50 miles a day and frequently ventures off course to 'see the sights'. Fascinating group of people usually but boy they are out there a long time.

Next on the list is the 'supported section or thru hiker'. These people hike... like on their feet... crazy I know. Some hike without a pack as fast as they can while a car meets them with food, water, etc. at regular intervals. Section hikers take years to hike the entire continental divide trail, and thru hikers do it in several months. These folks tend to look more like runners than hikers and they are on a mission.

Then we have the 'Divide Racer'. That's me. You get it so I'll keep going.

Yep... They get crazier. Nearing the top of our crazy list is the unsupported 'Thru Hiker'. So get this... These guys usually hike (on their feet again...), along the same continental divide trail in one go WITHOUT ASSISTANCE. They usually leave New Mexico in April or May, and hope to make Canada before it starts snowing. Just reflect for just a moment of how amazing their feat is. Crossing New Mexico on foot through the desert is taking your life in your own hands. There is no food and no water. It takes amazing planning and a little luck. When these guys arrive in Pie Town they look ROUGH. I met several this last year in Pie Town, and they were amazing. I'm not sure if they made it all the way to Canada but I sure wished them the best.

And at the top of our list is the 'Other' category. This group is reserved for the unicyclist, the tandem cyclist (yes... two cyclists acting as one), the fixies, and all the other sorts of individuals requiring extra mental training because of an intentionally added level of difficulty. For this group... the Divide is too easy and they require additional stimulus to grow. Many who fall into this category are the likes of 'Fixie' Dave Nice, who through multiple attempts rode a fixed gear bike on an ITT! And Justin Simone who in the 2011 'snow year' said, 'no way' to the advised detour and crossed Red Meadow and Whitefish Divide COMPLETELY COVERED IN SNOW. He tied his bike to an inflatable boat and towed it like twenty something miles. Others I call the 'Stoics', including Matthew Lee, Jay Petervary and the like. These guys raced the divide when you had to be tough. No cell phone, no music. My impression is these guys really don't need or want your opinion on their race, as they are in it purely to improve themselves. Their style, however, winds up improving the rest of us. These guys are the true heroes of the Divide.

So now back to the story... Watching the evening sun set over the desert I look over and behold! Tourists! Not only are they tourists but they are fellow Texans. Recently graduated from this small community college in downtown Austin, Texas, they come to challenge their spirits along the Divide (it is okay to laugh at the previous statement). We talk for a while and I ask why they are starting in New Mexico. "Easier northbound, we figure" they say. So let's discuss this for a moment.

Northbound, or NoBo as its known, is harder. I should know. The route northbound starts at the same elevation as Banff. It's hot and dry. Every day you gain an additional 1,000 feet or more, so altitude becomes a real problem really fast for someone who lives at sea level. This year I actually wound up with a moderate case of high altitude pulmonary edema from the rapid climbing on my NoBo. I was fortunate to fight off infection, but in Southern Colorado I really wondered if it would end my race. So very quickly I realize that these guys need information. We bust out the maps and I pour as much Divide wisdom as

I can at them. I did this multiple times throughout the race just to make sure that the areas that tried to kill me in 2012 didn't kill anyone in 2013. The brief usually sounded the same. There's no water here, there is water here, if you go here and ask for Pam she will give you watermelon, etc. Several parts of the Divide are really easy to underestimate. The Gila Wilderness is exhibit A, which the tourists would hit by Day 3.

My two most important instructions:

1. While in Silver City LOAD UP. You cannot carry enough food for this section. No matter how much you carry, you will run out.

2. There is only one place to get water and that is the Beaverhead Work Station (a mountain fire station), a VERY difficult 65 miles from Silver City. It will take you all day to cover that 65 miles and maybe more and there is NO WATER. So in the bags you have already stuffed with food, you might want to stuff some water too.

Finishing out with the rest of the intel, we part ways to prepare for the day ahead. The plan for me includes a 02:30 a.m. wake up and meal, with a departure at 03:00 a.m. I take my last shower for awhile and don my cycling attire so as to save time in the morning. This attire will soon become part of me so I might as well start now. And as I search for my why, I'd like to break it down into sections as the total of my race is way too long for a single chapter.

Brush Mountain

Hamburgers... I can smell them. They are right over this next pass. A pass I can't ride because it is covered in feet of snow. Slushy snow. One step, two steps, push the bike. One step, two steps, push the bike. I repeat this over and over. "Northbound is just weird" I say to myself, as I wonder if I will actually find food anytime soon.

The Brush Mountain Lodge is Tour Divide lore. It's between Rawlings and Steamboat Springs, home to Kirsten. Kirsten is the original Blue Dot Junkie, Trail Angel above all Trail Angels, doctor, psychologist, therapist, cook, cheerleader, and overall amazing person. Kirsten sits in a critical spot on the divide. Most riders who make it to the lodge will finish, but many are in rough shape. She sees the positive ones, the negative ones, and the breakdowns. Riders who are southbound just recently crossed Wyoming's Great Basin, then a terribly lonely stretch of southern Wyoming, only to be followed by a 14 mile climb before arriving. They are cooked. In 2012 Matt Lee took the helm because she was gone for the summer. And while Matt and Scott did make some amazing pancakes, they are not Kirsten.

Cruising down the backside of the hill I am on final approach to the lodge when I hear "BILLY!!! Over here! What took you so long??? Your dot sure wasn't moving very fast up there! I hope you're not a vegetarian but if you are I can make you something else", she says, as she places a HUGE plate of hamburgers right in front of me! I made it.

We quickly broke down into story time like long lost friends. She of course wanted to know why, which I didn't exactly know. We talked about the route, the conditions, and logistics. But we also talked about the people. She told amazing stories about riders coming into the lodge, some amazingly optimistic, and others very broken.

I told myself that I wouldn't be there long. It's racing you know. But three hours later I found myself slowly packing up. Three hours of talking Tour Divide philosophy, exchanging crazy racing stories, and developing a lifelong friendship. There are several places on the Divide that I just couldn't wait to return to after leaving them northbound. And the funniest revelation of all is that when people ask me why, the first thought that comes to mind, is because when you Yo-Yo, you get two helpings of Brush Mountain hamburgers.

Absolute

In 2012, I called a bike shop in Salida. I told the guy on the phone that I was racing the Divide and my drivetrain was a little sluggish, but that I would be coming through on a Sunday and needed their hours etc... He quickly said, hang on a minute, and let me get Scot. Scot answers, I tell him my story and he says something along the lines of, keep going, you're racing. I have 50,000 (or so) miles on my chain. You're good to go. Just lube it. I said okay and off I went.

Fast forward to the Yo-Yo. I'm northbound pulling into Salida. Bike is having a ROUGH time. It's late and the shop is closed so I have to wait until tomorrow. Waking early I go find food. A little later I notice activity in Absolute so I mosey over. "Have time to help a Divide racer?" I ask. "Ummm... the Tour Divide hasn't started yet" someone says. I laugh a little. "Yea, well, see, I had this idea of..." and the conversation begins. I take off all my bags, which is a real chore. Enter Scot.

"Just give me the bike. I don't need a report. I'm a professional. Go eat and I'll handle this" he says in a rather impatient manner.

"Hmmmm, well, my rear tire..." I try to say, when I get interrupted.

"I know...rear tire is bad, front tire is going to be bad, who messed up this wheel? Rear hub is loose, it's going to go out on you, derailleur hanger is bent, these cables are all wrong, and your brakes need adjustment".

Uhhh.... "I'll go grab some coffee" I say as I walk out. He looked at it for like 3.5 seconds to come up with all that. I figured he had it. After returning it looked like a new bike. Every issue I had been having up until then had been resolved and he told me of a few issues I would have (and did). Wrap your head around the logistics of changing out an entire wheel set in Eureka Montana, or having a broken seat post in Sargents. The Divide is hard on riders, but it is even harder on bikes.

You see, like Kirsten, Scot is not normal. Scot is the collection of a few unique circumstances rolled into the idea that defines what a 'Trail Angel' is and what a world class mechanic is capable of. Not only is he an amazing individual, he has the expertise of seeing most bikes come through town with 2,000 divide miles on them. This is the same guy, who kind of as a joke, suggested to me that a single drivetrain, one chain, one cassette, etc, could complete the Yo-Yo. And it did: 5,500 miles, one drivetrain.

Island Park

I find myself on the Idaho railroad trail. Another one of those moments where I act like an eight year old because I know that somewhere, not far ahead, is a northbound racer coming toward me. Not just any NoBo, this one. It's Cjell. You might as well go back and reread that section about different levels of crazy out here. Cjell has built quite the reputation riding NoBo on the divide and just killing it. 18 days is his norm and he does it not on a state of the art modern mountain bike, but on his own designed and built steel frame SINGLE SPEED built loosely around cyclcocross geometry and 3" tires. This thing is a beast and it suits him well.

He turns the corner ahead of me, his long locks of hair blowing in the wind. He pulls up next to me to ask how things have been going and starts giving me intel on the upcoming trail. "I know" I say, "I was here a couple of weeks ago". "BILLY!" he replies and the typical 'long lost lifelong friends that we didn't know we were' conversations begins. We talk for a while. We talk about route conditions up north and that he has decided to stop at the border. A real shame as he would for sure have set a course record. We also talk divide philosophy and I absorb every word. While I learn from every racer I meet, I really appreciate and listen to folks of Cjell's experience. He has a different take on the whole thing and that differing perspective out here is invaluable.

The sun has set, its cold, and it is raining. The beginning of that sentence is all that really changes. Dark, cold, and wet has been the norm for me since leaving

Banff on the return trip of what has now been affectionately dubbed the 'Yo-Yo'. So far, this thing has been amazing. I feel fantastic, have no issues, and other than being tired and cold, it really couldn't be going much better. I am now at the end of my day, rain soaking through my rain jacket, and because I am traveling light, REALLY LIGHT, I am looking for shelter out of the rain. I slowly make my way into the town of Island Park but to no avail. Motels are full, and the porch at subway looks like an amazing spot to snooze minus the blazing porch light. I make peace with the light but then get a tip that there is a vacant cabin several miles up the road, in the rain... It's worth it I say to myself and pedal on, in the rain.

Arriving at said cabin I find three young teenage boys manning the cash box. It appears that I interrupted a pretty fun sleepover.

"Why are you on a bike in the middle of the night in the rain?" they ask.

"I'm racing."

"To where?"

"Mexico... sort of."

And the conversation continued as predicted. By the time we finished they were expert blue dot junkies telling me all about Mike Hall was out front and that I better get moving if I was to catch him. They went over my bike like a TSA inspection asking about every detail. After they finished I realized I couldn't stand and talk any more. It's crazy on the divide. When your body is done it's done, and now, mine was done. Getting light headed I politely excuse myself and they pointed me to a rickety cabinish building with a heater and a bed... and Wi-Fi. Wi-Fi... a double edged connection with the world. Opening the Tour Divide news (the blog Half Past Done) it hits me.

"Bad news for record seekers in this year's Tour Divide" Jill Homer writes in her blog. She goes on to talk about the forest closures in New Mexico and that racers will not be permitted to enter. See, part of this whole gentlemen's race we call the Tour Divide includes the rule that course records must be run on the course. No detours. Sounds simple, but on a 2,745 mile race, one closure, one missed turn (go ahead, you can laugh... I went back) and your time on the route does not count. I'm now falling asleep near the 4000 mile mark with the news that this will not count. I didn't come out here to set a record but now that it looks like it is going to happen, I'm told I can't. Cue the emotional breakdown.

Emotions can be crazy and totally unpredictable. The draw of the Divide taps into this internal emotional strife that can't be tapped in our normal existence.

Sometimes it's sadness that tries to overtake you, but sometimes it's a complete and absolutely amazing feeling of completeness.

Whitefish

I'm northbound at the northern end of Whitefish preparing my bike with food for the next section headed toward Eureka. A jolly older gentlemen approaches, asking if I am Billy. This conversation has become somewhat routine as the story of the Yo-Yo has grown. A tad reluctantly I say yes, as I am really ready to go. He says his name is Tim and that he's a fan of the race, and just wanted to meet me. We talked for a few minutes before I had to go, as I rode off I knew this guy was different. Didn't know why exactly until later.

I'm now southbound on top of Red Meadow pass. All hell has broken loose. The hail is unrelenting; trees are blowing over and toppling around me. When it's not hailing, the rain is coming down sideways and I have found shelter in a forest service latrine. I would later find out that this is the same storm that destroyed the northern end of the course and washed towns away in Alberta. This was bad. Knowing that I couldn't stay up there forever, I set out for the long cold descent into Whitefish.

My brakes squeal but I can't let go for fear of getting colder. Rain has soaked through my rain jacket and I am shivering uncontrollably. I have never really liked descents on the Divide. Sure, you cover ground more quickly, but the problem is that you can't control your temperature. You only get colder as the cold air whisks away the heat you worked so hard to generate. Sometimes I would even stop and do jumping jacks on the side of the road. Really tough mentally when you get cold. My Scoutmaster from Boy Scouts always used to make fun of me because I was always cold on campouts. I had to learn early how to stay warm so I guess it paid off.

Passing the lake, the dirt turns to pavement. I'm really focused on finding a warm place to dry off. Looking ahead at the approaching town, I'm looking, looking. I see a restaurant that I am way too wet to go into, a gas station, a little food mart, some people in the road with beer and towels, another gas stat... Wait! People in the road with beer and towels! It's Tim! It turns out that Tim knows a great little lodge called the Hidden Moose and they saved my bacon that evening. He told me they had been watching me on the pass and knew I would be in some trouble.

I was able to shower and warm up. I enjoyed what I would consider divide delicacy that night, pizza with friends I didn't even know were friends. There was also a honeymooning couple, recent graduates from Texas A&M University in fact, who still lived in my town in Texas. They had no idea what their night was in for, as I answered hundreds of questions about the divide and told story after story about my experiences. You don't usually have time to sit around with friends on the divide. This was unique. The storm continued to blaze long into the night as we talked until the wee hours.

Heart Shaped Mattress

Viacitos (devil dogs) make me crazy. These are a group of famous dogs on the route. They live in a small alleyway in an old settlement town in northern New Mexico. I use the term 'town' loosely. There is only one road and you can't go around. I'm pretty sure that at some point, rabid dragons bred with hormonal werewolves, leaving behind flying, fire-breathing chupacabras which ate all the left over town folk and now run the place. This will be my third trip through, if I survive. It's uphill for the southbounders which makes it a tad harder. As evidenced by me actually telling this story, I made it through. All I want is to make it to Abaqui so that I can get an early start on what is probably the worst part of the Divide.

Polvedera Mesa... When I first posted that I would be riding the closed section of route known as the Sante Fe National Forest, a friend of mine messaged me "I'll enjoy watching you climb the mesa!" The mesa is serious. It's a long slow climb on really bad roads with no water. There's even less water now. The whole place will be extra amazing as it's closed. This is one of the sections of the route that was closed to the 'blue dots'. There will be no other people on it. I have permission to go in tomorrow and have to set myself up strategically. This is also the scene in the famous movie 'Ride the Divide' where Mathew talks about a rider almost dying. Climbing the mesa in the afternoon is just bad. I have to push on late into the night to make Abaqui, so I can climb the mesa in the morning.

But wow it's late. I fall into my usual trance. Music up, lights to bright, and pedal off into the forest that looks right out of a horror movie. And the lights turn off... dead batteries. I stop the bike and proceed with changing them when I notice I'm surrounded. Blinding lights in my face, I'm under attack. I'm trying to make out what they are saying but Justin Bieber is blaring in my ears and I can't think straight. Turning my music off I discover that it is Greg and Scott Thigpen. I met Greg briefly last year. He rides for the US Navy Seal Foundation and did not finish last year due to injuries. This year he rides strong and is planning on riding through tonight. Scott is different though...

Scott apparently didn't take very good care of his bike early on as it appears someone stole all his gears... Scott is single speed... (Please see list previous describing the differing levels of 'crazy'...) He has chosen to race the route in the simplest form. The single speed guys always amaze me, as they are usually just as fast as me with twenty or so gears. We talk for a while as we speed off towards Abaqui. With 20 or so miles to go, my gears are just too fast and I am too sleepy to hold back. I tell Scott about a nice little place I'm staying for the night before the rough stretch to the border and invite him to stay. He takes me up on it, but as I ride off I am doubtful he will follow up. Promises and commitments on the Divide have no place for a lot of reasons. One mechanical, missing the place, or change in mental state can all lead to last minute plan changes, so I think 'if I see him, I see him'.

Arriving at the little inn, I find a note taped to my door with a key to my room and a nice note from the US Forest Service. I plod over to my room in the darkness and quickly move through my late night ritual of clean and dry gear, scarf down calories, and get cleaned up. I throw my helmet on the outside of the door in case Scott shows up but it is way past my bed time so I crawl in bed. Sometime later Scott shows up and I'm not sure of the details. Scott describes a heart shaped mattress and pillow fighting...

The End

There is a frog in the road. In fact there are several frogs in the road. Odd, I think to myself. At least they are not arguing. It's the rocks that always argue, the trees try to grab me, and the bushes just tend to stare at me. This is new though, the frogs. Thousands of them now. They illuminate in the constant flashes of lightning as I am still getting pummeled by rain and hail along the last stretch of pavement approaching Antelope Wells. It's raining, a lot. That's certainly not new for me in this race, and at least it's warm rain.

I try the best I can to dodge the frogs but they are everywhere. The weirdest thing is that they appear to be real and not the typical late night hallucination. I'm not sure what I think about the end of the Tour Divide. I was hoping that I would finish during the day. Last year I finished around 3:00 a.m. and this year seems to be the same.

The end of the Tour Divide is odd. Most of the Divide is rough forest service roads, trails, and conditions that require planning and thought to remain safe and efficient. The last 70 miles or so is just the opposite. Flat, straight, pavement. No more resupplies, no more route finding. Just point the bike south and go until you can't ride anymore.

You also have the very real issue that life is seriously about to change. I've been away for 44 days. Feels like a week maybe, but to the kids and family at home it has been a very real 44 days. I haven't slept for more than an hour or two at a time since Cuba. In fact, staying awake now is next to impossible.

From behind I notice lights approaching. I don't think much of it as the border patrol is out here in force. I always wonder if they laugh at us out here in the middle of the night. These lights are different though. They slow and pull up next to me for a moment. It's the kids... a few minutes behind them, my boss, and just a little later, the research team from Texas A&M. Looks like it's going to be a party at the boarder if I can stay awake that long. I jokingly wonder if they would be annoyed if I took a quick nap which the map clearly says is unsafe on this stretch. Now there are lights ahead in the rain. Windows rolled down; it appears to be other racers yelling congratulations to me as they head home. I wanted to stop but I'm soaked to the bone at this point and having a really hard time staying awake.

Twelve miles to go and I can't do it. Those who know me know that I have a really large dislike for mile markers. I'm trying to be positive about mile markers but it's really hard. Turns out there is one every mile on the mile for the last 70 miles or so. I'm also pretty sure the state of New Mexico saves money by placing them just a little further apart than your standard issue mile. Kind of like how a microwave minute is just a little longer than your regular minute. They taunt you... So I'm at mile 12. I know this because, well, there is a marker...

"Okay Billy, time to strategize. I will ride one more mile and stop, and eat gummy bears." So I set off looking into the distance for mile 11 and try desperately not to fall asleep. 11! I quickly indulge in my late night snack and come up with the next plan to get to 10. "I'll pick an audio book." I'm off again, fighting the heavy eye lids. I make it to 10 and stop. I start my book, and fiddle with my shoes then head to 9. I do this over and over, assigning myself some ridiculous task at each marker in an effort to stay awake. Mile 4... "All I have to do is get to 3", I tell myself. You see, at 3, you can see it. Antelope Wells is a pretty big, and a very empty, 'shovel ready project', complex with lots of light. You can't see it until mile marker 3. But at 3, you can see it and it calls you in.

Pulling into the gate, you would think I would be, and I'm sure some are overtaken by emotion. I'm not really that way. The whole thing becomes almost another hallucination. A very foreign and almost out of place experience. Kids, family, and some of my closest friends are there which is amazing and totally weird. I'm still on no sleep and glad to be there, but sad in a way as I'm about to leave the route which I have grown quite fond of, like an old friend. Processing what is going on around me is difficult. I always tell people on the Divide that when things don't seem to be going well, you need to evaluate and fix the problem. It's clear to me, that my problem is sleep. So we hug and celebrate as the rain has finally ended. We take lots of pictures and then move to the research facility. A lawn chair and some needles. They are doing their thing when I look over and see what I had been dreading for some time.

They are being helpful I know, but the bike, my bike, is being pulled apart, bags taken off, disassembled, and cumbersomely being loaded on the bike rack. It doesn't seem right. No more miles, no more missed turns or mechanicals, no more rain, snow, or mud. No more trail angels or 11 course meals. My bike did its job and unavoidably, it is done.

Invictus

I get a lot of questions about what advice I would give potential racers. What are the best tires, what handle bars do you like? Mostly silly stuff like that. Gear and equipment is certainly important, fitness is important, but the best advice I can give is certainly more important than that, so listen up.

DON'T HAVE ANY MORE NEGATIVE THOUGHTS, EVER. THEY HAVE TO END.

Train yourself to see the positive in all things. That doesn't mean to ignore the bad, it just means don't react negatively. Enjoy the rain, the cold, the climbs, the running out of food. It's all the hardships of life in one race. Be happy in the moment and you can get the Tour Divide done. There are a lot of different names for this. Mathew Lee called it "getting it tight", William Henley described it in the famous poem 'Invictus', and the early stoics described it as an entire philosophy. Whatever you call it, you must separate yourself from the society norm of negativity provoked by events. Learn to be positive from those same events and you will be successful.

2013 Result: 1st So-No-So: 22:18:41 NoBo 20:08:00 SoBo 43:02:41 Riding

"No Offence, but What Are You Doing Here?"

Chris Culos

So, how does the average guy go from never doing an endurance event to riding the Tour Divide? Okay I have run a marathon which is an endurance event in its own right. I've also ridden a few long one day rides, but nothing which I could consider ultra endurance or distance.

It happened like this. I saw a magazine article, read a book or two on the Tour Divide, watched a movie and thought this could be cool. All of those got me hooked on the epic adventure and life changing challenges I was sure to experience. That being said, I remember two days in, pushing my bike up 'the wall' and saying to one of the riders, "They lied to us in that movie! They only showed the good parts." This section happened on the same day (day two of what would end up being 22) as my falling in a creek crossing. Side note: if you're going to attempt to run the creek, go for it, don't hesitate in the middle or half ass it !!!!!

I set out a game plan for how I was going to execute finishing this ride. I first thought about how many miles a day I could realistically cover. The ultimate goal was to ride just over a hundred miles a day guaranteeing a finish in less than 25 days to be considered a racer. My original idea for sleeping was to camp three nights and stay in some form of accommodation on the fourth. The second part blew up fast as by night two I was in a motel in Eureka. After only six days I had camped a total of twice, and was getting into what is called the 'town draw'. The mileage was coming so I wasn't overly worried and I quickly got into a routine of having a good breakfast before moving out, which I felt gave me a good base for the day.

My thought pattern was always to be smart about what I was riding into as I had never done this type of event nor knew the areas. I remember day seven and my right knee was starting to tighten up from some IT band issues. I was coming off a pass just outside of Polaris in the Pioneer Mountains, and as I came into the valley I could see this large storm moving down the valley towards me. I had read on the map that the Montana High country lodge was coming up and decided to head in there to at the very least eat dinner and hopefully miss the storm. I arrived just after 5 p.m. and soon realized I was going to spend yet another night in lodging. I had a great dinner and relaxed working on my leg trying to relieve some of the tightness.

The lodge was a stop for a few riders, some of which decided to head out after dinner as it was still early. I never felt the urge to join them as I decided the weather wasn't favourable to lay down any good miles. I decided that night I would stay for breakfast at 7 a.m., meaning I wouldn't get away until closer to 8 a.m., but the next resupply town was another 100 miles so I thought it best to fuel well. That morning I woke up to better weather and after breakfast got on the bike and right away was feeling good. I knew a couple of hours in that I had made the right choice as I was making good time. I pulled into Lima for lunch, 100 miles down (160 km) and met some of the riders that had moved on the night before. As I heard their stories about freezing and being wet I knew I made the right call staying. Before that day was done I had covered 180 miles (nearly 300 km) and was feeling good, staying at Red Rock RV and camp ground with Kevin, Sean and Ryan.

I often rode with or reconnected with the same group of guys at the resupply stops, and we began to talk about racing and the different thought patterns on how to get the miles done in a given number of days. The pattern I fell into was to get up hopefully with a source of food nearby before I left for the day. This commonly was around 7 to 8 a.m. which was funny to some of the riders because in their eyes I would be sleeping in and wasting good morning hours.

This whole race for me was about growing as a person and pushing the limit of what I could accomplish. As I got into it, it became what I called a holiday race. I wanted to be competitive and push myself but was enjoying the experience of not only the beautiful landscape, but meeting great people. What started out to be the event all about time became something a lot bigger. Early on in the race (day two) I met Serge, a rider from the 2012 Tour Divide and the last thing he said to me was "make sure you look around and take some of it in" and I believe I really tried to do that every day.

The Cordillera V5

I was two weeks in when I rode out of Kremmling and caught up to Kevin, Sean and Ryan climbing Ute pass. This was the common theme of the last couple days. I would see them sometime during the day and either have a meal or ride along together and then off we would go at our own pace. I entered Silverthorne with Ryan stopping for a junk food fill up at 7-11 and after sourcing some new arm coolers I was on my own again until the summit of Boreas Pass where I met Chris Bennett taking pictures and as we were talking Peter, Kevin, Sean and Ryan joined us. That afternoon I found myself riding with Kevin as we had split up with the others on the descent. We arrived in Hartsel to a town that had a gas station (closed) and a saloon-restaurant.

As it was past dinner we decided to eat there (like we had a choice) and before we finished we were joined by the whole gang from Boreas Pass. As a storm was approaching, we all decided to stay at a ranch close by.

As we sat in the common area of the ranch house waiting for our accommodations to be ready, Chris said to me "no offence, but what are you doing here ?" I guess by the puzzled look on my face he thought he should expand the question. He continued with "I mean, are you nursing an injury or is there something wrong?" I still didn't quit understand so he said "you seem like a strong rider and when I saw you the first couple of days I thought this guy will put down a good time and here you are still with me". I have to admit I was happy that he thought I was a strong cyclist, but never thought of myself and still don't as anything but a guy riding his bike. I explained to him that I had been tending to a sore knee but didn't think it was slowing me down. I wanted to beat the 25 day mark and was on a schedule to do that and I was also having a lot of fun. I explained that I get up early for work every day at home and here I get up a little later and have breakfast (some mornings this part got skipped due to location) and ride my bike as fast as I can for a given time and when I feel I'm done for the day I stop.

I didn't feel I needed to ride 16 to 20 hrs a day to meet my goal if I just rode faster. I appreciated being asked this question as it made me realize what racing meant to different people.

The thing I like about endurance racing is all these different strategies on how you are going to reach a common goal. I just know from this one experience that I probably could have pushed myself harder but I got out of it what I needed at my own pace. Chris on the other hand was what I called "the Energizer bunny" this guy could go and go...... It became a bit of a game for me to see if I could catch not only him but some of the other riders that left before me in the morning. I found playing these types of mind games made the days more interesting and entertaining. I know towards the end of the race there came a point when everyone started to look around and wonder who was going to go for the finish in one big push. I have to admit I never really wanted to change what was working and towards the last couple of days almost didn't want it to end. Chris on the other hand made a huge push on the last day and rode over 26 hours to beat me to the border.

So I guess to the question "no offence but what are you doing here?" I'd have to say, "Having a great time meeting amazing people and enjoying an endurance race holiday away from all the everyday stuff. There isn't a day that goes by that I don't think about how or when I am going to get that feeling again". On the last day I was asked if I would do it again and I said "No I'm good with once". But now with time to reflect, and knowing in life you can never say never, you just might see my name on the starting list again someday!!!

Thanks to these great riders I met who made my Tour experience AMAZING!!!!!!!!

Peter Haile
Kevin Campagna
Ryan Sigsbey
Prentiss Campbell
Peter Maindonald
Don Gabrielson

Ezra Mullen
Sean Putnam
Greg Thompson
Ron Babington
Christopher Bennett

2013 Result: 31st Place - 22:06:59

Reflections on the Tour Divide

Christopher Bennett

Having finally completed the Tour Divide after three attempts[1], I thought I'd put down some thoughts/suggestions which may help those who want to race the Tour Divide in the future. It may also help me should I ever suffer from acute memory loss and decide to race the beast again …

Preparation

I have a seriously dysfunctional life which makes any form of proper training for a race difficult. My job sees me travelling to different countries for over six months a year. In spite of owning 16 bicycles (yes, 16—I've a very understanding wife who prefers a bike in every port to a girl!) strategically placed around the world, it still makes following a training plan challenging at best.

For the Tour Divide there is a basic truism: you simply cannot train enough to be ready to ride 200 km/day every day. I recall Scott Thigpen sharing his really heavy training regime with us months before the race and I was quite impressed. As for me? I just maintained my fitness (running, swimming, biking when I could) and then did a good training block of six weeks or so before the race. The training program consisted of some of Jesper Bondo's work. His site www.training4cyclists.com is the singularly best resource that I have found for cycle training. It probably helps that I'm into interval training. It basically saw me riding 3-4 hours a day 3-4 times a week, with some long days as well.

---

[1] My first attempt in 2011 was northbound from Antelope Wells. I got a severe asthma attack and had to get a ride ahead to Gila hospital so was disqualified. Didn't matter. My lungs were fried. In 2012 I got to Brush Mountain Lodge where I learned my 90 year old mother had broken her hip that morning so I withdrew to go and help my parents.

In the end, the best advice is ride as much as you can, preferably with a loaded Tour Divide bike, and accept that you will suffer for the first week until your body adapts.

The Bike

This year I ran a 29er Titanium Motobecane from www.bikesdirect.com. The complete bike only cost $2199, but in hindsight I would have been better off just buying the frame and then building it from scratch as I ended up swapping out a number of parts. Two years ago when I first did the Tour Divide, a 29er were a relative rarity. Now with places like Wal-Mart selling them they are very mainstream—as shown by the results of our 2013 'Gear Survey' where all respondents bar one used a 29er. For a race like the Tour Divide the reduced rolling resistance of the 29er make life much easier.

While the bike is more than adequate for the race straight out of the box, I made a number of modifications which I think improved what was already a good bike.

Most importantly—always start the race with new chain, cassette, pedals and bottom bracket. If you don't (particularly the cassette/chain) you will regret it. Be prepared to replace them all again at the end of the race (unless you run a Rohloff—in which case replace the belt before the race). I also replaced the bottom bracket with a new Hope ceramic bottom bracket.

I replaced the front shocks with a White Brothers carbon fork. This is about one kg lighter which may not sound like a lot, but every gram counts. I had no numbness in my hands this year at all, and the ride with the fork was very smooth. There is a good reason why more and more Tour Divide riders are running carbon forks.

I chose a SON front generator hub from www.peterwhitecycles.com which was connected to a Tout Terrain 'Plug 2', also from them. The Plug 2 mounts to the top of the steering tube and has a USB plug on it. This was connected to my GPS or cell phone to power/recharge them. It worked okay but the problem was that I did not have a cache battery which meant that at slow speeds the GPS would give the message 'Power Lost'. Very annoying! A cache battery is essential with a setup like this. I ran a USB cable from my Garmin 800 and the phone (which was in a pocket on the handlebars) into the case on my top tube, where I had another cable connected to the Plug 2. This meant I only needed to swap the plugs in the bag, rather than fiddle with the Plug 2 (which I waterproofed with tape). Having the plugs in the bag also kept them protected from the elements. Using different colours for the GPS and phone cables made it easier to be sure that the right one was being charged.

I used the Supernova E3 light which was great. With the light on there was no power for the GPS so I made sure it was fully charged before any night riding. There are now some other options on the market, such as the new Busch and Muller Lumotec which contains both a USB connector and a cache battery so I'd probably not go for the E3 again. I supplemented it with a Fenix LD22 torch on my helmet. I used the latter mainly when going uphill at slow speeds. I also had a flashing red light on the back of my helmet for night riding on roads—very important! The one from www.roadid.com is the best I've found, tiny and bright beyond belief.

My wheels used Stan's Arch EX rims. Absolutely bullet proof. They were built for me by Tristan at www.wheelworks.co.nz and were as true after the race as when I started. We used a DT Swiss rear hub. I highly recommend this combination—especially when built by an expert wheel builder like Tristan. Worth the investment. After the race they were as true as when I started.

On the advice of Ollie Whalley (who won the 2012 Tour Divide) I was going to run with WTB Vulpine tyres. He didn't have a single problem and used the same tires the entire race. WTB are renowned for quality control problems and the tyres that I bought were absolute junk. Two punctures in not difficult riding conditions. The photo to the left is a piece of wood that punctured the Vulpine when I was cycling the C&O Canal in Washington D.C. a few weeks before the race. If they couldn't handle such an easy ride they sure weren't going to last on the

Tour Divide. Then there are those who used WTB Nanos. I know of two riders who cut the sidewalls during the first week of the Tour Divide. It is exceptionally hard on tyres and it just not worth running with light weight ones. Or WTBs.

At the recommendation of Absolute Bikes in Salida, I went for the Specialized Fast Track Control tyres and they were magic. I did not have a single puncture and they lasted the entire race. By the time I reached Antelope Wells the tread on the rear was a bit thin—should probably have swapped the front and rear tyres in Steamboat Springs. I used 2.2 tyres rather than 2.1—the extra width is helpful in the sands of Southern Colorado and in New Mexico.

I ran them tubeless and used lots of Stan's fluid in them—and added more in Steamboat Springs. It can evaporate in the heat so you want to make sure you use more than you think you need. Of course you could avoid this problem entirely by running proper UST tubeless tyres—my riding buddy Peter Maindonald extolled their superiority every chance he got during the race, and I'm convinced he is right. But most of us had a tubeless conversion and Stan's.

I used the Ergon G3 handlebar grips again, with additional tape wrapped around the edges for further padding. I really like the fact that with their integrated bar ends you have so many choices for hand positions. I also put on a pair of the Profile Design T3 aerobars which gave my hands a rest.

The first two times I tried the Tour Divide I used standard SPD pedals and I had a lot of numbness in my feet. The third time I used the SPD XTR Trail M985's which have a larger platform and absolutely no numbness. I put the cleats as far back on my shoes as possible which helps prevent Achilles problems.

As mentioned above, use a new chain and cassette for the race—and consider new chain rings if they have a lot of miles on them already. I recommend SRAM as they are available at every bike shop along the way. Plan to replace your entire drive train by the end of the race, and the chain half way at Steamboat Springs.

I put on new brake pads before the race, and took two as spares. I should have had three. I think the jury is out on hydraulic vs. cables. I prefer the former but if something goes wrong you want the latter. Since my Motobecane came with hydraulic, that is what I ran with.

I highly recommend the Thudbuster seat post (www.thudbuster.com). Yes, they are heavy, but the extra damping they offer makes a huge difference—at least if like me you are on the wrong side of 50. I ran the 'Long Travel' (LT) version but this had the disadvantage that on some very bad sections the seat bag would hit the rear tyre. This depends a lot on the geometry of your bike. For my set up the 'Short Travel' (ST) would have been better. I just put some leather on the bottom of my bag and made sure not to bounce too heavily on those bad sections.

After crashing a number of times on previous races, I realised that having water bottles close to the wheels was a bad idea. Mounting the 1 Litre 'Magnum' water bottle on the top tube worked really well, and I had the Topeak oversize bottle cage on the down tube for putting in a 2 litre bottle for long desert runs.

For navigation I used my same Garmin 800 Edge as before, with my Sony Xperia cell phone as the backup GPS. I've done a post at www.tri-duffer.com

on my navigation setup. Next time I'd be tempted to skip the cue sheets entirely, and put the maps on my mobile phone by scanning them (although that would be a copyright infringement). I almost never used my maps or cue sheets—the maps were most useful to show me supply/sleeping options in the areas. I used a Specialized Speedzone Wireless trip computer for the odometer to supplement the GPS, but it was really not needed. Having power from the hub let me run the GPS all the time so I just followed the GPS track …

Bags

My frame and seat bags were from Revelate Design. Before the race I waterproofed them again using silicon spray, but since they will always leak to a degree I also used the 'Sea to Summit' microlight dry bags to hold everything and keep them dry, and these were then put in the seat bag.

I used a 35 litre dry bag for my handlebar bag, which was held by the Revelate Design handlebar harness. The bag contained my tent, sleeping bag, and sleeping kit. I could also stuff in my jacket and rain gear during the day. I added two extra tie down straps wrapped around the handlebar ends for extra lateral stability. You can see them in the photo below running over the brake lever. I had a 3 litre Camelbak 'Unbottle' which I mounted over the top of the dry bag. I used two clips to hold it to the handlebar which allowed me to unclip it for filling. You can see these just to the right of the aerobar.

I ran some REI Velcro straps through the bag as well. These were handy for when having to carry extra water—the photo below shows the two 1 litre water bags I used for desert runs (giving me a total of eight litres).

While on water, I used Aquatabs for water purification. They are very effective with one tab/litre of water and it only takes one hour. To offset the taste, I used Camelbak Elixir tablets which also provided electrolytes. I would say that 90% of the time or more it was not necessary to use Aquatabs, but I was glad to have them when I needed them. I stored them in the Camelbak at the bottom where there is an access zipper. This made it easy to locate them when needed.

Finally, I had a Carousel Design map and cue sheet case on the top of the bike. As I mentioned, I could probably have done without it having used the GPS full time. In the photos above I've got my MP3 headphones rubber banded to the case (my cell phone was also my MP3 player).

For the first time in three attempts I did not wear a hydration pack and I was so glad I didn't have it. Not only does it give you more freedom when riding, but it forces you to take less. I did have a small 'Sea to Summit Ultralight' day pack. These are about half the size of a soda can and very light. I used it to carry extra food/water when necessary—i.e. until I could consume it so never more than a few hours! I also dispensed with my Revelate handlebar bag this time—at the suggestion of my riding buddy Mike Kerley. He drilled into me the less bags, the less gear, the lighter and more pleasant the ride. Thanks Mike for the great advice!

Clothes

Keeping with Mike's philosophy, I minimized the clothes I took.

My jacket was a Paramo Quito Cycling Jacket. It was great last year—which was a cold year—but I found it too hot this year. I would have been better off having a light weight Gore-Tex jacket, and a super lightweight windbreaker. I could have then layered them (my Paramo has two layers—you just can't remove the inner one). Make sure your jacket has a hood that fits under your helmet. Quite useful—especially during a hail storm. Easier than worrying about a helmet cover, or having cold water running down your back.

When not wearing the jacket I wore my Pearl Izumi Elite Series wind vest. This is one of my favourite pieces of kit as it is so comfortable over a range of temperatures. My Gore Bike Wear rain trousers were great. I really appreciated the almost full length zip. I wore them even when not raining—especially when the mosquitoes were heavy!

For my hands I had Specialized fingerless cycling gloves. I used a lightweight Merino glove for cool days, which I put on before the regular cycling gloves. I had Gore Bike Wear winter gloves for the cold days. A real blessing was my Extremities Gore-Tex over mitts. They were super light weight and waterproof so I could keep my hands dry without overheating. Highly recommended. I used them even in cool dry conditions—just slipped them on over my gloves. The winter gloves were hardly used and I could probably have done without them, but it was a warm year.

Along with your hands, keeping your feet in good condition is essential—there is a reason why it's the first thing they teach you in the army!

Here was my solution, from the inside out …A pair of the BRD Sport Achilles Braces (www.brdsport.com). Achilles problems are the #1 or #2 physical problems riders have and these braces are magic. I had Achilles problems the first two years but this year not a single issue—even though I rode longer and harder. Absolutely essential. Trust me.

Merino wool socks keep you warm, even when wet. Ground Effect from New Zealand (www.groundeffect.co.nz) makes them specifically for cyclists.

Rocky Road Gore-Tex socks as an outer layer. Your feet will be warm, dry and comfortable. I even wore them in the dry desert to keep sand away from my skin.

Be sure that you can walk five kilometres in your cycling shoes pushing your fully loaded bike uphill. If it is a snow year this is what you will end up doing. And make sure you have broken in the shoes before the race. I used Specialized Body Geometry shoes, but it's really whatever is comfortable and not too rigid.

I wore a Ground Effect 'Rock Lobster' long sleeve jersey. During training I tried a short sleeve jersey along with the Pearl Izumi arm coolers for extra hot days, but it just was not worth the hassle of having the extra pieces of kit to worry about. I pulled up the long sleeves when necessary. They were coupled with Ground Effect 'Exocet' shorts, which really are by far the most comfortable that I've ever cycled in. And over the years I've tried many.

For cold days I used a pair of winter weight cycling trousers. I've found it impossible to hold up leg warmers for hours on end and the extra weight of the full trousers was negligible compared to the comfort. I also carried a Mont-Bell under layer down vest which came in very handy at night after finishing riding for the day. I took along arm warmers, but only used them once or twice so could have done without.

My 'sleeping kit' consisted of a pair of lightweight triathlon shorts—which can also double as a replacement for your regular cycling shorts if needed—and a lightweight T-shirt. When cold I included Merino socks and warmer clothes like my down vest and winter cycling trousers. When doing laundry I was able to wear my sleeping kit while my other clothes were cleaned.

An often overlooked item is a hat. When it gets really hot you don't want to wear your helmet (in 2013 it hit 45C/113F one day). I always wear a 'Drymax' runner's hat under my helmet as it not only keeps sweat from my eyes, but sunburn from the top of my head. However, this didn't work well in the extreme heat so Peter Maindonald and I stopped in Silverthorne at Columbia and bought hats which had 'flaps' on the sides and back. Looked quite silly but were wonderful for keeping the sun at bay. Peter mentioned that Simon Kennett created something like these flaps from an emergency blanket during a previous race so there are other options … but suffices to say that something like this is useful to have.

Finally, and importantly, once you've got your kit together pack your bike with all your gear, and then get rid of at least 20% of it. More sage advice from Mike!

Race Strategy

I **really** needed to finish the Tour Divide this year. After my two earlier failed attempts it was this cloud hanging over me. Not only that, my longsuffering wife Lis was becoming fed up with my Tour Divide obsession and having a big chunk of the year blacked out for this race, and a modicum of training leading up to it.

The logical thing to do was to aim to finish in sub 25 days and ride conservatively enough to just meet that goal. But I had unfinished business with this blasted race so rather than be logical, I decided that I would ride the race to the best of my ability and go as hard as I could, hopefully without blowing up or hurting myself.

Now "hard" is a relative measure, and different to fast … as I soon learned.

There were so many strong and fast riders this year, that very early on I realized I had no chance of keeping up with them and finishing. I would blow myself up after only a few days. But one thing I did notice was that because they were riding so much harder, they seemed to require more time to recover. And recovery is the key to finishing the Tour Divide.

Don took this photo outside of Helena. Left to right is Prentiss, Peter (NZ), Peter (USA), myself and Ron. Prentiss and Ron were riding single speed bikes. It's a sign of how strong they are that after 800+ miles they kept up with fast riders like the two Peters, especially Peter (USA) who rides like he has a rocket under him (as evidenced by his crushing Cjell Money's 'La Manga Pass Challenge'). Me? I was only there because I could ride more hours in the day than the others …

And that was my basic race approach. I would be up and on the road most days by 6:00 a.m., take short meal breaks of 30 minutes or less, and ride until dark or afterwards. Peter (USA) gave me a complement when he said that after 12 hours he didn't want to be on a bike. For me 12 hours was a short day—most were 15-17 hours of riding.

I ended up riding 'with' about seven others. I say 'with' because on a typical day I would start around the same time or earlier, they would then blast past me. At lunch I would arrive at the restaurant after they had finished a leisurely meal and were recovered. If I was lucky I'd stumble upon them in the evening at a campground, restaurant or hotel. They were good natured about this 'plodder' catching up with them, and often we rode together for a while, but in the end I couldn't keep up with them and we would bid adieu until later.

Riding as late in the day as possible is really important in the Tour Divide, especially if the weather conditions are favourable. More than once I covered an extra 20-40 miles in the evenings continuing until I couldn't ride any further. I then crashed next to the road, or if I was lucky, in a town where I would treat myself to a motel room. That's one thing for the Tour Divide: you have to have the confidence to be able to sleep in the wilderness on your own. If you don't have that, then you'll not do as well as you could have. I slept everywhere from under signs to a few metres off the edge of the road. When you decide you can't go any further that's it...

One advantage to averaging some 200 km/day is that I was more often than not able to spend the night in a town. A good meal and sleeping in a good bed is the best way to recover. One just has to be able to set the alarm for 5:00 a.m. and be on the road by 6:00 a.m. at the latest—in other words, overcome the temptation to succumb to comfort.

Another skill which is good to develop is that of the power nap. The sleep monster will rear its head at the most unexpected times, and it is often best just to pull off to the side of the road and sleep for a short time. It does wonders. A month after the Tour Divide my wife and I were mountain biking in Switzerland. She fell

behind and since I had a wait just parked the bike and did a power nap. She snapped the photo below. At least I now know what the motorists who passed me during the Tour Divide saw!

Of course there are times when you don't want to power nap and then caffeine pills come in handy. I don't drink tea or coffee and so they probably have a greater impact on me than others. I used them very judiciously at absolutely essential times. The other useful thing is the '5 hour' energy drinks—which last about 29 minutes on the Tour Divide.

In the end, you just have to be able to spend as many hours on the bike as possible, irrespective of the conditions and focus on the finish. For me that not only meant riding through rain, but towards lightening storms (I counted between the lightening and the thunder and as long as it was over five seconds I didn't worry), and through very hot parts of the day. You just keep on going until you feel you can't ride any more.

And that was how I managed to finish so well in the race. After a long day I arrived in Silver City with some 200 km to the finish line. I suspected that a number of the riders I had been catching up to were going to overnight in the city. After eating and resupplying I hopped on my bike and headed for the border. After 392 km of riding over some 26.5 hours I ended the race, and moved up some seven places to manage a 27th. I was shattered at the end (especially having to really haul it for the last 1.5 hours as Nathan, Nick and Hugh were kindly waiting for me to join their ride to Tucson) but it was worth it.

So the best race strategy? Eat, sleep and ride. Eat lots. Sleep little. Ride long and ride hard(ish).

2013 Result: 27th Place - 22:01:26

The La Manga Pass Challenge: Tour Divide 2013

Cjell Money

Does Cjell Money really hate south bounders? Not really. Does he believe there is much too little trash talking amongst Tour Divide riders? YES.

Enter the La Manga Pass Challenge, a remedy to the ho-hum camaraderie of extremely like minded folks who have devoted themselves to bike racing 3,000 miles along the Continental Divide.

I feel like instead of creating strong bonds and relationships, riders of the Tour Divide fall victim to a common problem amongst bike racers—kicking dirt and pretending not look at each other's bikes, instead chatting and chatting with a group of people that are so extremely similar, it's sickening.

That's why there needs to be much, much more trash talking on the Tour Divide.

The idea for the La Manga Pass Challenge came to me while touring down to the start of the Tour Divide. I saw a few options for getting from the east side of the divide to the west side in a geographically efficient manner. La Manga Pass was labelled and it seemed like a no brainer. I remember coming down that pavement climb the year prior and contemplating what it must be like heading the other direction. Now was my shot to find out.

Evening time, just before the base of the La Manga climb, a few short miles before Horca, CO, I see a man standing on the side of the road with something in his hands. It seems to be a sign. I can't make out what it says until I get very close. "Go Cjell Money". YEA! It's a divide fan Spot stalking. Yea!

Bob invites me in for a bite and a beverage. A real divide fan, Bob talks about Eric Lobek and Jay P from the early days of Great Divide Race. He has owned this cabin close to the route for years and followed the race. He had spotted (pun intended) me on the computer as I had turned my Spot device on for the tour down to the race start.

I tell Bob about my aspirations of climbing La Manga SoBo, a feat Bob has accomplished many times before. He shows me his GPS tracks and times up the pass. Together we hatch a plan to record a time up the pass and see how it stacks up. That plan grows and blossoms and I see it as a great opportunity to so some serious trash talking to the SoBos that will soon be riding this same stretch of road up the mighty La Manga Pass.

The next morning Bob makes a big breakfast of eggs and sausage. Well rested and fully fuelled I go at La Manga with everything I have. I ride with all my gear and little water or food, because who needs that?

The climb is pitchy with certain sections that are very steep. A few of the switchbacks have a good amount of exposure with awesome vistas of the lush Carneros River valley below.

I remember hitting my top speed for the entire route on La Manga Pass the year prior, racing down it at 51 mph. Boom!

Towards the end of the climb the grade lessens a good deal and I concentrated on keeping a good speed here because I knew it was a spot where much time could be lost or made up. I would like to say that the single speed was a big disadvantage here but I was so spent anyway, it didn't matter.

I stopped the clock when I touched the La Manga Pass sign at the crest. Very pleased with the effort, I was pretty confident that it would take quite a rider to best it. The more I thought about SoBo riders, fully loaded for the Brazos section ahead, just having come up and over the Tour Divide's tallest pass, Indiana, this, presumably into their third week of solid riding, would have to spend energy that no one could possibly have at this point in the race. My lungs burned but I smiled knowing that a few of those idiot SoBo'ers would have to try it.

A few minutes later Bob showed up. He seemed almost excited as I was. I put it on him to post the feat to the bikepacking.net forums for the other riders to see. I also instructed Bob to add a heavy dose of salty trash talking to the post to entice, entertain and belittle all the Southbound Tour Divide starters.

The original plan was to tape a dollar with my time on it to the La Manga Pass sign, allowing anyone who bested it to replace with their own dollar, but Bob had a much better plan.

The next time I heard from him, to my absolute delight, he informed me that he had set up a drop box chained to the sign. Along with the drop-box he had left instructions for SoBo'ers to leave their signed dollars with times in the box. Hell yes Bob! He also told me he had relayed my heckling which I was chuffed about as well.

The next time I saw the summit of La Manga Pass was on my NoBo run. I saw the lockbox chained to the big green sign at the top. I smiled from ear to ear. I was hoping it would also upset some purist on the forum. Nothing like upsetting those who fear change, banter, good times, etc.

A few days after I had completed my divide race I made it to a computer and checked bikepacking.net and was delighted to see that Bob had orchestrated the whole thing beautifully and there were a number of riders who indeed had joined the fun by submitting their dollars. There also seemed to be other third parties who enjoyed the whole thing and were offering prize money to the winner. Sweet!

A few days later I was notified that an effort from another rider had been posted. I was told I was bested by a Cat-something racer. I logged on and saw it for myself. Peter Haile bested my time by a few minutes. I could hardly believe it.

I snooped his Facebook account and found out that he had attended Lees McCrae University somewhere on the east coast. I remembered Lees McCrae from racing at collegiate mountain bike nationals. They had to be the largest and most successful team there. Their school had double the number of kids who were at nationals than the entire Midwest conference...point being, his effort was indeed plausible.

I read that he had shorted himself on supplies for the long difficult Brazos section and had given everything he had. His story added up. Kudos Peter.

Bob called and after another week we sent Peter the prize loot with our congratulations on his effort.

The La Manga Pass challenge turned out to be a great success and I think added a little spice and camaraderie to the 2013 Tour Divide. I hope that future idiot SoBo's will attempt the 'La Manga Pass Challenge' for years to come.

Editors note. I was riding with Peter to Horca and told him about the challenge which he had not heard of before. He was totally into it. He inflated his tyres, spun the wheels to check the brakes, took a drink and focused. I cycled ahead of him. To say that he blasted past me was an understatement. Sorry Cjell. If he had been as fresh as you the record would have been broken by a greater margin. Here is the photographic evidence of Peter's assault on La Manga Pass. And yes, you are right Cjell. He did suffer afterwards—I actually got to Cuba before him! But that was mainly because he wimped out in a lightning storm...

An Interview with Eric Foster

TC: Tell us a little about yourself

I grew up in Phoenix Arizona for the first 18 years before moving to Flagstaff for college. Growing up I was really active outdoors, always out riding bikes, playing in the sand and doing what kids used to do back then. We didn't have cell phones, video games, or iPods growing up in my generation, we had to make our own fun. Not having those modern gadgets and having to make your own fun is why I grew to love the outdoors and the risky adventures that make for great life experiences.

I began riding bikes at the age of three, and only stopped for a try at other sports and lifestyles along the way. Two years later I began racing BMX at the local racetrack. Eventually I stopped racing BMX and did other sports like cross-country, and then my true passion, rock climbing at the age of 17. It wasn't until 2010 that I started mountain biking. And like every other sport I had done, I obsessed over mountain biking for a decent chunk of time before burning out. And that is where I am now, looking for my next adventure.

TC: How did you first hear about the Tour Divide and what made you want to race?

A friend of mine who rode the Tour Divide route back in 2009 told me about it. I thought it sounded crazy and wondered why anyone would want to do something like that. I distinctly remember having a conversation with him discussing why I thought the Tour Divide sounded totally ridiculous. Sooner than later I was at the starting line for the Arizona Trail Race in 2011, and 30 miles later wondering why I got sucked into this crazy sport. Eventually one day I woke up and decided I would race the Tour Divide, it was definitely an impulsive decision, but one I will never regret.

TC: What experience did you have with long distance racing before the Tour Divide?

My first mountain bike race was the Arizona Trail Race 300 in 2011, which kicked my ass. I did a few others shortly afterwards, such as the Dixie 200 in Utah, where I was also shutdown—this time by foot deep clay mud. The first race I finished was the Coconino 250, which was in my backyard. Finishing was a confidence booster.

I then came back and finished the AZTR 300 in 2012 and finished in three days 14 hours. I had such a great time out there that I decided to try the AZTR 750 the following year, but with no ride time at all for the eight months prior. I took all that time off the bike because of my knee injury on the Tour Divide in 2012.

So that's about it for long distance racing experience prior to my finish of the Tour Divide in 2013. Not a ton, but enough experience to really have stuff dialed and be confident that I could finish.

TC: How did you train for the race?

I actually didn't train at all. I spent eight months trying to rehab my knee then went for the Arizona Trail Race 750. The month in between races was spent off the bike because I was finishing my senior year of college for my Geology degree. In spite of not training, I really just went for it. I wonder if it would have been less painful had I trained. Not sure if it would have made much of a difference had I trained for a couple months. Maybe I could have done it faster, but what it really comes down to in the end is just finishing.

TC: Tell us a bit about your rig and gear

I rode a custom Titanium Guru Cycles 29er hardtail with a 100mm front Fox Fork. My entire group kit was Shimano XT with a 3x10 drive train. My pedals were just your standard Shimano SPD's.

TC: How did you handle the nutrition and hydration challenges on the ride?

I really just ate everything in sight. When I had time and was passing through a town, I would definitely hit the diner and rack up 50 dollars easily. I tried to eat healthy, but I was just more concerned with getting enough calories. Sometimes I would spend 80 dollars at a convenience store; most of it was just junk. At times during the Tour Divide I felt really tired, could have been my diet or it could have been the consecutive 120 mile days.

TC: All riders eventually hit a rock bottom, a new low during their race. Could you tell us about your darkest hour during the race?

There were two very distinct periods of total exhaustion mentally. They were both only a day apart. The first was the Idaho 'Rails for Trails' section. I never saw this section coming, nor had I heard about it. My Achilles tendonitis had just recently subsided the day before, but then the endless whoops of six inch deep volcanic cinders (some 25 miles worth) flared them up again. It was demoralizing to say the least, but I ended up pushing through it. Looking back makes it seem like it wasn't so bad, but pain fades as time passes and I am no stranger to the cyclic nature of ultra racing.

The only time I really wanted to quit was on Union Pass in Wyoming. My Achilles tendonitis was at its all time high. I was also extremely exhausted and the 50 mph headwind the entire day didn't help. I made slow progress but eventually made it to Pinedale where I got a big steak dinner and a hotel, which I enjoyed with another friend racing the Tour Divide. That lifted my spirits and the next day my luck changed. I awoke to a 50 mph tailwind and sailed through the Great Basin. Just like life is full of ups and downs, so is the Tour Divide. Pushing through them is more gratifying than the good times during the ride.

TC: What advice would you give to future Tour Dividers

Just make sure you have fun out there from beginning to end. Be careful not to get caught up in all the little details, because once the adventure starts all the nitpicking over the little minor things about what gear to buy and bring, how much to train, and how fast you plan to ride won't matter. You can show up with the latest and greatest bike and gear, but that's not what gets you to the finish. Sure all that nice stuff might make it a bit more enjoyable and easier, but we all eventually hit rock bottom. What matters the most is having the heart and determination to finish. Make sure you prepare yourself mentally and look deep inside to find what drives you; it will be your greatest tool when the going gets tough. And before you know it you are back home yearning for the next adventure. Hope you enjoy the ride as much as I did and good luck.

TC: Will we see you again on the Tour Divide or are you going after other challenges?

I don't think I will be back and there are a couple reasons. One, there are so many other adventures I still want to do that there's just not time for another Tour Divide. The world is full of new experience so why not try something different? Two, I had a great experience this past Tour Divide and if I did it again it just wouldn't be the same. Maybe some of the veterans could relate to this. I want to remember the Tour Divide as it is now. Three, I think the Triple Crown really burned me out on ultra racing for a long time. And the last reason; I want to create my own adventure. I have a few ideas up my sleeve and I hope to make them a reality in the next ten years. You'll have to wait to find out what that is.

My next challenge is the military. I am shipping out on the 21st of January 2014 for my basic training. Decided the desk job in the private sector was something that could wait. I am looking forward to leaving and wish all the future Tour Divide riders the best.

2013 Result: 44th Place – 23:12:06

Headwindsandhills.com

The First Time You Race The Divide You're Not Racing, You're Learning. When You Come Back You're Racing

Erick Armentrout

I remember the first time that I saw the film 'Ride the Divide'. It was a cold, well cold for Houston, December night and I had returned home from a night out with friends to my small apartment. At the time my apartment living room was overrun with two road bicycles, various bicycle tools, pumps, and several other boxes of materials. By the end of that evening I would have a new goal, to ride the Tour Divide.

Having never ridden a mountain bike, and not knowing anything, I spent the next week reading everything I could. I ultimately took a page out of Matthew Lee's book and being a Cannondale man, I bought a Lefty Flash 2 29'er and then the fun began. Living in Houston, the highest 'mountain' is effectively a bridge over that I-45 that's about a two percent grade. Saying I wasn't able to properly prepare for mountain terrain is an understatement. Yet I wouldn't let that stop me, so I chose to concentrate on distance.

As my training, studying, and preparing continued, I learned of fellow Texan Billy Rice who was trying to do what had never been done before: a 'Yo-Yo' of South-North-South. It also happened that I would be moving to the Bryan/College Station so I was able to meet Billy. It wasn't until the afternoon that I sat down with Billy that I began to think I'd probably made a stupid mistake in deciding to attempt the Tour Divide. The guy is a Tour Divide encyclopedia and knows the route as well as anyone! He freely shared his advice and guidance.

So the time came in June to move from Houston and then travel north to Banff. After making sure that everything was safe and secure in my new home, my girlfriend, her daughter, and I headed north. It took a few days before we got to Banff, yet when we did I found myself sweating as I was looking at the mountains. I kept my fears at bay, and looking at the terrain around me I was transfixed by its beauty.

The night before the Grand Depart, a party and race information meeting was held where we got last minute advice and guidance via a phone call from Matthew Lee. I found myself and some 140 of my new favorite cyclists at the YWCA for a group photo prior to heading to the trail head. My nerves were up and I kept trying to find a way to chicken out. Not being able to do so, everyone started to push off. After a quick hug and kiss to my girlfriend and a hug to her daughter I was off.

As with most races the push off was crowded and congested. I chose to sit back and enjoy what I'd been dreaming and desiring for a year and a half. The racers began to string out as the terrain changed leaving me behind, I wouldn't let this bother me at all as I was still on a high just being out there. By the end of the first day I'd only covered 46 miles, met three other guys whom were of my experience level, and slept in the most amazing campsite I could have imagined.

The next day we all got off to a slow start and found ourselves in Sparwood. The biggest surprise for me came when around midnight I ran into Billy Rice riding by himself. We exchanged information with one another and then left. That was the first and last time that I'd see Billy on the trail, I'd see him again at Aggieland Bike shop a month and a half later.

Now the in between moments have gotten a little blurry as time has passed since the Tour Divide. I've held onto specific moments and am going to continue this story by giving the highlights I recall.

After passing Billy in Sparwood the group I was with headed straight on to Galton Pass, which would lead to an awesome downhill and American side for the first time in five days on the trail. The group chose to stop for the night, not wanting to attempt Galton Pass in the middle of the night. I on the other hand felt too good and continued on. At about 3 a.m. I chose to lay down for a brief nap, and three hours later I was up and on the bike again. At around 10 a.m. I crossed back into the United States laughing the whole time as I crossed the border on bike. All the people in cars were looking at me like I was crazy. Two days later I found myself crossing the pass over Whitefish and into the city of

Whitefish only to be reunited with my riding mates that I'd left behind at the base of Galton Pass.

We rode out the next day from Whitefish in a rainstorm that we were trying to outrun. After about 25-30 miles two of the guys in our group fell back as the remaining four continued on. When we realized this we were shocked at how far we'd gone: riding a mountain bike on pavement is thoroughly frustrating because you can't go as fast as you can on a road bike! .We texted our friends and found out one of them had fallen while crossing a set of railroad tracks and they had chosen to bail out together. Once we had this sad information we continued onto the next town. As I had done previously, I left my travel companions and headed south to Seeley Lake. Once in Seeley Lake I was able to make an important phone call for a position with a company in College Station.

My next big event occurred on the 4th of July. I left Atlantic City and rode straight through the Great Basin into Rawlings, Wyoming in one 15-hour stretch. I stayed the night and received an email from my mother saying I'd done what took some people two days to do. Needless to say this bolstered my spirits. By this time I was starting to suffer from loneliness. Despite this I continued to push on.

The next big place I remember was Brush Mountain Lodge. I'd texted Billy earlier telling him I was going to drop, he insisted I had to get to this lodge then I could drop. Here I was able to tick off a big milestone I wanted to reach. I later found out that Billy had reached out to a co-worker to ensure that I'd gotten to Brush Mountain Lodge. Let me tell you it was amazing! Kirsten is the most gracious and loving hostess; she supports every racer out there no matter how fast or slow. At this point in the race I was second to last overall in the race.

Steamboat Springs was the next stop and with that Orange Peel Bike shop for a lube and bleeding of my brakes. In hindsight, it was here that my bike started to slowly die. I had the rear brakes bled only to be told that they couldn't fix it 100%, this process I repeated in Breckenridge and later in Gunnison.

My next big moment was rolling into Hartsel, Colorado and stopping by the mercantile. I didn't even realize it until I walked in that I was going to meet my first and only person that was in the documentary. The owner of the mercantile was amazing and we chit chatted a bit. She gave me the best advice I'd received on the whole ride, "The first time you race the divide you're not racing, you're learning. When you come back you're racing".

She encouraged me onto Salida, which was some 50 miles away. I reached Salida the next day after sleeping next to this amazing old cabin that was marked on the maps. Sadly, I found out my rear derailleur which had been plaguing me for

over two weeks was cracked. The guys at Absolute Bikes tried their best to jerry rig it and I was on my way up to Marshall Pass. The paved climb to Marshall Pass was horrible and I hated every moment of it. Then after crossing onto dirt I met a few other bikers who had climbed Marshall Pass earlier that day and were telling me what to look out for. Then it was my turn to start climbing Marshall Pass. Now I never got to the really big climbs but Marshall Pass nearly killed me emotionally and mentally. If I had cell coverage I'd have quit right there and then, but being in the middle of nowhere and with nowhere to go but south, I kept riding and I loved the downhill more than anything.

The next, and what was to be my last, big climb and final stretch was going over Cochetopa Pass. I started out from Gunnison after a really amazing fire fighter, who had picked me up the day before when my bike broke down, drove me back out to where I had been picked up the day before. Since I was unsure if this had disqualified me according to the rules, I decided to continue on just for me, but I didn't get very far. I soon discovered that my crankset was so worn down that the chain was slipping and wreaking havoc as I pedaled forcing me to use my granny gear. I knew this was the end of my ride as I was nowhere near a bike shop and Tomichi Cycles didn't have anything that could help me. After several hours I had made it up and down Cochetopa Pass. At the top I took a good deal of time to myself knowing this was it and that the Tour Divide for me was over.

Finally after 30 days and 2,000 miles I reached the bottom of Cochetopa Pass and sat on the road and cried a little. All the preparation I'd put in and this is how I was ending the race. It wasn't a freak bear attack, or a crash (I'd already survived one crash that was caused the first week by a rampaging elk). It simply came down to the one thing I'd not even considered: a worn out crankset with over 4,000 miles and barely a year old. I was lucky enough to have my girlfriend nearby as she was wrapping up her national parks tour, and she was able to pick me up.

The race for me ended the second week of July. On the drive home I did nothing but look forward to doing it again. I told my girlfriend that the next summer I wanted to be dropped off in Del Norte and continue the ride south so I could "complete" the journey.

As of this writing I'm dead set on returning to Banff in 2016 to race the Tour Divide this time. I need that picture of a dirty, tanned, tired, and jovial me at the border of Mexico. The Tour Divide is more personal to me than any long distance race I've ever attempted. The day after I left the trail I wanted nothing more than to get back on my bike and continue the race. I've held onto this feeling and carry it with me every day. I can't say anything more about this experience as words don't seem to sum up the experience of what the Tour Divide can take away from you and what it will give to you.

34 year old male from College Station, TX

Rookie Year

Riding a Cannondale Flash 29'er 2

All my bags were Relevate Design other than my frame bag; this was a homemade job that my girlfriend made for me

Trail Angels

Fred Arden

It is hard to explain the Tour Divide to anyone other than those who have been there. It is even harder to sum it up in a brief story for this book. When thinking about all that transpired, all that I had seen, done, been through, experienced and survived, one thing stuck out—it is the people that make the difference. And that is what I want to share.

My pace in the Tour Divide had been pretty well matched with another Tour Divider—Mike Arenberg, a rider (and now friend) I had met in 2012. Mike and I had left Del Norte, Colorado to head through the final miles in Colorado, including the huge climb up Indiana Pass. Both of us were looking forward to being in New Mexico soon. For us it was Day 21—three weeks on the Tour Divide. We were dirty, a little beat up and trying to hold everything together for what would hopefully be another six or seven days to the finish.

We camped in the woods a few miles beyond the New Mexico border. After an early start we encountered what every Tour Divide racer who makes it that far experiences: the unbelievably rough, washed out, brutal roads/paths/trails of New Mexico. To say that the welcome to New Mexico is grueling is an understatement. It was a long day on the Tour Divide and we were hoping to make it to Abiqui which seemed at the time to be a hell of a long way away. It was raining. We were cold, wet and, yes, a little more than starving.

Knowing Tour Divide lore pretty well, and of course never saying no to some good Mexican food, Mike and I planned a stop in the town of El Rito at a restaurant called El Farolito. Now El Rito is a pretty isolated town whose better days are definitely in its past. El Farolito is one of the few places in the town that even had lights on. What we found in this little restaurant, in this little town, in the middle of nowhere was pretty amazing.

First, let me say the food was ridiculously delicious. And then, unbelievably enough, the people there knew all about the Tour Divide and even had a guest book for us to sign. When we walked in we apparently also drew the interest of some fellow diners—a couple with two kids and a grandmother. The family asked us tons of questions and were really interested in our adventure. Genuinely interested.....like 'in awe' interested.

We were dirty, grungy, wet, starving lunatics and this family treated us like we were rock stars. When it came time for us to pay our bill, I went up to the cash register and found out that the family who had chatted with us had quietly covered our check along with their own. When the waitress let me know they had paid our bill it actually brought tears to my eyes—me the 225 lb big guy on my tough and rugged mountain bike covered with mud, dirt and who knows what else. Yep made me cry. The waitress also.

And that is what the Tour Divide is really all about. It is the unexpected kindness of people you don't know, who you will never see again and for some reason are moved to do something kind for you—a mud-covered, crazy Tour Divide racer. It happened over and over again and that is what makes the Tour Divide a very special and unique experience, and one that I am so privileged to have taken part in and ultimately finished.

2013 Result: 60th Place - 27:05:29

Mike and Fred

Fred Arden is a 54 year old endurance athlete with a great love of mountain biking and anything that pushes the limits. He is the father of two adult daughters, Sara and Laura and has been married to his wife Caroline for 34 years. After competing in the Tour Divide in 2012 and not finishing, Fred came back in 2013 to have a great ride, great weather and a great finish in 27 days! Chronicles of his journey are available at www.2745epicmiles.com.

My "Brutal but Beautiful" Tour Divide Race

Greg Andre-Barrett

"Brutal but Beautiful" became my mantra for surviving and indeed enjoying the 2013 Tour Divide (TD) race.

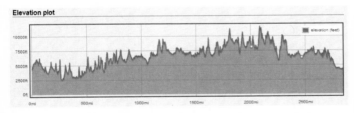

.The T D's 2,859 miles are brutal on both body and mind. However, what makes the TD route both really brutal as well as so beautiful, is that it follows the Rocky Mountains, criss-crossing the Continental Divide 34 times, resulting in some 200,000 feet of climbing, the equivalent of climbing from sea level to the top of Mt Everest seven and half times!

I survived the TD's brutality by focusing on the beauties of it—a big sky mountaintop view; a fire road vanishing into the distance of a vast desert; colourful flowers; a bear blocking the trail; antelope 'flying' across the plains; a trail angel's kind support; and sharing the experience with fellow TD racers. I also focused on enjoying the current moment and day, not thinking about yesterday or tomorrow. Only thinking ahead to conquering the next peak, the joy of the next descent, and the destination goal for the night.

Leading up to the race I trained as well as I could for someone who is married, working, and living in flat Ontario. I commuted year-round 3-4 days/week to work, a 60 mile round-trip. I did five two-day overnight bikepacking trips of 200 miles. Last summer I competed in several races, including winning a 24-hour 200 mile solo race. I knew that this did not make me fully prepared for riding the TD, especially as a rookie, and so figured that for the first week of the race I would still be training, so that I could survive to the end. With this in mind I set my goal for the TD's 2,728 miles at 27 days or 102 miles/day. A couple of last minute re-routes increased this year's distance to 2,859 miles.

I arrived in Banff the Tuesday before the Friday start and stayed at the YMCA. Luckily I met Marco Nicoletti, a world 24 hr solo winner from Italy, and he shared many useful tips, including helping me tether and setup my GPS. He even tuned my shifting so well that it worked flawlessly for the whole race.

Day 1: Cold rain started about mid-day, and by the time I reached Elkford I could not feel my hands or feet. I had completed my daily target of 100 miles, so I decided to stay overnight in a house that the owner—surely a beautiful person—opened up for TD racers.

Day 2: I felt great and the weather was fine so I pushed hard...too hard and too far as it

turned out. For a while I tried to keep up with Sara Dallman (first place woman). Sara practically ran up the 'cliff' trail. By the time I struggled to the top Sara was long gone. I topped the last peak as it got dark. The ride down in the dark and cold was fun, although I wish my light had been brighter so I could have seen the corners coming. When I reached the highway I decided I might as well try for the USA border. At the border, I caught up with three others and rode with them to Eureka and shared a motel room. This day's 155 miles was probably the hardest day of cycling I had ever done.

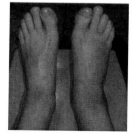

Day 3: When I woke up I was really worried as my right Achilles was very swollen and painful. I remembered reading how many TD riders drop out because of Achilles tendinitis. Lesson learned—don't do much more distance than your planned average in the early days, otherwise your body will break! To reduce the strain on my Achilles I tried to lower my seat post, but discovered it was seized in the frame. Another lesson learned—make sure everything works on your bike. I wrapped my ankle with medical tape, took the first of many Ibuprofens, crossed my fingers and pedalled out of Eureka.

I didn't get far out of town before I had a huge nosebleed. I stopped and sat under a tree until the bleeding stopped. I would get a nosebleed almost every morning for the next several days. Probably this was caused by a combination of the elevation, dry air, and exertion. While I waited for the nosebleed to stop I called my daughters Merike and Annike to tell them about my Achilles tendinitis and for some emotional support. As they did many times throughout the race, they provided me with sound advice and inspiration: see a doctor and get some anti-inflammatory drugs, slow down until its better, keep going if you can, and we're rooting for you! I got back on my bike and pedalled out of Eureka with my daughters' words of encouragement in my heart and my focus on my cycling rules and the Tour Divide's beauty all around me.

My swollen Achilles made climbing difficult. However, I was still enjoying the climbs as the views from the peaks were breathtaking, such as this view from Richmond Peak, and the climbs (which were breathtaking in another way) were always rewarded with an exhilarating descent.

Day 6: I rolled into Helena with my Achilles screaming at me to stop. So I went into a medical clinic to see a doctor. Here I learned another lesson—make sure you have travel medical insurance. My workplace health benefits had been changed and no longer covered travel outside of Canada. Luckily both the doctor and pharmacist, upon learning I had no insurance, charged me very low amounts for the visit and drugs. That day I did buy medical insurance for about $70 for the rest of the trip…which I luckily didn't have to use.

In Helena I also visited the GravityGuildGarage.com and they managed with great difficulty to wrench my seat post out and replace it with a new one. I then visited the Great Divide bike shop to have the owner do a quick bike fit to accommodate my sore Achilles. Unfortunately no adjustment seemed to be helping my sore raw arse!

Helena is very biker friendly as indicated by "Welcome Tour Divide Riders—Apple and Water?" sign.

Days 10 through 14: These were probably my lowest, toughest days, as on top of the sore Achilles I was experiencing bad diarrhoea, possibly caused by the anti-inflammatory drugs. I was getting little sleep as I had to get up almost every hour. During the day I made several trips to the bushes or washrooms. My speed, especially on the climbs, was reduced to an exhausted painful crawl! I was managing much less than my target 100 miles per day. I

wasn't going to quit, but did think I might have to request an extension to my vacation so I could finish. To keep going I continued to focus on the TD's beauty such as the Grand Teton Mountains and Jackson Lake.

Day 14: I bought some Imodium in Pinedale and felt much better the next day. Lesson learned—pack Imodium! Although my Achilles hurt like hell for the rest of the trip, the rest of my body and mind felt pretty good, and the rest of the race went by almost too quickly! So let me tell you about some of the TD's beauty.

I found beauty in occasionally being able to share with my fellow racers climbs, descents, food, beer, and life stories.

Here are a few TD racers with whom I was lucky enough to ride at least briefly: Sara Dallman who showed the men how to race; Brian Steele

'Creature Boy', a Hollywood creature-actor, who on Day 2 climbing 'the cliff' chipped his wrist, had a cast put on it, never complained,

and finished the race; Richard Costello, who used to weigh 325 pounds when his full-time 'job' was as a highland games strong man, and whose 'enjoy the journey' attitude helped me get through my low energy days; J.D. Pauls, a local friend, whom I saw shortly after he had a bad crash, but I knew from his smile and spring in his step, that he would finish well...which he did even though his frame broke; Billy Rice, the super-human racer that completed the first south-north-south ride, who took the time to give advice to me, a sub-human racer;

Brian Jett with whom I shared Wyoming whisky in Atlantic City when he had to scratch because both Achilles were shot; Mike Cleaver of CleaverBikes.com who built his own titanium bike, with whom I enjoyed riding and sharing life's stories.

There were the beautiful 'Trail Angels' whose acts of kindness put a smile on my face and spring in my pedal strokes—someone who left five bottles of cold water on the road for me and four other riders, a sign beside the road saying 'you rock' with my name and others, the woman who let me sleep in the Atlantic City community centre, Kirsten at Brush Mountain Lodge who sang "O Canada" to me for July 1st, a SUV driver who gave me bug spray when I was being eaten by mosquitoes on a slow tough climb, the Skyline Lodge owners who gave me Ibuprofen and replaced a broken bungee cord holding my water bottle, Roger who picked me up from Antelope Wells…and many more acts of kindness.

Community Health Worker: Wilson Banda
Wilson is a Community Health Worker in Malawi, Africa.

There were the beautiful people that donated $4,000 to the 'Bikes Without Borders' charity for which I was fundraising. This money will provide 26 bicycles to health care workers in Africa, enabling them to reach many more patients…and probably on trails and roads worse than those of the Tour Divide! This thought made me smile and gave me the energy to finish the race for them.

The Tour Divide's beautiful landscape was decorated with beautiful flora: Fir trees providing a partial green cloak on a snow covered peak; 'Aspen Alley' made you feel special riding along it; and finding cheery wild flowers outside your tent in the morning.

There was also the beautiful fauna with which we had to 'Share the Road'. Cows that would wait until you were almost on them before getting spooked and stampeding,

a couple of times almost running into me. On a descent coming around a corner to discover a bear blocking the trail; seeing deer and antelope "flying" across the plains; having to carefully ride around or through herds of elk and big horn sheep that seemed used to cyclists (a benefit to being 64th); and on my last night a scary but still beautiful tarantula!

Despite having painful Achilles tendinitis since Day 2, four days of diarrhoea, a couple of flat tires, and a broken pedal 30 miles from the finish, I feel very blessed to have limped to Antelope Wells in 28 days, 4 hours and 8 minutes, or 101 miles/day—64th of the lucky 79 that finished, out of the 143 starters.

Rudyard Kipling wrote "Something hidden. Go and find it. Go and look behind the Ranges." Well I went and looked behind the Great Continental Divide 'Ranges' and found them to be 'Brutal but Beautiful'. The 'Brutal/ will disappear when my Achilles fully heals, but the memory of the Tour Divide's 'Beautiful' journey will always be with me.

P.S. A special heartfelt thanks to my daughters Merike and Annike for their special emotional encouragement and their Bikes Without Borders fundraising support. I would love to do another Tour Divide to apply my veteran lessons learned and experience the beauty again—perhaps in 2019 when I'm 65 ☺.

2013 Result: 65th Place - 28:04:05

Greg was born in 1954. He works as an IT Change, Configuration and Release Process Manager for the Ontario Government's Ministry of Health. He is a proud member of the Cyclepath Oakville Race Team and has won three 24 hour solo races. He loves to combine his passion for cycling with travelling, with some memorable journeys being Camino de Santiago Pilgrimage (with his wonderful wife Anneli), Trans Portugal Mountain Bike race, and now the Tour Divide!

greg.andrebarrett@gmail.com

GregRidesTheDivide.Wordpress.com – blogs and links to photos and Bikes Without Borders pledge site.

Photos: https://plus.google.com/101928407697579153511/posts/J9EHeMrckJi

Hail to the Elder Statesmen!

Greg Strauser

The Tour Divide racer demographic is nearly as diverse as the terrain that defines the route. The youngest rider on the 2013 unofficial list of racers has yet to experience his twentieth birthday, while the oldest rider has seen his seventy-second come and go. The bikepacking.net and Trackleader blue dot junkies were even given a rare treat in the form of the Peter Kraft duo, senior and junior, that is. Since Peter Junior is a full-grown twenty year-old, one would think Peter Senior would be grouped in the ranks of the oldest competitors this year. Nope. If all the competitors lined up in Banff according to age, Peter Senior would have been standing behind 26 other racers.

The Tour Divide 2013 posts on the Ultra Racing forum of bikepacking.net were loaded with great posts highlighting the trials and tribulations of the Kraft father/son pair. There was no shortage of accounts showcasing their tenacity. That's a trait every Tour Divide racer must possess if he or she has a shot at making it from one end of the course to the other. One would assume tenacity would be the hallmark trait of the racers with more than five decades of life's lessons under their belts. But that wasn't the case for the Tour Divide 2013 competitors. If I had to choose a one-word descriptor for the Elder Statesmen I competed with along the Great Divide Mountain Bike Route that word would have to be 'Grace'.

At this point, I'm sure there are many readers out there who are thinking 'Grace?'... Yes, grace. It's not the descriptor one would expect when chronicling the traits of any Tour Divide racer, let alone those with so many years of riding experience. But that noun appropriately describes the physical attributes I witnessed as these mature riders repeatedly left me in their dust on countless ascents. That noun also nails the generosity I witnessed from these racers on multiple occasions.

Hal Russell, a 64 year-old racer from Missouri, was my first encounter with the Tour Divide '13 Elder Statesmen. I was introduced to Hal two days before the Banff Grand Depart by my good friend and fellow Navy veteran, Ed Fogarty.

We flew to Calgary and shared a car together on the way to Banff, but once there, Ed did the YWCA scene while I stayed further downtown with my family. Once I got my bike assembled, I took a ride to the YWCA to see how Ed and the other racers were doing. He introduced me to Hal briefly while I was still astride my bike. The next morning, we ran into each other at breakfast where I had the pleasure of engaging Hal in deeper conversation. Too humble to outright brag, I was able to pry enough information out of Hal to identify him as someone to watch. The guy was no stranger to adventure racing. While I'm on the subject of Hal and Ed, I should mention Ed is no slouch when it comes to mountain biking. He's got his own adventure racing pedigree. Over the past couple years when I was making my transition from mere athlete to ultra-endurance cyclist, Ed has constantly demonstrated the grace (refinement, style, kindness, charity) I've found as the hallmark for the Tour Divide'13 Elder Statesmen. But, alas, Ed's just a punk kid who just recently turned 50. He doesn't make the grade.

Fast-forward to the second morning of the Tour Divide, on the long stretch of British Columbia blacktop between Sparwood and Corbin. It was a cool, sunny morning, and I was enjoying a relatively flat course where my bike's higher-than-average gear ratios had me steadily passing other racers at a fairly good rate. Two such racers were Coloradans Robert Orr and Kent Davidson. I exchanged pleasantries as I overtook them, eager to find the next set of racers to reel in. Well, the terrain and road surface soon changed. The pavement gave way to dirt, and the flat valley road gave way to the Flathead Wilderness. I'd shifted gears, and shifted my riding style to what I thought was an efficient climbing mode. Then along came Robert and Kent. I encountered Robert first. It was a fairly steep section that saw Robert climbing out of the saddle. It was like he was dancing up the mountain. Damn graceful. Kent wasn't far behind. He came rolling up on me, seated square on the saddle, but spinning effortlessly. Not as elegant as Robert, but clearly a refined climbing style. Despite his rapid ascent, Kent was fully prepared to engage in conversation. My flatlander lungs were burning, so I was having none of that. Kent diplomatically disengaged without calling attention to my suffering... Grace!

My encounters with Kent and Robert would be numerous throughout the race. I'd manage to regain contact with these veteran Colorado mountain bikers by pushing hard on the flats and being aggressive on my descents. I managed to distance myself from them owing to the favourable terrain in southern Montana, Idaho, and Wyoming. What I should have done was shadow Kent and Robert to learn a thing or two about mountain biking. If I had, perhaps I could have saved myself from the bodily harm that nearly ended my race on my first morning in Colorado.

Typically, I was trying to make time by flying down the descents near Meaden Peak, about 30 miles north of Steamboat Springs. I crashed in spectacular fashion along a steep, rock-strewn section. Rookie mistake #1: I was picking out the rocks to avoid rather than looking for the "clean line" to follow. Rookie mistake #2: After inevitably hitting one of the rocks I shouldn't have been looking at, I learned my weight wasn't far enough back for the steep descent. Of course, I wasn't aware of this mistake at the time, so my front tire stopped at the rock while the rest of the bike and I kept going. Face plant into the rocks! It was through Kent's grace that I learned these lessons, after the fact, during discussions we had after finishing the race.

Branded a mountain bike novice by the unforgiving Colorado High Country

Another veteran racer made quite an impression on me during the race. I was very fortunate to cross paths with Fellow Virginian James Hodges. I'd met James briefly last fall when we were competitors racing the inaugural Allegheny Mountains Loop 400. I ran into James, Robert, and Kent in Wise River, Montana. I stopped for dinner just before dusk and found the three veterans already enjoying their supper and looking forward to their night's rest on-site. I was hoping to keep going after dinner, but a look at the storm clouds further along my intended path, coupled with the irrefutable wisdom of the trio had me reconsider. A few racers in our immediate vicinity chose to press on while about half a dozen of us remained for the night. The following dawn was beautiful. Dead-calm, cold, and dry. I don't know where they stopped, but those who chose to continue didn't fare nearly as well. We moved right through them that morning.

Later that day, I took advantage of Russ Kipp's hospitality at the Montana High Country Lodge. My late breakfast/early lunch stop was a bit too leisurely and several racers passed me in the interim. Along the route between Polaris and Lima, I'd caught up to the pack and moved through them owing to the relatively wide-open terrain. The only exception was James. He was riding as if Antelope Wells was just on the horizon. The relatively benign grades were getting steep as we neared the Medicine Lodge-Sheep Creek Divide and James was really attacking the climbs. I didn't really understand his sense of urgency until he explained where we were and the impending doom associated with the rain coming our way. Sure enough, a glance at the map told the story: "Road might be mucky when wet." James told me of his encounter with bike-stopping mud in that very stretch of road on a previous Tour Divide. Needless to say I made great time all the way into Lima, Montana, thanks solely to the grace of James.

I'd be remiss if I didn't mention the freshman class of this year's Elder Statesmen; Fred Arden and Jeff Mullen. They're both only 54 years young, hence their freshman status. I recall seeing Fred briefly in Banff before the race, but my lasting memory is one of Fred blowing by me like a runaway Montana logging truck. It was not long past sunset and I was heading off-route towards Condon to find some food after a long day's ride. Just before Fred shot past, I started to make out the outline of a restaurant in the distance. I found Fred in the parking lot, clearly disappointed. It turned out the place had closed within the past hour. Fred explained how he reached the restaurant last year around the same time. They'd stopped serving, but made an exception for Fred. He was hoping for a repeat. No such luck.

Like James Hodges, I met Jeff Mullen last year at the Allegheny Mountain Loop 400. Although his physical fitness belies his status of Elder Statesman, he most certainly qualifies for the distinction. Jeff and I crossed paths on numerous occasions throughout the race, just like we did last fall. The great equalizer that bonded us was Jeff's mountain biking skills and my lack thereof. Jeff was on his own race, sure and steady throughout, but not at all slow. In that respect, Jeff's race reminded me of Robert and Kent. Those three were the tortoise to my hare, but that's a horrible analogy because these guys were anything but slow, and I was only fast when the terrain suited.

My hat's off to Mike Hall and the rest of the Tour Divide 2013 contenders, but the Elders are my new heroes and role models. I'm sure there were other racers this year worthy of inclusion as an Elder Statesman, but I can only comment on those relatively few racers with whom I interacted. They ran their own race, on their terms, and those of us who were fortunate to share space and time with them along the route couldn't help but be touched, and inspired. When I grow up, I want to be just like them; skilled mountain bikers and gracious competitors. I like to think I'm halfway there. Hopefully, my mountain biking skills will improve with more time in the saddle!

Pristine Load-Out, Shortly before Packing for Banff

2013 Result: 51st Place - 24:08:42

Greg is a retired US Navy Officer, six years into a second career as a US Navy Civilian. An avid endurance athlete, he purchased his first mountain bike two years ago after being exposed to the Colorado Rockies through his wife's recent career posting. Owing to her outstanding performance keeping friends and family abreast of his racing antics after Greg crushed his Smartphone in the Colorado backcountry, many mistakenly assume she is a full-time publicist. Like Greg, she is a government civilian, employed by the Department of Homeland Security. As noted in the narrative, Greg looks forward to the day when he's proficient in the use of his mountain bike in its intended operating environment.

gstrausermtb@gmail.com

Spirit Divide

Greg Thompson

In an April post on my blog, I wrote about my latest training for the Tour Divide and talked a little about the inspiration for 'Riding the Divide'.

"So—about the inspiration... Yesterday was freezing when I was out doing my ride around the Lake Minnewanka loop in Banff. On my way home, the wind was ferocious from the North East and I was having a bit of a suffer fest. Thought I had frozen my feet, my hands were like clubs but I was okay.

In September, our older son Peter died in a kayaking accident near Whistler, B.C. One of his many hare-brained ideas was to pack up his bike, pull along his kayak and paddle all the rivers to which he could cycle. When I think of Peter, especially when things are tough, his spirit is inspiring and I physically get a warm glow. I imagine him smiling and being part of the action. I believe the Tour Divide will be his way to see all the spots he could have gone. Know that he will be with me all the way as he is with so many of his friends and family."

That was in April, about two months before the start of the Tour Divide. As I think back to that entry, and in answer to all of the questions after completing the ride, inspiration and motivation is the key to having a great ride. Being on the Tour Divide, enjoying the challenges, and being open to any and all experiences turned the Tour Divide into an incomparable mental and physical journey—time to reflect, time to mourn and time to laugh were part of this ride for me. These and other emotions and thoughts would ebb and flow and the Tour Divide was always an amazing backdrop and inspiration. I often close my eyes and think back to the Tour Divide. We are all on a journey—know that there are places and times out there that transcend description. This is the inspiration for riders and for those who are riding along with us in Spirit.

2013 Result: 47th Place - 23:15:10

http://spiritdivide.blogspot.ca

I Didn't Ride Alone

Hal Russell

Can I ride and finish the Tour Divide? That seemed to be the main question I was asked when I would tell people what I had planned for the summer of 2013. In the past 15 years my family and friends have gotten used to following my yearly adventures. I have run a number of marathons, including the Pikes Peak Marathon (several times) and have ridden in a number of mountain bike races, including the Leadville 100 mountain bike Race four times. So it has become a question each year "Hal what is your next adventure?" Only this time when I told them I was planning to race my mountain bike from somewhere up in Canada down to the Mexican border, most people gave me a look of doubt. "It sounds neat, but I don't know", was a typical response. More than one person mentioned the word "crazy". Probably in part because of my age—I'm 64 years old.

However, the people who know me well knew that something pretty drastic would have to go wrong for me not to finish. I had my share of setbacks, as I am sure most of the racers did. In my mind, no matter what happened, I was going to make it to the border at Antelope Wells.

For this race I wanted to be viewed as a racer, not just someone touring. In my mind my main competitor was Father Time. For someone my age the clock is ticking on how many more adventures you may have left. This race was my Mt. Everest. I wanted the whole thing, the complete adventure. I wanted to travel all the way from Banff Alberta, down through British Columbia, Montana, Idaho, Wyoming, Colorado, and to the border at Antelope Wells, New Mexico. I had three main objectives. I wanted to meet people, see the country along the continental divide, and come to peace, if possible, with a few past ghosts from Vietnam.

I started the first day riding with Ed Fogarty. After several cold wet days we arrived at Lincoln, Montana. Here Ed decided to hole up at a motel. I was hoping to have some time riding alone to reminisce about past memories that have been with me since Vietnam. As I left Lincoln alone in the rain I called my wife while I still had cell service and told her I was cycling on by myself. As I headed up Fields Gulch I received a text from my wife Linda, who said "please be careful out there by yourself". I texted back and told her I was not by myself, I was travelling with a couple of old "Nam buddies". She would know these were memories of friends I had lost in Vietnam. I heard my phone ring again, but I was already back in Vietnam with my old friends. In a steady rain I turned and headed up South Fork of Poorman Creek. I was fully alert with the ghosts of my friends beside me. We topped out on Stemple Pass in a misty evening fog. The meadow on top of the pass was beautiful with multitudes of wildflowers. Straight ahead of me and to my right a huge mountain storm was moving in. There was no panic as I watched the lightning streaking across the sky. I looked around for cover and slid my bike and myself under a large spruce tree where I was dry, and warm out of the cold driving rain. I was still in Nam; I was with my old friends. I needed to say bye to them though—that is why I was here.

My first thought was just to camp there for the night, it was a very peaceful beautiful place. As the rain eased up I came out from under my shelter to check on the storm. I looked up the trail where the road forked to the right, the sky in the distance was very black and menacing looking, to the left on the Tour Divide Trail (FR 485) the sun glowed brightly down in the Marsh Creek Canyon. I knew this was the place. I looked around and found a polished rock. Under a steady rain I pushed the rock down into the ground by an old stump. I sat under my spruce shelter near the stump for a while thinking about those days in Nam that seemed moments ago. To the Northeast the sky was still very dark and black, to the West the late evening sun shone brightly. I looked around at the beautiful high country meadow with the wildflowers and green grass. With one last look at the stump and rock I quietly said goodbye. Then I slowly climbed on my bike and alone headed west down the Marsh Creek Canyon Trail. That night I camped at the fork of Marsh Creek Canyon. With a waning moon shinning outside the opening of my bivy tent I lay there peacefully somewhere in Northern Montana trying to put it all in perspective.

I rode on alone for another day and then hooked up with other riders. For several days I rode with Mike Komp and off and on with Andrew Stuntz. Mike, Andrew (Drew) and I rode across the Great Basin together. At the amazing Brush Creek Mountain Lodge, Drew decided to spend the night while Mike and I continued up the trail and bivied for the night so we could make it to the bike shop in Colorado Springs the next day for bike repairs. Drew said he would catch up with us there. However, when Mike and I reached the store at Clark, Colorado, we checked Drew's progress on the web and found he was off route. We stopped at the Orange Peel Bike Shop in Steamboat then decide to head on after having our bikes tuned. As we reached a parking area near a fishing stream at the Blacktail Conservation Area below the dam we stopped to use a park restroom. I deposited my Camelbak on a rock. After resting a bit and visiting with a fisherman, Mike and I continued across the dam and up the next mountain road. After about an hour of riding all of a sudden I realized I had ridden off without my Camelbak. Just about everything that was of any importance to me was in it. All of my ID, credit cards, passport, driver's license, money, Spot tracker, maps, cell phone, even rain gear and warm clothes. I will admit I panicked a bit. I told Mike I had to find it. Mike continued up the trail figuring I would catch him later that night. I rode fast and hard back to the parking area, only to find nothing there. Where there had been several fishermen and a Camelbak now there was nothing.

I remembered seeing a guy at the dam fishing with his young boys so I cycled back there and the fisherman helped me contact the rangers' office and report my stuff missing. With their help and phone I was able to contact my wife to cancel my credit cards and start figuring out how to have stuff sent to me to regroup. The fisherman told me "you have nothing left, you're done!" I told him "no, just slowed down, I am still heading to Mexico!" I knew Drew was behind me and I still had my GPS on my bike for navigation. So I went back to where I had lost my Camelbak and just as I arrived Drew popped up over the hill. He was worn out from riding hard trying to catch up with Mike and I after getting off route. I told Drew my dilemma and we decided we would bivy there for the night and head out in the morning. It had been a long day for both of us. Drew was having a few problems with his bike and I needed to resupply. Therefore, we decided to head to the border together. We were sort of an odd pair as Drew, from Durango, Colorado, is 20 years old and I am 64 years old.

Over the next couple of weeks it was the "Colorado Kid and the Old Dude" making our way down through Colorado into New Mexico, experiencing the many ups and downs of the Tour Divide. We met a number of really nice people and had some awesome experiences. Needless to say we had a few rough times, especially travelling through the Gila National Forest. One day we got off route for a while, then Drew's derailleur failed and he had to cycle single speed with quite a bit of pushing. Then he had a flat and his spare tube also leaked. If all of that wasn't enough we ran into a heavy rainstorm which played havoc with the roads. Worn out we eventually called it a day somewhere up in the Gila. After 31 days we finally made it to Antelope Wells riding through one last heavy thunderstorm to the border. The last five miles were amazing!

As one friend told me, "we thought you were crazy at first, but after following your daily progress during the race we know you're not. What an adventure!"

Note: Thanks to my family and friends for their support! The Tour Divide was an awesome experience! I have been asked what my favourite part of the race was. What part of the country did I like best? The truth is I liked all of it. It was all beautiful in its own way. I wanted to see and experience all of it, the weather, the mountains, lakes, rivers, wildlife and the people. There is so much to see and experience out there. It was all great! It was great meeting different people along the way. Thanks to those I rode with, it was a blast! I especially thank Andrew Stuntz, for riding with me the last couple of weeks. Looking forward to 2014 to try to ride the Tour Divide in a more competitive time.

2013 Result: 74th - 31:08:09

I was born September 2, 1948 in rural Missouri, USA. I grew up on a farm where I would dream of many far away adventures. One of my biggest adventures before racing the Tour Divide had been a tour with the US Army to Vietnam, 1968-1969. My wife and I have two children and we have been married for 40 years. I was a self-employed farmer for 20 years. I started college at the age of 38 and obtained degrees in elementary education and counselling. I have been an elementary teacher and counsellor for the last 21 years.

russell.hal@gmail.com

An Interview with Hamish McKee

TC: Tell us a little about yourself

I am 38 year old eye surgeon from New Zealand living in Australia. I don't particularly like cycling but I do like adventures.

TC: How did you first hear about the Tour Divide and what made you want to race?

I read about it in Outside magazine in 2008. It sounded like one of the ultimate adventures. Long, hard and self-supported.

TC: What experience did you have with long distance racing before the Tour Divide?

None at all. I didn't even own a bike until I decided to start training.

TC: How did you train for the race?

Firstly I decided to ride across Cuba as a holiday and preparation in long distance cycling. I was running fit but had done no cycling. I quickly worked out that going from 0 km to 100 km a day of cycling would likely end in knee pain. A third of the way across the country my chain broke and derailleur ended up in my spokes and the trip was over. That was the start of a lifelong hatred of external gears, so I made it my mission to find an alternative.

For the six months leading up to the race I'd do a long ride in the weekend (about 120 km) then do a couple of sessions on my indoor trainer during the week. Also some running and exercises that I do anyway. Not great training but it turned out to be enough for my 26 day finish.

TC: Tell us a bit about your rig and gear

Belt driven Rohloff on a titanium 29er (Lynskey Ridgeline) with rigid carbon fork (Niner). The usual bag setup. Tubeless.

TC: Tell us about some of the highlights of your ride

Montana High Country Lodge, Brush Mountain Lodge in Colorado, and Como Depot B&B in Colorado. Loved these places and the people who ran them. Gave me the warm fuzzies.

The ride from Silverthorne to Hartsel. Just a great day. Boreas Pass was a breeze, constant gradient, just didn't feel like I was riding uphill.

I saw a bear too. That was cool. I love bears.

TC: How did you handle the nutrition and hydration challenges on the ride?

With difficulty. I don't eat anything from dead animals which made it even more challenging. I think I was getting protein deficient until I discovered Muscle Milk which they have at most gas stations which helped a lot.

TC: Did you have any major mechanical problems during the race and, if you did, how did you deal with them?

My rear tyre started going a bit flat riding in to Grants. So put some more Stan's in the tyre then pumped it up at a gas station then that was it. Other than that, nothing. With a belt drive and Rohloff hub there isn't a lot that can go wrong.

TC: All riders eventually hit a rock bottom, a new low during their race. Could you tell us about your darkest hour during the race?

Riding from Togwotee Mountain Lodge to Pinedale. It was just taking so much longer than I thought it should. I rode over the pass expecting a nice downhill, but it was really gradual with crappy terrain and a solid headwind. I was getting nowhere. I decided to quit the race so threw my bike down and just lay on the side of the road. Then I got ravaged by mosquitoes so I had to get up. There was no phone reception and there was no traffic so I had no choice but to keep riding on the route. Eventually I hit a sealed section with a slight downhill and tailwind and made it to Pinedale that day as planned. So it worked out in the end, but it's a special sort of race when you can't even quit!

TC: What advice would you give to future Tour Dividers

Pearl Izumi Sun Sleeves are a must. Most riders didn't have them but when they saw mine wished they did. They also make leg sleeves which I wore. I also had this cover for my nose which attached to my sun glasses. Looked stupid as hell, but kept the sun off.

Get reliable kit if you can afford it. As an off the shelf bike that has Tour Divide written all over it, I would go for the van Nicholas Zion Rohloff 29er with belt drive. However I would put rigid forks on it. Suspension just isn't worth the extra weight. You'll spend pretty much all day every day riding up hill, so carrying extra kilos uphill to make the quick downhill easier doesn't make much sense to me for the terrain.

Also make sure you can pack up quick and easy. I had a little too much stuff that was really hard to fit in my bags so it took me extra time each morning that I should've better used sleeping.

Be very careful pushing your bike up hills. Your foot needs to be able to bend or you will overload your Achilles. Loosen your shoes so your heel can lift up. Alternate the sides you push the bike from to even the load.

Use low gears and take it easy on the uphills or your knees will be wrecked before you leave Montana.

Try and work out a rough plan of what riding you want to do each day. Have a couple of options, one with your target time and an easier one if you have to back off. Most people I rode with thought they were going at a much quicker pace than they were and really had no idea. You need to base your goals for each day on riding time **not** kilometres. This is difficult information to get and most people just post about kilometres and not hours on the bike. It can get very depressing when you think you'll cover a leg quickly due to the distance, but then find out it's going to take twice as long due to the terrain. Here are my details if it helps:

The Cordillera V5

Date	Start	Finish	km	Ascent	Moving time	Stopped time	Moving Avg	Overall Avg
14/06/2013	Banff	Elkford	178	2179	11:41	02:34	15.2	12.5
15/06/2013	Elkford	Butt's Cabin	140.5	1050	8:32	03:19	16.4	11.8
16/06/2013	Butt's Cabin	Eureka	113	1598	8:34	03:17	13.2	9.5
17/06/2013	Eureka	Columbia Falls	170.4	1729	11:18	04:26	15.1	10.8
18/06/2013	Columbia Falls	Holland Lake Lc	164.3	1907	10:08	03:30	16.2	12
19/06/2013	Holland Lake	Lincoln	160.6	1947	11:39	04:28	13.8	10
20/06/2013	Lincoln	Helena	102.5	1459	8:09	03:36	12.6	8.7
21/06/2013	Helena	Butte	109.2	1646	8:45	03:44	12.5	8.7
22/06/2013	Butte	Polaris	147.9	2077	10:32	03:44	14	10.4
23/06/2013	Polaris	Lima	158.8	1134	8:29	01:26	18.7	16
24/06/2013	Lima	Warm River	194.7	949	12:15	03:36	15.9	12.3
25/06/2013	Warm River	Togwotee Lodg	151.2	1638	9:25	03:35	16.1	11.6
26/06/2013	Togwotee Lodg	Pinedale	186.1	1738	11:20	03:14	16.4	12.8
27/06/2013	Pinedale	Diagnus Well	175.4	1332	10:48	04:30	16.2	11.5
28/06/2013	Diagnus Well	Rawlins	178.8	800	10:10	03:20	17.6	13.2
29/06/2013	Rawlins	Steamboat	223.2	2619	14:15	04:06	15.6	12.1
30/06/2013	Steamboat	Past Kremmling	156.3	2162	10:51	03:19	14.4	11
1/07/2013	Past Kremmling	Hartsel	169.5	1583	10:40	06:08	15.9	10.1
2/07/2013	Hartsel	Past Sargeants	205.4	1992	12:48	04:33	16	11.8
3/07/2013	Past Sargeants	Platoro	206.6	2635	14:24	03:55	14.3	11.3
4/07/2013	Platoro	Hopewell Lake	143	2041	11:01	02:48	13	10.3
5/07/2013	Hopewell Lake	Cuba	185.2	1862	10:27	03:22	17.7	13.4
6/07/2013	Cuba	After Pie Town	263.3	1240	12:24	03:46	21.2	16.3
7/07/2013	After Pie Town	Just before alte	148.1	1108	9:22	04:10	15.8	10.9
8/07/2013	Just before alte	Silver City	196.2	1971	12:46	03:13	15.4	12.3
9/07/2013	Silver City	Antelope Wells	201	570	9:45	02:03	20.6	17

TC: Will we see you again on the Tour Divide or are you going after other challenges?

Hell no. It was just too hard. Not just the race but the demands of training. However I am thinking about the Transcontinental race. It's got to be easier.

2013 Result: 58th Place - 25:07:58

A Spot of Defiance

Hugh Harvey

I could write about riding through amazing scenery or meeting brilliant people but instead have written about some of my emotions. I have done this perhaps because it isn't that easy to fit back into the big city again with the people, concrete, and constant dulling noise. It is only a soft melancholia but it replaces the joy of being and feeling and experiencing what I did out

there. The people in the cities are less interested and probably for very good reason. To them, at best I am a small opportunity and nothing more. They see a million others just like me ambling through their space. Out in the wilds of Wyoming and Colorado, the people were truly interested. Those you interact with in the supermarkets, outside restaurants, or wherever they have caught you, genuinely want to engage and learn. You are something a bit left of centre and not usual to their world. But not in a threatening cheesy moving kind of way.

Firstly, I want to say sorry to all of the Spot watchers out there for my frustrating ride. With hindsight, having been an avid Spot watcher in the past, I can see where you make the mistake of filling in the blanks, I now learn, usually very incorrectly. I did have an action packed ride where things did indeed go wrong and my Spot either didn't move or went backwards. In the worst instance, 20 miles back out into the Basin. There were other times however where my Spot didn't move for all of the right reasons.

My experiences along the entire route have given me cause to believe that the American people are some of the most generous, open and friendly people on the planet and in race terms it cost me dearly.

My 4th of July, American Independence day, shall always be remembered. Robin and I started the day just short of the infamous detour down Bursom Rd, FR 159. I was a broken man at this stage and Robin left me well behind very early in the day. I had to struggle on without enough food and water and not really knowing where I was without the comfort of my GPS's thin blue line to follow. Sometime in the early afternoon, I was lucky enough to have a car stop and offer me a couple of muesli bars and an assurance that I was actually on the correct road. Whoever you were, thank you again, so very much.

After bouncing along the top of the divide on a punishing dirt road in really threatening weather for the day, as I arrived in the historic mining town of Mogollan, the heavens opened properly and let forth sweeping monsoon rains complete with angry thunder and lightning. Rejoining the highway at Glenwood, with it still belting down rain, I at least was able to refuel a bit at the gas station with more chocolate, chips and cherry pie washed down with copious amounts of root beer. There were some very drunk people in that gas station paying for fuel for the long drive home.

Although it was late afternoon, I knew I had had a bad day and was intent on grabbing a proper hot meal in Silver City and making a push for Antelope Wells that evening. My Spot watchers know that isn't what happened. Instead, what they saw was my Spot stopping several times along the highway before finally setting up camp in the tiny town of Cliff for the night much earlier than had become my custom. Why on earth would you stop there? The answer of course is Deb Nordquist.

I had been cycling along in the terrible storm, looking like a drowned rat when a very concerned motorist stopped and after introducing herself as Deb, attempted to convince me that I was a fool in terrible danger, my rear red blinking light wasn't bright enough, on July 4 all the motorists were going to be driving intoxicated, they wouldn't see me because my coat was too dark, the gates of hell were about to open up, and…

Well anyway, I did manage to convince her that I was in a little bit of a bicycle race and it was important that I do continue on rather than accepting her lift back to the little town of Pleasanton where she was offering me a room for the night. As always seemed to be the case, we chatted some more about the race and the logistics of it all and the fact that one of the hardest parts of the whole Tour Divide was living on gas station crap for three weeks.

Deb left me with a rain jacket of vastly inferior quality to that which I was already wearing, but she felt much better about me having it because it was luminous yellow in lieu of my navy blue coat that apparently rendered me invisible to all but the keenest eye in the pretty ordinary weather I was riding through. I was far more concerned about the thunder and lightning which I don't believe cares what colour my coat may be.

About 15 miles down the road, a car horn emanating from a familiar looking vehicle draws my attention and out jumps the same manic full-of-life Deb. Totally unsolicited or expected, she had raced back to her place and put together the most amazing vegetarian organic pasta dish including the best cherry tomatoes from her own green house and a bottle of some craft Porter style ale. Now, I am not usually one to drink at all, and I will put my hand up as the Australian that turned down free beer at Como Depot and copped a ribbing for it, but it was just too difficult to refuse the hospitality that was being offered. It was like the celebratory meal you have after completing the ride.

I wasn't even able to pay Deb any money as I had used every last red cent in Pie Town so many hours ago and only had plastic on me. So we sat there in Cliff, I was so shattered at this stage, I cannot even really recall what we talked about but I am pretty sure I wasn't the one doing most of the talking. I do know that by the time everything was packed up, it was pretty close to dark and I hadn't been cycling for well over an hour and all of my body was saying "enough for the day already."

So I set up my bivy, bunkered down and got the reasonable night's sleep that allowed me to enjoy the following day's fantastic ride all the way into Antelope Wells.

I wish I had a Go Pro camera just to show everyone that followed me how happy I was over those last few miles. Every turn of the pedals over the preceding 4,500 odd kilometres was worth it for those few precious minutes of absolute joy. I did have my arms raised, punching the air. I yelled "Yipyah" at the top of my lungs from quite a long way out. Out of necessity, you do keep a lid on it until you know for certain that the finish line is yours, but I did let go of a fair few emotions in that final run in.

It was very interesting in terms of the big picture evolution of the psyche stuff. The first couple of days were a blur and for me just happened. I suspect the climbing and roads and everything in Canada makes it the most difficult cycling in the entire race. All of the planning and thinking pre-race is still clear in your mind and you can push through. You still have visions of greatness and all of the motivational material you started with about just riding your bike and staying strong.

When things get difficult it is still possible to think you are on this massive journey and it isn't supposed to be easy. For me, Canada was the most awe inspiring ruggedly beautiful part of the trip with big snow capped mountains.

A couple of days after Canada were really super hard mentally. You have depleted any residual glycogen stores and your body is eating itself. You have not yet adjusted to a new sleeping pattern and the finish is so far in the future that it isn't really possible to imagine it. The only way to survive is to ride from one resupply point to the next. Perhaps I made some mistakes here. I didn't have the course knowledge and didn't know how hard I could push myself. I probably went heavily introspective there for a bit, and a casual observer may have thought that I dug too deep too early.

Even then I was worrying about wasting 45 minutes waiting in a restaurant for proper food when we could have grabbed three footlongs from Subway and kept riding; worried that we pulled up stumps too early or missed out on an hour's sunlight by sleeping in until 5:00 a.m. in the morning. You do make the conscious effort to look up and around and admire where you are riding. Part of the positivity was being amazed and thankful for where you were. That certainly helped, but nowhere near as much as the food did. You have to eat constantly and it doesn't matter what it is you eat so long as the fuel is going in. The body stops very quickly if you stop fuelling it.

I don't know which day it was but I remember with absolute clarity the moment things started to improve from a macro level. Coming down off Fleecer Ridge after having walked the last quarter mile up that beast, and then having to walk down it because it was just stupidly steep. The weather was really harsh. We had a bad hail storm briefly with big chunks of ice falling from the sky and also some snow, but when I jumped back on the bike, for the first time in the race I had a small flash of "I am going to finish this thing!" It was not a moment of determination; it was a joyful celebration kind of thing. The unconscious smile breaking out on the face kind of moment. You just realise you have done some really hard stuff and you are making some serious progress. Now please understand, coming off Fleecer this was only a fleeting flash of whatever that super positive emotion/feeling was.

At least a couple of times a day, things were really dark and you think very much about quitting. One's mind went so sour that you only want to keep going so that you can reach the next town where you are going to scratch. Again, food was the only answer. The down moments stay with you for as long as you are pushing yourself too hard. I reckon it was only on the last day that I didn't have those really dark moments.

What should have been the toughest day was probably psychologically one of the easiest. I need to run through some of the events that were difficult to explain.

I had been riding with Walter for the first eight or nine days and he met with some misfortune roughly 20 miles short of Rawlins. We had been pushing into a really strong headwind all the way through the Basin and finally reached Mineral Road X which was paved. For the first time that day were streaking along downhill with the wind at a pretty reasonable clip making a good push for Rawlins. It was mid afternoon and we were really looking forward to a big feed in a proper town for the first time in a couple of days, probably thinking that we could push on well past Rawlins later that night. I was maybe 40 or 50 metres behind Walter when he was clipped by the mirror of a pickup truck. And that was the end of the days riding.

After Walter was hit, I didn't know if I was going to continue or not. After visiting Walter in hospital I paid way too much money for a crappy hotel room in a crappy town I never want to visit again. The first half of my race was over and it had been tough on me physically and emotionally but, other than my mate being cleaned up, super tough in a way that really appeals and excites me.

So the next morning after visiting Walter again and making sure he was being looked after properly, I had to cycle back into the basin for 20 miles to the scene of a pretty traumatic event in my race. My progress over those 20 miles was made even more difficult by a really strong headwind and then I had no frigging idea how far out I had to go. There were no trees and no real reference points to find out where the hell you were, and quite frankly it wasn't a priority the day before. One sage bush looks exactly like the next. I remembered the Sheriff saying it was 20 miles back to Rawlins so I cycled back that far and then gave it another mile for luck. All of this was done against a backdrop of knowing that I was losing time and places as I cycled backwards against the flow of other riders which of itself was heartbreaking.

Things improved markedly as soon as I left Rawlins. Bizarrely it was good just to be back on the bicycle and making forward progress. The landscape improved dramatically. I cannot provide words appropriate for the Basin—it is a barren, desolate hell. You cheer when you see the first tree and then pretty quickly full grown Aspen forests appear. Probably the old fashioned prettiest part of the ride. No more wind, and the further I got from Rawlins the better I was feeling.

For the first time I was cycling on my own and I really enjoyed that far more than cycling with others. It did change the way I managed my race and although I was hoping to make it to Brush Mountain Lodge that night, I got a bit cold during one of the descents and I found the best camping spot about nine miles short. It was all but dark when I stopped. I'd had a big day and did not want to risk cycling past Brush Mountain Lodge which I know is a mistake others have made. I certainly found I slept much better bivying than I ever did in any hotel room.

There was a mix of emotions for the remainder of the ride. I felt really bad when I had days that weren't long enough or I was aware of not having pushed hard enough. Every hour you drop is an hour that you cannot get back. It is gone and there were some days where those hours really added up. That weighed heavily on me and I was acutely aware of them. It was great to catch Robin again between the top of Boreas Pass and the start of the Gold Dust Trail. I loved the top of Boreas as I am a real train buff and the historical depot meant a lot to me.

I didn't really ride with Robin after that as we had different paces. We did catch up at every resupply point and did all we could to look after each other. The camaraderie of shared experience was far more important than any under lying competitive aspects. I'm sure Robin always thought he was going to finish first but I was pretty happy with that as with all of the amazing and good people I met out there. Robin was one of the best.

I was at the end of my super hard race and being very reflective. One of the final divide crossings is a great spot to stop and see the importance of the Tour Divide and all that it means. Not just the divide of the nation's watersheds but also everything that created the nation. What the divide had meant to the settlers, the railroads, the miners, the loggers and those that live there now; the receding and evolving natural environments and the harsh and rugged splendour, the beauty and the terror that I had experienced over the three weeks.

Right now, I would love to do it again. I would love to do it next year but I really owe Michelle a lot as it is. It is a very selfish thing to do. The training alone is a big time commitment given that I have a full time job, and I know a lot of people worried about my welfare when I was out there.

I did better than to just be a finisher and I was never out there to beat people in the first place. You learn so much doing the race for the first time. The best possible preparation must be to have the word "veteran" next to your name. I find myself obsessing far more about the race now than I did before hand. I am stuck on the things I did wrong and things I could do better; the extreme good fortune I enjoyed and maybe some of the bad luck. The event, course and knowledge of self that I have now mean that I am constantly wondering "what if?"

I constantly had stuff go through my mind: the entire route, good thoughts, bad thoughts, and pure evil genius thoughts. When the mind turns sour, I contend that there is nothing better than being able to sing along at top voice with no one else around to lift you from the dark matters that can inhabit the mind. Fortunately with all the different voices riding shotgun inside my head, I never suffered boredom and at no stage did I find myself wishing that I had my old MP3 player.

Then you finish, is that all there is? I have read many people talking about the fact there is nothing at Antelope Wells and it is all a bit anti-climactic. For me it is the perfect way to finish and other than perhaps having someone very special there to meet me, I cannot think of a more appropriate way to complete the adventure. In many ways, the entire race is the ultimate in selfish endeavours. The finish should really be about self as well.

I hope you understand how desperately proud I am of what I achieved out there and just getting to the starting line was a big part of that. If anything I have proven to myself that it is okay to start something big.

2013 Result: 23rd Place - 21:12:38

Hugh is the naughty school boy who turned up for the exam without having done the study before hand.

Course knowledge? Wouldn't have thought so.

Resupply strategy? Make it up as you go.

Race experience? Never been in a race before in my life.

An Interview with Ian MacNab

TC: Tell us a little about yourself

I'm a 57 year old, from West
Yorkshire in the UK. I have been
involved in competitive sport and
outdoor pursuits from the age of 8.
Professionally I have been teaching
Sport Science, and instructing outdoor
activities. Cycling has always been a
recreational passion. Just prior to the
Tour Divide 2013 I had spent 5 years
living and working in Antarctica. I had
no opportunities to pedal other than in
the gym on station. Our summer
temperatures ranged from 0 to -30°C
and in the winter -10 to -50°C. So
when I returned to the UK I was keen
to challenge myself with something
involving cycling, preferably
somewhere nice and warm.

TC: How did you first hear about the Tour Divide and what made you want to race?

I was a blue dot-junkie following Mike Hall's round-the-world cycle race in
2012 and read in one of his blogs about the "Tour Divide". I had never heard
of it before but this sounded like a great challenge that would fit into available
holiday time.

TC: What experience did you have with long distance racing before the Tour Divide?

I have done several multi-day adventure races, the longest being 7 days with little to no sleep. The Tour Divide was my first multiday bikepacking event.

TC: How did you train for the race?

In the months leading up to the Tour Divide I did a few audax/randonneur road events here in the UK, mostly 200 – 400 km. Through the winter months I also rode out and back to many mountain bike navigation races, often coming home late at night both tired and hungry. I ate lots of food and went to Banff a bit overweight. Did I mention I like pies?

TC: Tell us a bit about your rig and gear

My setup was fairly lightweight, comfortable, and proved to be very reliable.

Bike … 29er rigid with internal geared hub. Details … Van Nicholas Redwood titanium, built up from scratch by myself including wheels. Rigid 26" carbon forks. Wheels: ZTR crest rims; DT Revolution spokes; tyres WTB Nanoraptor tubeless; front hub SP dynamo; rear hub Rohloff. Brakes Avid BB7 cable.

Contact points … Flite saddle, straight bars with foam grips extra tape wrap, ergo bar ends, XT pedals.

Navigation/lights … Dynamo hub powering Exposure front light and charging Garmin Edge 705. Powerful Petzl Myo XP head torch on helmet. Two el cheapo cycle computers, one of which failed mid-route. Rear blinky LED. Carried cue notes and profiles only.

Luggage … Revelate bags: front Sling with 8L dry bag containing camp kit; 2x Mountain feed bags; Gas tank; rear seat pack Pika. On the frame 2 large drink bottles.

Camping… fairly lightweight setup: Gore-Tex bivy bag; Neoair Thermarest; down bag; silk liner, plastic groundsheet.

Hydration … packable rucksack used with 2 litre bladder when needed. Extra 2 litre bladder attached to tri bars. Two bottles on bike.

Note … I had too many clothes. Stuff I wouldn't take again: tri bars (too low for comfort); synthetic duvet jacket and long sleeved cycle jersey (probably swap for a fleece top); spare cycle shorts.

Stuff I would take next time … 4 litre bladder carried in a backpack.

TC: Tell us about some of the highlights of your ride

Seeing a cougar on the second night, fortunately it was chasing something smaller than me.

Although I'm a slow rider I did some very long days and so was privileged at times to ride with faster riders who had a lot more sleep than I did. Those days spent with other racers, sharing stories, and picking up the pace together was a personal highlight for me.

Alone above 10,000ft in Colorado amidst thunder, hail, and lightning storms.

Iced coffee and chocolate milk.

TC: How did you handle the nutrition and hydration challenges on the ride?

Good until I hit the heat in Colorado … I suffered with mild heat stroke, and dehydration. I was expecting more water sources—Rookie error. After that I tried to avoid the hottest parts of the day by having extended lunch stops.

TC: Did you have any major mechanical problems during the race and, if you did, how did you deal with them?

Zero mechanicals, zero punctures. I bought a new chain in Steamboat and had a top up of sealant, but this was only an excuse to eat more and sit out the hottest part of the day.

TC: All riders eventually hit a rock bottom, a new low during their race. Could you tell us about your darkest hour during the race?

The last four days were dark for me, I wasn't eating well. I was ill, partly with heat exhaustion but also, stupidly, had given myself food poisoning by eating a 2-day old breakfast that I had "saved". I wanted to quit, wasn't racing anymore—just surviving. I lost over 12kg bodyweight by the end.

TC: What advice would you give to future Tour Dividers

This is also advice to myself for a repeat attempt as well as other racers …

- Sort out and practice extra water (and food) carrying setup
- If you want to save weight take only what's needed NOT what you want

TC: Will we see you again on the Tour Divide or are you going after other challenges?

I swore when I finished "never again". However … several weeks have now passed … I've eaten lots of pies … bodyweight back to normal … maybe 2015?

2013 Result: 49th Place - 24:05:11

A rookie in 2013 (finished in 24 days placing 49th), Ian's first experience of bikepacking has left him wanting more. He would like to do the Tour Divide again with the benefit of hindsight, wisdom, and improved route knowledge. He has now completely forgotten the pain and suffering endured on the miles of wash boarded gravel roads.

e-mail   ianmacnab@imap.cc

Man versus Machine

J.D. Pauls

In 2012 I came to the Tour Divide ill prepared. It chewed me up and spat me out. I was not physically prepared, mentally prepared, some of my gear choices were terrible, and I made a lot of mistakes during the ride. The weather turned bad, the snowy passes and the mud in the north were relentless and I was cold, tired and miserable as I navigated only a handful of miles every day. I pulled the plug in Butte succumbing to pain in my knees and a broken ego. It seemed like a hard decision at the time, but in hindsight it was actually extremely wise since I had so much to learn. I was averaging 75 miles a day and that was not going to cut it. I left the route with a promise to myself that I was going to take what I learned, train harder, plan smarter, and come back in 2013 to finish what I had started. Nothing was going to stop me.

Fast forward to June 2013. I was in Banff at the YMCA with a smile on my face. I wasn't pacing nervously like I did in 2012, I wasn't hiding in my room, but rather I was confident, happy and ready to roll.

I was certain I was in great physical shape, I was mentally prepared and I was quite happy with my gear choices this year. Funny thing though, the Tour Divide has a way of searching out your fears and weakness and poking at it, stomping on it and testing you for 2,700+ miles. For all my strengths this year my only concern was whether my bike would hold up. I did predict this may be the year of mechanical problems, but I hoped for the best and tried not to think about it.

J.D. vs. Divide Round 1: Day 1- Shifter cable, and Seat Post

After only about 40 miles my shifter cable came loose. I had it in my easiest gear climbing up the wide dirt road just past the Heli-pad. When I got to the top, nothing. It wouldn't shift. I had some issues installing my derailleur when I assembled the bike in Banff but I thought it would be fine. I ended up taking all the slack out of the back of the line but this only left me with less than half of the cassette in use. At least I was still riding. My amateur wrenching skills cost me well over an hour that first day, and a red face as rider after rider passed by.

At the last minute in Banff, I had switched out my seat post for a carbon post. I should have used a spray to add some friction. Every ten miles I had to stop to re -adjust the height. I had a quick release clamp on it and I couldn't keep it tight. The carbon kept slipping. In a moment of weakness and frustration I adjusted the tension and then tried to tighten the clamp with my hand but couldn't close it, so I did what every tired and frustrated rider would do: I stepped on it. I snapped the lever. I never once said I was the brightest racer. I was able to hammer the nub end of it closed with a rock and control the tension with my 'Leatherman A' wrench. As a side note that Leatherman was used every day. One of the best pieces of equipment I had. I solved a lot of problems with that awesome little thing.

The only other issues I had before rolling into Whitefish on Day 3 was a missing screw from a shoe clip which meant my shoe wouldn't come out of my pedal, a broken chain and some minor damage on the bike due to a downhill crash. I remember sitting on the patio at Glacier Cycle and being frustrated that I was behind a half day already due to bike issues but, unlike 2012, I was happy. Really, really happy. The Tour Divide was putting up a fight but I knew I was still in control.

J.D. vs. Divide Round 2: Steamboat Springs

A beautiful day. I had a great morning riding into Steamboat. I had spent the night at Brush Mountain Lodge after a battle through the Basin. It was a great place to recover. I was hoping to get into Orange Peel Cycle quickly, get my preventative maintenance, and be on my way. What I didn't factor in was that it was a Saturday at a very busy bike shop. They did their best to get the Tour Divide riders in ahead of everyone else, but I was the third rider in.

For six hours I anxiously waited to get a new rear tyre, a chain, and brake repairs amongst other things. When all was done, the shop was closing and my bike was handed over without a test ride. Ten miles out of town and the phantom shifting began. I tried to come up with a fix but I could not, so back to Steamboat I had to go. The original bike shop was closed. It was 6:45 p.m. on a Saturday night and I was already mad that I would have to wait in town and be at the bike shop when it opened at 10 a.m. on Sunday morning. I found a couple of people on bikes and asked them if they knew of a mechanic in town and they did me one better. They directed me to a shop that was open till 7 p.m.! I rolled in as they were closing and they gladly stayed late and went to work replacing the cassette and the front chain ring. Incredible really. They had me on my way at about 8:30 p.m. and I was able to salvage the wasted day with a few more hours of riding. Weird that after a painfully frustrating day, it ended with me feeling like the luckiest rider in the race.

J.D. vs. Divide Round 3: New Mexico—the Knockout Round

I had my share of annoying mechanical problems, all of which I felt able to deal with somehow even if they weren't always the best solution. The Tour Divide was doing a good job of trying to stop me this year, but I kept winning. It saved the best for last.

I was climbing a paved road somewhere between El Rito and Cuba when I first noticed a creaking noise. I would stop climbing, inspect the saddle and carry on. I thought maybe the saddle itself was failing or maybe my saddle bag clips were rubbing. It was driving me nuts as I couldn't figure it out.

This went on for about a day until I reached Grants. It was a 4 a.m. start and I had left Grants on my way to Pie Town when I noticed my seat post was twisting. I thought the clamp was loose again so I stopped to grab my wrench and check the clamp. I grabbed the saddle, pulled up and the whole thing came right out. The clamp was tight but the frame it was clamped to was no longer attached to my bike. I couldn't believe it.

I dropped it in place and continued on. My weight held it in place, but I had to ride out of the saddle for several miles until I reached Pie Town. As I sat on the porch of the Pie-o-neer, with my head over my knees, I went over a list of my options:

1. Hitch a ride to a lateral bike shop off route ;
2. Find a welder in town;
3. Quit; or,

4. Duct tape and crazy glue it in place and hope for the best and try to get to Silver City which was still over 175 miles away through a barren landscape.

I chose the last option.

I had worked way too hard for two years to get here. Nice try Tour Divide. I did find a man wearing a welder's mask in town, much to my excitement, but he could not weld aluminum so I continued on. Every bumpy road my stress grew and so did the hairline crack in the top tube. I had to walk several climbs since I could feel the flex and hear the frame grinding in pain when the grade steepened. The flats were okay as I could balance the seat in place and keep more weight on the pedals.

I rolled in to Silver City with Hamish McKee. It was great to have someone to finish this with. I knew now I would finish. Even if my bike failed now I could always get back to Silver City to have it repaired. As I got closer to Antelope Wells, it felt like a Christmas countdown as we watched the miles tick down, I remember discussing with Hamish how long it would take to finish on foot if I had to. When we got to the marathon distance of 42 km I thought "I've got this now, I can run a marathon if I have to—even in crazy heat and bike shoes". Then mile one.

My frame is unrideable now. It has since been replaced but I keep the old one as my trophy.

2013 Result: 57th Place - 25:07:56

Once I Was A Divide Racer

James Olsen

At the start of this year I set out to do something that I really thought was beyond me, but I went ahead anyway. It felt good to be quietly preparing for the task, realistic in my aims or not. There would probably be a get-out clause later down the line, there usually was. I wasn't good at committing to things. I liked to have aims that gave me a focus that suited me even if I didn't arrive. The journey, not the destination; an idea often taken to a fault. This time my aim gave me a reason to ride at all times of the day and night; stay out overnight in winter; devote the weekend to just riding and recovering; to arrive at work flat-out tired. At the time I just needed to do it and I wasn't sure if the destination was as important. I read McCoy's Great Divide book with casual interest and daydreamed.

Once I decided that many of my rides in previous years had been worthy trials for a bigger journey, Tour Divide daydreams solidified into something I truly wanted. This aim felt different, concrete. I felt ready to openly talk about it among a small group of friends, I had to 'call it' then so that there couldn't be any going back on my word.

I could start out, but circumstances along the Tour Divide would never be within my control and I thought about that often. Uncertainty is part of true adventure so I prepared for failure while I trained to finish. I simply wanted to try my best. But try is a small word that cannot express how this goal began to move me and how it shaped six months of my life. Maybe it's true that 'there is no try'.

I sent a letter of intent and mentally I was already in Banff, right there and then. I'd entered the Tour Divide. During the time between sending that email and lining up at 8 a.m. one morning in June, the Tour Divide was never far from my mind. My training wall-planner filled out and offered confidence to balance the fatigue. When I was fit and uninjured in May I booked a flight to Canada with a return from El Paso, and admitted to myself that I was as ready as I'd ever be; ready enough.

Once I felt the excitement of the start line dissolve into solitude, I settled into a ride that had almost no end. I didn't think of the route in terms of progress each day but simply rode on, going as far as I could. Each day was just that day, there was no tomorrow in mind. Thinking of the next day and the days after that was too much. The route was too big. It had to be reduced to a rhythm and the here-and-now. Each bivouac was something to look forward to, even in the rain. My sleeping bag was a respite and a comfort blanket and my home. I told myself every day that I'd find a perfect bivy spot that night but I never got it, I simply slept close to where fatigue got the better of me or where I found some element of shelter. A tub of ice cream insulated in my down gillet, or a foot-long sandwich, carried into the hills to my eventual bivy spot was an occasional luxury, no privileged lifestyle could match the value of my possessions then.

Other nights, dinner was the remnants of gas-station provisions, stolen from the next morning and gone too soon. Sleep was deeper than a view into the night sky that I enjoyed for only seconds before my body snatched a few hours rest from the mind that drove it on so much further than before.

Once I took a long wrong turn and silently cursed my race planning. A set of maps, a compass, cue notes and a computer, no phone or GPS; my choice and no-one else's and I was racing fairly; my way against others racing theirs. Ethics and ideals that suited me. Perhaps some cover-up for a lack of preparation compared to others.

My wing-it approach to life this time manifesting itself as accepting the route as it was to be; riding on-sight; just not interested in planning it to the nth degree. Race and adventure in balance. Other times, the cues and computer approach kept me focused and forced me not to drift far into my own world. Cue sheets fed me directions without the need to see elevation profiles and other useful information on the ACA maps. The trail then produced surprises that lifted me as often as they almost crushed me. After this turn, the realisation that it wasn't going to be the right way after all, hit once I'd spent too long kidding myself, enjoying the fast and flowing trail. I rode back, up, steeply, the burning effort of frustration in my legs. Failing to check some route information well had caught me out. Caught by a rider behind. Lessons learnt then of what the race meant that would come to mind often.

Once I rode into the hundred-mile wilderness with a familiar empty feeling, precious few provisions but not alone. I realised that as content as a rider with a hobo-life can be, shared experience with good company is worth at least as much as a solo traveller's insight into their soul..

I felt fear among the expanses for the first time and the loss of my confidence as energy ran low and I understood the ability of the mind to regain control over the fading physical self when there's nothing left inside. I walked with my bike and for a while the journey changed. Forced detachment from the vehicle that had brought me to this point, a

separation. A growing uncertainty for my position as well as confirmation that the Tour Divide is so much more than racing. Rankings were inconsequential to my experience in the then-and-there, and I wondered if I might have begun to understand Zen or something when I could stop thinking for a while and move onwards and just be.

Once I rode late towards the dawn on desert roads to avoid the heat of New Mexico days. It wasn't the first or last time I'd ride late. I was harassed by a pack of dogs in the night and saw movement and teeth and heard growls and barking only when they'd surrounded me. My eyes struggled during the small hours, mixed messages from the headlight's pool. Marks on the road turned into a linear kaleidoscope of light and dark as I dipped into a new mental place, moving between interest and detachment, on towards the unconsciousness of sleep. Shimmering layers of shade and pattern created by outlines of great cliffs in the dark. Waking, swerving on the road again after a moment's dream-state took me elsewhere—talking with friends back home. I stopped to look at a few clouds lit up by the sunrise after sleeping for an hour or two in the sand at the side of an empty road.

Most days I paused in awe of huge skies and the expanse around me and forgot that I was a meant to be racing. I defaulted to touring mentality with disabling ease. Settling on a fast-tourer-expedition approach where I moved fast, kept going and didn't stop too often and didn't forget to look around occasionally worked. Appreciation had to be through motion not reflection. Finding a number of hours of real non-stop flow through the Basin or later in tree-lined wilderness trails was wonderful but predictable discomforts made it a rare experience.

Many times I looked for a rider behind me in the distance or for tyre tracks in front, wondering where the other racers around me were, suspecting close by, never knowing for sure. I couldn't claim detachment from the ego-driven appeal of a top ten finish so I judged myself against others. My pre-race expectations had shifted in the early days and were re-evaluated daily, based on where I thought I was on an imaginary leader-board that had only a couple of confirmations during the race.

I tried to figure out who'd made the tracks in front of me. How tired are they? He took a fast line there. They're weaving here and I'm not. Yet I never caught up. Tracks of other cyclists became racers who had passed me as I slept. Three of us rode closer than I realised for much of the route. There was only the threat of being caught or chasing the same rider again in my race. Gaps made couldn't be held when the road was long and riders well matched. The more I pushed on and coped the harder I wanted to push, but still the temptation of a cosy bivy and a need for sleep beat me too often, too easily.

More than once I was moved to tears as extended solitary experience and exposure to the wild brought emotions to the fore. It was an outlet for something inside that made me able to accept this lifestyle without concern. There were simple happy-tears from singing songs along the trail and enjoying a life with simpler aims, a welling-up when thinking of loved ones that I couldn't speak to until I emerged from my tunnel at Antelope Wells. There was excitement of the circumstance, yet it felt natural, normal, on-going. There was nothing to do but 'do', as long as I was physically able to do so.

Once at the border of Mexico I realised my batteries were empty, a body deep in energy-debt with little more than momentum carrying me over the last few days. I was there—finished physically and mentally. I felt elated but I missed everyone at home and longed to call them. I read a message delivered by the Payne brothers—family well-wishes including a picture of my niece in a home-styled blue dot romper suit and I smiled widely with cry-eyes. I was silenced and brought to the verge of real tears when someone then asked about my family. I forget the question but remember the response. Only after returning home did I realise the extent of how my Tour Divide had become my family's Tour also, as the blue dots became more than markers. This time my pursuit of solitude by bike had become something that brought us closer together and their pride in my achievement meant more than the finish itself.

I sat in a restaurant but I was elsewhere. A month or two later the physical after-effects were fading but memories in great detail and range came and went, an intermittent slideshow in my mind set to random shuffle. Flashes of landscape and related emotions that I hold onto when I can. Now I struggle to say with any clarity where the race took me. Somewhere homely that I feel but don't see, a fuzzy dream-memory, a place that I miss and will find again elsewhere. Beyond the sense of place and being, the mixed feelings about a dream realised in such intense circumstances and a retrospective wonder at what happened this June. There was a shift in my perspective of life's challenges and I hope it stays with me. I look back to before the race and how I thought I'd feel about arriving at that border post and I smile.

Once, I was a Divide Racer.

2013 Result: 4th Place - 17:05:29

James Olsen, originally from Stroud, UK. 38 years old, professional bike-geek based in the Chiltern hills north of London.

Patience and Tenacity

Jean Louis Doridot

I come from France and learned of the Tour Divide race from Nicolas Senie, who completed the race in 2010 in 25 days. For two years I trained with Philippe Androuet, a friend who shares the same taste for adventure. Being at the Grand Depart on 14 June was a huge victory for us. Having arranged with our company to have five weeks off, trained, saved enough money, spending a lot of time on blogs, travelled with our bikes and gear from  France to Canada, we did not know at this time if the biggest challenge was behind or in front of us. Nothing was to be easy. But thanks to our deep motivation, we had transformed problems into challenges.

Seven days after Grand Depart, Philippe had to quit at Polaris Montana because of tendon problems with each leg. It was a hard moment for both him and me. He had pushed his physical and mental limits but could not ride anymore. In seven days we had ridden almost 1,200 kilometres (745 miles) together. It was already a good performance, but as any Cordillera reader knows, the goal is to reach Antelope Wells. And the way to reach the Mexican boundary is long and difficult.

Let me just focus on my lasts days to share what kind of adventure riders can meet, just to highlight Tour Divide moments.

I was at about 500 kilometres (310 miles) from Antelope Wells. I started to ride early in the morning from Pie Town with Ron and Greg. We had slept in a rider's refuge. This house is opened to any rider where you can find the kind of unexpected comfort riders love to meet during Tour Divide. It really exists!

That day, the temperature was already high and the sky perfectly blue. I was feeling tired since the previous days had been long and difficult, but I kept on going and following Ron as far as I could. Greg was behind us.

Ron and I decided to stop at a deep water spring, close to a windmill. I did not need water at that time but having some rests was a good idea. Once ready to re-start, we saw a rider behind us. We thought it was Greg but finally we saw Sara coming toward us! It was very amazing to see her there. The last time I saw her was at the beginning of Colorado, seven days before, at Brush Mountain Lodge—another lovely place to stop. She does not ride fast, but she never stops. For instance, the night before she arrived at Pie Town at 1 a.m.!

We rode together and the sky quickly turned dark grey. Within ten minutes we were in the middle of a thunder storm. The track became unrideable, as the mud was getting sticky. We pushed our bikes off-track, with strong winds and thunder all around us. Our situation was not good: services were far away, I was

low on food, and the reroute in front of us was not covered by the map. Sara said to me: "Don't stop here! Better times are in front of us!"

She was right. Two keys to keep in mind for Tour Divide: patience and tenacity.

One hour after the beginning of the storm, we reached another track which was rideable, and we started the reroute. It was very tough, with many uphills. I focused on the food I was still carrying. One sandwich in the front bag, peanuts in the frame bag, and I was hoping for more! Two Snickers Bars in the top bag... Ron and I stopped at a desert fire station. No one could offer food or water.

So we continued climbing. At 7 p.m. we finally started downhill. I had lost a bottle of water. Ron was ahead from me. The descent was very technical and darkness was coming. Sometimes I lost my way as the river came onto the track. I was alone on my own at this time. I reached Mogollon ghost town. Pavement at last!

I did not see Ron's bicycle. The road was so steep uphill that I had to push my bike. I switched off my light in order to save the battery. I was not feeling safe at all. I could not explain why. I was very tired, and had no place to sleep. I watched backwards and saw a light—probably Sara. In fact it was Ron who had stopped at Mogollon. We continued to push our bikes with the lights off. Then Ron stopped and switched on his light: a rattle snake was one meter in front of us. God! One meter more and we would have walked on it. I could not imagine if I had been alone, and was bitten by this snake, in the night, far from any service. At that moment I felt really lucky, and said to myself that Tour Divide was an adventure in which chance is a huge factor.

After that, we both switched our lights ON and reached Glenwood by avoiding big spiders on roads…

We slept at a gas station. Exhausted by all this adventure! Antelope Wells was still 300 kilometres (186 miles) in front of us.

Ron had very few hours of sleep and started riding at 4:30 a.m. He wanted to finish that day. Once he left, I only saw his red lights far down the road. I was too tired to get up and ride. Finally I started this new day at 6:30 a.m. and reached Silver City alone at 12:30 p.m. I continued and rode across Chihuahuan desert up to Separ. There, I saw Ron's bicycle in the firework shop close to Interstate 10!

We rode together up to Antelope Wells, which was the best moment of this Tour Divide, like a nice gift. We arrived at the border, on Sunday 7th July at 00:45 a.m., finishing in 22 days 16h and 45 minutes, in 36th and 37th positions. Four hours later Sara reached Antelope Wells confirming her huge endurance skills. Greg finished the day after.

Jean-Louis Doridot   33 years
        Rookie Lille FRANCE

jldoridot@yahoo.fr

2013 Result – 36th Place 22:16:43 with Ron Babington.

I am a test engineer for Oxylane, a French sport and leisure company. I spend my free time between Lille and Paris, where Clara and my family live. The big issue now is to find another adventure after Tour Divide!

Confusion in Pie Town

Jeff Mullen

It was July 5th (day 22 of the Tour Divide) and I was heading to Pie Town, with less than 400 miles to go to the finish at Antelope Wells. The Tour Divide had been all that I had hoped it would be, but I was ready to be done. I had held up well mentally—never once thinking of quitting—but the long miles of pavement in New Mexico (partially due to the required fire related detour between Abiquiu and Cuba) and the constant threat of oppressive heat were starting to get old. But mainly I was looking forward to seeing my wife and the experience of getting to the finish of such an amazing event.

I was also holding up well physically, although I had suffered earlier in the race. Problems included excruciating knee pain that would occur in the middle of the night. Fortunately my knees never bothered me on the bike and the night pains eventually went away.

The biggest physical problem that I faced early on was saddle sores. I only did one multi day training ride (220 miles over three days including a 102 mile day) and this ride confirmed that my current saddle wasn't going to cut it. So I got my butt measured and three weeks before the start of the race and I bought a new saddle. I started developing saddle sores early on—due to not being used to the new saddle and, aided by the weight I was carrying on my back, there were a few days where it was extremely difficult to find a comfortable riding position. Eventually calluses developed and the pain went away.

By Day 22 these physical problems (mainly attributed to not enough training hours on the bike) were mostly behind me and I was feeling ready to push to the finish. I had started this day camped by the side of the road 50 miles north of the towns of Milan and Grants. Six miles after Grants—just before crossing I40—there is a gas station which is the last chance to grab food/drink before the 65 mile stretch to Pie Town. There I unexpectedly reconnected with Eric F and Scott T.

I had originally met Scott in the airport at Calgary. We both arrived late in the evening and slept in the airport. I had run into him several times on the trail but not since Montana. Scott had been behind me but was finishing impressively strong on his single speed. I also met Eric early on as we had biked from Cochrane, Alberta to Banff together before the race. Both of us were avoiding the cost of the shuttle from the Calgary airport to Banff and it was also a good opportunity to make sure the bike and gear were working well. I had never expected to see Eric on the trail, but he experienced a few bike problems in Wyoming so surprisingly I ran into him on the long/hard stretch between Union Pass and Pinedale, Wyoming. I kept meeting him every day or two from that point on and we always enjoyed interesting conversations which helped the miles go by.

Eric reminded me that this might be the last good spot for resupplying before Silver City (over 200 miles away) so fortunately I added more food/drinks to my stash. We had very little information about the 100+ mile fire related detour that would start 70 miles south of Pie Town. At least we didn't need to worry about the infamous stretch through the Gila Wilderness which included the challenging C.D.T alternate. Or did we??

Early into the 30+ mile rough gravel road stretch that would bring us into Pie Town Eric checked his phone and discovered that we had been sent a text message from Matthew Lee. The detour was now supposedly closed due to severe road damage that was caused by heavy rains a day or two earlier. Possibly due to these same rains, the regular route through the Gila Wilderness was now open and we were told to take this. We weren't sure if this was good news or bad news. Eric was excited about the opportunity to ride this classic section of the trail but I had reservations. I didn't feel mentally prepared for this likely tougher section and was now concerned that I didn't have enough food to get me through. However, I still expected that there would be food available in Pie Town. I also felt that the ideal situation would be for all racers this year to ride the same course.

We soon met up with Ian M and then Mike P and told them about Matthew's text message and the discussion of what that news meant continued. I was still hoping that the detour might be a possibility as we pedaled into Pie Town with thunderstorms about to hit. We were met at the junction with Route 60 by Bruce Creg, the chief of the Pie Town volunteer fire department. He explained that everything was closed in town (no pie!) for the 4th of July weekend but we were welcome to stop by the fire station where we could get out of the rain and check e-mails. We gladly took him up on the offer and Bruce and his wife Lisa were fantastic hosts. They had only recently learned about the Tour Divide going through Pie Town (when a rider looking for the local campground stopped in at the fire station for directions) and immediately became fans and enthusiastic supporters of the race. They provided food and drinks for us and pulled trackleaders.com up on the overhead projector. There we could see the riders on the detour ahead of us and we would likely be the first southbound racers to ride through the Gila this year.

A little while later Taylor K, Kristin A, Ty H and Joseph H joined us. They had arrived in Pie Town earlier and caught a ride to/from the grocery store three miles out of town. The four, each in their twenties, had been riding together for a while and were finishing strong. Discussions again turned to the route issues and Eric made a call to Matthew Lee. Mathew said that it was acceptable to ride either the regular route through the Gila or the detour though the condition of the detour was unknown and rough sections could be expected (based on an MTBCast call in from Chris A which we listened to in the fire station).

I was relieved that I would be able to ride the detour and tried to convince others that it was the right thing to do, again thinking that it would be best if we all rode the same route so that times/places would be more meaningful when comparing to other riders. Later I saw this comment from Matthew on the Tour Divide forum he wrote in response to a question about what riders should do if closed sections were reopened : "The general idea with a grand depart is to compare one's efforts to others under similar conditions. For this reason, back markers have been encouraged to run the same course as the front runners unless additional closures force additional detours (which is more likely than closures opening up). I think if I were not on record pace, I would personally be deferential to my fellow grand departees and take the same course." But I think the decision—based on the unique circumstances—to allow us to choose which route to ride made sense and we each had to make our own route decision.

It was still fairly early in the evening but based on the rainy radar pictures Bruce was projecting on the wall for us it seemed prudent for everyone to stay in town. We biked a couple blocks to the 'Toaster House', basically a free, unstaffed hostel open to bikers and hikers. Scott T was already there. That meant there were ten of us in Pie Town, with several different strategies on how best to get to the finish line over 300 miles away. I didn't know it at the time but we were competing for finish positions 40-49 as there was no one in front of us that we could catch and no one behind us that could catch us. We all started fairly early in the morning and I believe that four of us took the detour (Scott, Mike, Ian and myself) while the rest rode the Gila.

For some reason it turned out to be my hardest day yet, as the confusion over the route and the frustration that we weren't all riding the same route took a bit of a mental toll. After making the turn for the detour I immediately wondered if I had made the wrong decision. The road was very rough, included some very tough climbs and the section that was washed out was very challenging (though almost completely ride-able due to quick rebuilding efforts). On my Facebook fundraising page (I was raising money for the Vermont Cancer Center) I wrote the following after getting up the next morning: "Toughest day yet yesterday. Tired physically, fried mentally and very rough roads. Thankfully it never got too hot and no mechanicals - or I might have cracked! Expected a day like that though and it ended well. Evening riding was fun - curvy, rolling and smooth mountain road with a long descent to a nice bivy site."

When I arrived at the Magollon Historic District, a cool little former mining town that I hope to visit in the future, towards the end of that long day's ride, I knocked on the door of the Silver Creek Inn which was closed even though it was a Saturday night (as no rooms were booked that evening). Fortunately someone was home and I had a nice chat with the innkeepers and was able to purchase a couple of sodas and they also gave me a couple of other snacks. Hearing about the café in Glenwood that I would hit the next morning was exciting as it meant that I could stop rationing what little food I had left. I rode another 5-10 miles before finding a good roadside campsite which made for about a 112 mile day. Not bad but others that had left Pie Town that morning put in bigger miles and I was now slipping in the rankings. My recent hope for a top 40 finish was now out of the question.

I managed an early start the next morning (Sunday July 7) with the expectation that I wouldn't finish until sometime on Monday afternoon (24 days and ?? hours) which was a little above my goal of 23 days. I felt all along though, mainly due to the fundraising that I was doing, that the only important goal was to finish so I was happy with how things were going. I arrived at Silver City in the early afternoon after 75 very hot pavement miles and spent way too much time at the local Dairy Queen (Blizzards were a treat that I always looked forward to) and neighboring grocery store. I had internet access in town so checked trackleaders.com and noticed that 8 of the 10 from the Toaster House 2 nights ago were already way south of Silver City and likely finishing today as they had made good time (on both routes). Only Ian was behind me but I was still satisfied to think that I would finish sometime on Monday afternoon.

As I was getting back on my bike around 3:00 p.m. I noticed another racer heading down the road that I didn't recognize so I jumped out to catch him. It turned out to be Billy Rice and he explained that he hoped to complete his 'Yo-

The Cordillera V5

Yo' Antelope Wells to Banff and back to Antelope Wells ITT (individual time trial) that evening. He had started the ride at 3:00 a.m. on a morning back in late May so hoped to finish the ride by 3:00 a.m. that night to make the round trip record look as good as possible. I first saw Billy near the top of Cabin Pass (me riding south and Billy riding north) a day and half out of Banff which meant that I had a three day head start on him on the south bound portion of his ride. One goal was to not have him catch me and now he had done it.

While leaving Silver City the clouds thickened and I had to duck under cover to avoid a passing thunder storm. This cooled things down considerably and when I resumed riding the winds were in my favor and I was making good time. Thinking about Billy finishing that night, and how good I was feeling with the favorable conditions, I decided it made sense to also try to finish that night, hopefully beating Billy to the finish and coming in under 24 days. I stopped to let family members know via a text message. My wife Leslie received the text just as she had booked into her hotel in Silver City after four long days driving from Vermont where the current plan had been to meet me at the finish the next afternoon. Learning of my new plan meant that she wouldn't have much time to relax before hopping back in the car for the three hour drive to Antelope Wells.

Shortly after I reached the turn for the final 65 paved/straight/flat miles to the finish it started to get dark. I've heard this section can be fairly mind numbing so it seemed better to be doing it at night. But would I be able to avoid major thunderstorms? At one point I could see lightning in front of me, in back of me and on each side, but I was still staying dry. It made for a truly epic feeling which was enhanced by listening to my favorite music on my iPod (a lifesaver on the tough sections of the race). It was a little spooky riding that stretch at night with only the occasional border patrol car going by and the occasional tarantula crossing the road in the light being put out by my handlebar light.

The miles continued to fly by, although I was starting to get tired. I would be finishing with a 200 mile day which would be my longest day ever on a bike. I was getting closer to the finish and hadn't yet seen Leslie (she has her own story of trying to get to the finish which includes an exploded Red Bull and being stopped by the Border Patrol!) but finally with 15 miles to go she went by and tooted the horn. Shortly afterwards it started to rain, but soon after I could see the glow of the lights at the border. I biked those last ten miles as hard as I had any of the previous 2,800+ miles and what an amazing feeling it was to finish! I missed out on the Popsicle given to those that finished during the daytime but in retrospect it seems like the perfect way to have finished.

I later found out that Scott T was the first of the ten riders who spent that night together in Pie Town to finish. Scott nabbed 40th place with an incredible 300 or so mile push to the finish on his single speed without sleep. Hats off to him!

I wish I had had it in me to make a bold move like that but am already thinking about returning within the next couple of years with hopes of knocking a couple of days off my 23 day and 17 hour finish time. Though while riding there were times I would have sworn that I would never do it again!

2013 Result: 48th Place - 23:17:11

Jeff Mullen – Richmond, Vermont, USA

Rookie – 23 days, 17 hours

Jeff is an avid hiker/backpacker, cross country skier/racer, ex triathlete and now an enthusiastic bikepacker (he finally found the perfect sport!). He rode this year with the additional goal of raising money for the Vermont Cancer Center (VCC) where he had been treated for stage three colon cancer in 2008 (surgery and six months of adjuvant chemo therapy) and told that there was a 30-40% chance that cancer could return and he wouldn't be around in five years. Now five years out and no longer needing to go back for follow ups this fund raising effort was a 'thank you' to the wonderful doctors, nurses and support staff that he worked with at the VCC. Thanks to many generous supporters over $7,500 was raised in this effort.

jeffmullen@gmavt.net or find me on Facebook. Great riding in Vermont if anyone is ever up for a visit.

The Beauty of the Tour Divide

Joseph Holway

"This is the most beautiful place on earth." As stated by Edward Abbey, "There are many such places. Every man, every woman, carries in heart and mind the image of the ideal place, the right place, the one true home, known or unknown, actual or visionary. A houseboat in Kashmir, a view down Atlantic Avenue in Brooklyn, a gray gothic farmhouse two stories high at the end of a red dog road in the Allegheny Mountains, a cabin on the shore of a blue lake in spruce and fir country, a greasy alley near the Hoboken waterfront, or even, possibly, for those of a less demanding sensibility, the world to be seen from a comfortable apartment high in the tender, velvety smog of Manhattan, Chicago, Paris, Tokyo, Rio, or Rome—there's no limit to the human capacity for the homing sentiment."

It is for these few weeks in June and early July that the Tour Divide becomes home. The Tour Divide is unlike any view down Atlantic Avenue, any cabin on a blue lake, or any swanky Manhattan apartment; it is the vast wilderness that lies between Banff and Antelope wells. The Tour Divide is a collage of the endless herds of cattle, good vibes, kindness, rolling hills, fawns, unpredictable weather, great people, and forever climbing. The open road becomes your only focus, what you wake up for. At least what you try to wake up for...with a few inches of hail, fog so thick you can hardly see the ground, and sub freezing temperatures it's not at all easy to wiggle out of the sack before the sun has made its glorious debut.

On the other side, sometimes it was equally as difficult to stop riding. Early on in the race, Day 4, June 17th, the sun was low on the horizon. Edward Turkaly, Ty Hathaway and I peddled up to the base of Richmond peak determined to make it over the pass and into Seely Lake, Montana in time to find some food. It had been a long day of eating trail mix and Snickers bars—a staple food along the way—so a good meal was much needed. A storm was brewing to the east and blowing our way. We tried to pedal faster but to the best of my recollection our speed only fell.

As the dark clouds rolled in, lightning and thunder took over. Making our way up the switchbacks we came around a corner only to find ourselves in a valley quickly filling with smoke. Having not much of a choice we continued on only to later find out a forest fire was started by lightning when we were up there. The sun was now setting, casting vibrant reds, oranges, purples, and every shade of yellow across the sky. Mixed with the smoke it was truly a sight to see. It is at this time of day the Tour Divide transforms. As darkness sets in, the wilderness around shrinks to what is visible through your light, yet it remains equally limitless and transcending knowing anything awaits you. We arrived at what appeared to be the top only to find a portion of single track that continued along the crest of the pass for a few miles. Signs stating bear danger were all over the place. There was bear fur stuck in tree branches and tracks in the mud. For some reason my fear of bears was tremendously exacerbated come nightfall. Beginning the descent down in the dark was quite fun. As hunger set in, town seemed as far as ever—the descent everlasting.

Finally we reached town between midnight and one a.m., still with the hope of finding an open restaurant. We wandered into an empty, dimly lit bar only to find a closed kitchen. However, the kind woman assured us we were in good hands. She had a few bags of potato chips as well as a full selection of drinks. What the hell we figured, and ordered a round of Makers Mark, followed by a number of beers and of course a few potato chips. At this point I was fairly intoxicated, still hungry and most of all, ready for bed. It wasn't the best recovery meal, but certainly took the edge off. Finally she surprised us with a piece of cheesecake and we were off. A few more miles down the road and we called it a night.

The following morning was rough, perhaps the toughest throughout the adventure. I felt horrible, like nothing I had felt previously. No hangover, or sore muscles, simply weak as though I had aged 40 years overnight. My body was punishing me for not consuming the proper nourishment. However, I am still convinced there is a sandwich in every beer. So with all the time in the world we slowly wandered off to the nearest restaurant, and feasted! With each entrée ordered I felt my body come back to life. I'm pretty sure I ate half a dozen eggs, a few pounds of potatoes, and a number of fat stacks of pancakes. By now it was noon, not the greatest start but much needed recovery time. And off we went, forever southbound.

It is not a specific event, but the entire journey that makes me happy. Not only do I miss the open road, the amazing descents, and friendships along the way, but I've also grown to miss each and every climb, thunderstorm, and all 23 long days. The simplicity of riding day after day brings unparalleled bliss, everything else falls from your mind, and you are able to connect with the beauty that surrounds.

With that being said I would very much like to thank Jeff Stroot, Edward Turklay, Ty Hathaway, Kristen Arnold, Taylor Kruse, and Scott Thigpen for being a part of my home along the route. I would not have had as much fun without you all. I will always hold the Tour Divide in my heart and mind as a home—a place that just feels right. The Tour Divide is truly beautiful.

2013 Result: 46th Place - 23:12:24

Highlights and Challenges

Markley Anderson

A journey that was filled full of smiles, tears, rewards, suffering, joy, laughter, emotion and pain. Oh how sweet it was to roll into Antelope Wells and fall off the bike. Thanks to each and every family member and friend that supported and cheered me on. The incredible amount of belief and support truly overwhelmed me. Thanks to all of my sponsors for their support. Money was raised for the BRS Mountain Bike Program—nice! An 18 day finish on a busted quad for the last 2 full days isn't too bad. I shall now recover for a few weeks and plan to kick it up with some 24 hour racing in a month. Cheers!!!!!!!!!

I wanted to wrap up my Tour Divide experience from this year by listing the top ten highlights and the top ten challenging moments:

The Cordillera V5

Highlights:

1. Making it to Butts Cabin the first day. Not many have managed that.
2. Staying in the top ten the entire race. Multiple 200 mile days. 154 mile average/day.
3. 18 Day Finish.
4. Overcoming and pushing through my leg injury for the last 2 days.
5. Single track on Richmond Peak, MT.
6. Descent off Union Pass, WY.
7. Descent off Galton Pass, Canada Flathead Valley.
8. Gold Dust Trail, CO.
9. Amazing support from my family and friends.
10. Ovando Stray Bullet, Brush Mountain Lodge, Pie Town Toaster House.

Challenges:

1. Lightning Storm on Elk Mountain as I descended to Lima scared me for real.
2. Leg injury preventing me from a quicker finish.
3. Climbing Silver Creek Pass in New Mexico with busted leg.
4. Running from lightning out of Platoro to Horca.
5. Breathing smoke up Indiana Pass.
6. Outhouse sleeping.
7. Never enough rest to recover.
8. Always hungry.
9. Getting up early, never could master this task.
10. Recovering from a 40 Hour push without sleep in MT.

2013 Result: 11th Place - 18:14:42

My Tour Divide Bear and Cow Stories

Michael Arenberg

I was fortunate to ride with Chris Bennett up Red Meadow Lake climb and he took a photo of me adding "Mike, I'll only send you this if you write something for the Cordillera". As he rode off into the sunset all I could think of was I sure hoped something would happen that would be worth writing about.

The Bear Story

After crossing the rail road tracks near Blossburg (between Lincoln and Helena) I started up Priest Pass road when I suddenly and uncomfortably became aware of a peppery odor and taste in my mouth and nose. I had thought it a pretty smart idea to hook my bear spray on one of my aero bars using the looped plastic holder on the bear spray canister. It was easy to get off and readily available just in case. In the photo below the bear spray would have been located under my aero bars resting on the harness that held my sleeping bag. In the photo, you can also see where my Camelbak bite valve was located.

My first reaction was to not only wonder what this odor was, but where it was coming from as it just did not register that I may have sprung a leak in my bear spray. After only a few seconds I knew it had to be my bear spray. I came to a quick stop and unclipped from my pedals, leaned over and looked closely at the canister. I saw a thread-like line of brown ooze on the container. I knew I had to get rid of the container so I grabbed it with my gloved right hand and tossed it down the hill. Problem solved, problem over, or so I thought.

A few minutes down the road, Mother Nature called (can you see where this is going?). So I stopped to take care of business, pulled down my bike shorts, did my duty and continued down the road. A few seconds later I started feeling this amazing sharp pain you know where, and you know from what. Seems that little brown ooze had got on my bike gloves which I did not take off to go to the bathroom.

The pain got worse and worse and I was in tears, yelling out loud obscenities that would make a sailor cringe. I had to stop, I had to do something. The only fluid I had left at this point was Gatorade, grape to be exact. I laid my bike down, grabbed a water bottle, pulled my shorts down and sprayed Gatorade everywhere down there! It did little to ease the pain so I just lay there on the side of the road, clutching myself (having taken my gloves off as I had figured it out by then) in so much agony my stomach tossed out its contents. I don't know how long I lay there but after a while I knew I just had to get on the bike and deal with the pain. I was afraid someone might ride by and see me lying on the ground, clutching myself in a spot where you're not supposed to be clutching yourself in public. So off I rode. Now I had another issue to deal with. A groin area soaked in sticky Gatorade. This was getting to be very unpleasant.

I also knew I had to drink as this had taken a lot out of me so I reached down and took my bite valve in my mouth and started drinking (can you see where this is going?). A few moments later, the burning pain in my you know where was matched by the same burning sensation on my lips! It just did not register that the bear spray had been spread over the front of my bike cockpit. Now my lips were on fire, along with that other area. When was this going to end? Getting to Helena I was able to wash off in the bike shop restroom and cleaned off the front of the bike. I did a good job of cleaning, except for one thing, which I would only find out the next day.

I was riding up another long pass and wanted to use my GoPro camera to get some footage. I did not want to stop so I put the camera on my aero bars and at one point I had to put a bolt that holds the cameras brace in place in my mouth as I was riding. Yep, you guessed it, the bolt had some residual bear spray on it and my mouth was, once again, on fire.

My Cow Story

Toward the end of a long day that started in Wise River, I was heading up Medicine Lodge Sheep Creek Divide. Tour Divide racers will all tell you about the free range cows that you see along the route, some of them right on the path as you ride toward them.

Most of the time the cows would see or hear you coming and move off the trail. Well, here I was riding on this gravel path when I looked up and saw a large cow grazing right on the side of the road. As I approached it, it struck me odd that this large cow wasn't moving. This particular cow had a mean look in its eyes so I kept my distance. As I rode past, from the corner of my eye, I saw the cow move from one side of the road to the other, passing behind me. I turned my face forward but then sensed something weird and looked back.

Here was this cow running right at me on the path. I stood on the pedals and took off...or not! The road was muddy and I was heading towards a small steep hill and realized I was not going to out run this large speedy cow. I dismounted and started to run with the bike up the hill, the cow closing the gap. I remembered reading somewhere that appearing much larger than you are is a way of stopping said animal from attacking. So I stopped, turned the bike around and pulled it up on its rear wheel and started making animal noises. This didn't work and the cow was closing fast.

This is almost exactly what that cow on the side of the road looked like! The photo (obviously not from the Tour Divide) really gives you the feeling what a cow looks like in full flight!

I turned to run some more when I looked down and saw a stick in the road. I stopped, picked up the stick and threw it at the cow. Throwing things has always been something I have been good at, but a few days before I had cracked a rib on my right side as well as torn some ligaments, so my stick throw looked like a very un-athletic motion, accompanied by a scream of pain. The stick still grazed the cow right on its ear but this did nothing to stop the cow.

I dropped the bike and started running but then realized this was stupid! I had to protect the one thing that was going to get me off this mountain pass, so I stopped and right when I did I saw a rock the size of my fist on the road. I picked it up and fired it with the same un-athletic painful motion, but still good enough to hit the cow...........on its HOOF!!! Well, this stopped the cow in its tracks just as it would anyone walking barefoot and stubbing their toe.

I was so drained after this encounter I decided to camp for the night a couple miles further on. The whole encounter had taken less than 30 seconds but for the remaining weeks, every time I approached a cow I made all kinds of animal noises and remained paranoid about free range cows.

2013 Result: 61st Place - 27:05:38

Editor's Note: I think you've earned your photo Mike.

The Emperor's Rubbish

Michael Grünert

A story about missing carbohydrates and how the Tour Divide cuts you slowly into small pieces.

Day 7: Butte

Thirty miles to Butte. There was the imperceptible ascending terrain plus some strong headwinds paralleling Interstate 15. I crept along at 7 mph and less toward the city. My legs were done. My mind was done. I was done. There had not been many situations in my life where I felt so down. This was the first time I seriously thought about quitting the race.

After a very tough week I had decided that Butte, just a 65 mile ride from Helena, would be my final destination for the day. After the first climb out of Helena, and finishing the wretched Lava Mountain Trail after what felt like an eternity, I had a premonition that this day would turn out to one of my darkest days during the whole race.

This was confirmed when I saw the gravel ramp located near the Interstate. You can't get off your bike while climbing the ramp, because everybody on the Interstate is watching you. I mobilized my last energy and climbed the ramp in one push. But I paid with a total crash of my carbohydrate deposits. After that, I fought tooth and nail getting closer to Butte. Other riders caught up and showed me how slow I was. No chance to keep their pace.

I don't know why, but for me Butte was the first milestone on the Tour Divide I really wanted to reach. As I started the downhill on the Interstate shoulder and the city came into the view my eyes were filling with tears. What is this race doing to me? I didn't know, but I guess it was a mix of joy, relief of the torture, and looking forward to some hours of rest before getting on the bike again the following morning.

Visiting 'The Outdoorsman' bike shop in Butte is a must. My bike was just fine, but obviously it needed a new rider. The other MUSTS for me—Starbucks and checking into a decent motel. Having dinner with my German buddies Thomas and Mirko, who were also in town and who had suffered a similar misery to me, was a great relief and gave me the power to go on.

Day 13: Rawlins

After the climb my eyes fell onto a bunch of buildings: Atlantic City, population about 17. The door to the Great Basin.

As far as the eye could see there were no typical indications for thunderstorms, just a few fluffy clouds. There was a very strong tailwind and the temperature at the end of the eighties (29°C). Just perfect!

Finding the one and only restaurant in town was not really a challenge. I just had to watch out for dirty fully loaded bikes in front of a building. As I stepped into the restaurant two tables were occupied with other riders. I gave myself more than one hour before I planned to go on. Several Cokes and a meal should arm me for the long push to Rawlins. I stocked up all my water to the top level, overall almost two gallons. As I left the restaurant I met Ed Turkaly at the mercantile store who was also preparing for the 140 mile ride through the desert.

The first climb out of the town was very steep but my legs still felt, even after the 80 miles from Pinedale, surprisingly good. The first ten miles into the Basin were almost all downhill and done in 30 minutes. The strong tailwind pushed me over the dusty and often very rough or wash board gravel roads. Yes, now I was really in the back of beyond. The only sign of life I saw were some pronghorns and mining companies who had their drilling facilities along the road. I ate the miles, a feeling that I had missed the days before.

Every time in my life when a day turned out to be a perfect day, I became highly sceptical. This day was too perfect. 60 miles in just four hours wasn't so bad. It was 8 p.m. and time for dinner. I climbed up a small hill with a fantastic all around view, sat down and ate my last sandwich. The light of the setting sun colorized the landscape in a bright shining orange. As I finished my evening snack I just wanted take a video of the scenery. I looked at my handle bar where my GoPro Hero 3 camera was supposed to be, but I looked at an empty spot.

I don't know for how long I starred at the handle bar, or how long it took to realize that the camera was really gone. The only thing I saw was the broken holder still fixed on my handle bar. I guessed the holder broke on one of the wash board sections. I panicked. Tears filled my eyes. I was not able to think clearly.

The camera just three months old with 110 videos on the card was simply gone. $400 flushed down the drain. First my $110 sunglasses that I lost on the downhill from Fleecer Ridge, and now the camera. I shouted my frustration into the Basin. Fortunately nobody could hear or see me. It took ten minutes until I was able to sort out my thoughts. No chance for backtracking and searching, because it was about one hour before dark, I would run out of water, and the camera could be anywhere between mile 30 and 60 so any search attempt would be all in vain anyway. I was completely done. The only thing I wanted was getting as fast as possible to Rawlins and quit this bloody race.

One reason why I didn't quit arrived covered in a cloud of dust: it was Ed. He woke me out of my stranded thoughts and we agreed to continue together until one of us would fall off his bike. I guess Ed was happy finding someone sharing a night ride with him, and I was happy not being alone with all my gruelling thoughts and having someone I was able to talk to from time to time.

The light was fading and in the meantime I had revised my decision of quitting the race into making a call to MTBCast to alert all those riders who would ride through the Basin in the next days to look for my camera. If there was a tiny chance of getting my camera back I had to grab it.

After some hours of riding in the dark we stopped for a short break. I switched off my flash light and saw this amazing starry sky. We made a good pace and near midnight a big orange moon was rising over the horizon just before we hit a paved road. What a relief after all this shaking. I didn't have a clue how many miles we were away from the highway. We saw the bright lights of the trucks in the distance but we rode and rode and didn't seem to come closer. For miles we were attended by a strange sweet smell and I startled briefly as the light beam hit a dead bull right next to the road.

When we finally reached the highway we both felt dizzy as we got off our bikes for a break. Desperately we tried to calculate how many miles were left until Rawlins. Apparently it was not so easy after 20 hours and over 200 miles on a bike to subtract 122 from 136 using our fingers.

Of course we first had a hill to climb until we crested at the Continental Divide crossing number 13. The downhill to Rawlins was similar to our earlier experiences getting to the highway. We saw the lights of the city but couldn't get closer. It was 3:30 a.m. when we finally crossed the city line. Ed and I had both started in Pinedale and in a single push covered the 225 miles (360 km) in 24 and 22 hours respectively.

Unbelievable! Totally insane! In Rawlings we parted company and after five attempts I got a room in one of the motels. I tried to call MTBCast, but neither my Smartphone, nor the phone in the motel, were able to make the call. Finally I wrote a post to the bikepacking.net forum and asked for someone to make a call. After a shower and some cold drinks from the vending machine, I switched off the light at 4:30 a.m. What a day/night! Unfortunately, once again my feelings about so called 'perfect days' had proven to be correct.

Day 14: Brush Mountain Lodge

I got up at 9:30 a.m. and hoped that the misery with my camera yesterday was just a bad dream, but it wasn't. I felt totally blue and I had no desire for another psychological day on the Tour Divide. I decided to think about it over breakfast before making an over-hasty decision.

Before the race I knew that I would struggle with a lack of carbohydrates. Unfortunately, the classical food on the Tour Divide is high in fat, but very poor when it comes to good carbohydrates. Potatoes, rice or especially pasta was an exception to our daily menu. Three weeks prior to the race I sent a parcel with some special carbohydrate-based nutrition to the post office in Rawlins. This would hopefully be an option to mitigate my permanently empty legs. Furthermore, Brush Mountain Lodge just 90 miles south of Rawlins was my second milestone on the route, and important from a nutrition point of view.

When I am on tour in the Alps there is a traditional dish called 'Kaiserschmarrn' that originally comes from Austria. Today it is a typical South Tyrolean dessert, but is also very common in the German and Swiss Alps and is served in nearly every alpine hut, café and restaurant in the valleys. If I had to translate the name I'd call it 'The Emperor's Rubbish'. 'Kaiser' means 'Emperor' and 'Schmarrn' is a Bavarian dialect and means something like 'Rubbish or Nonsense'. It's comparable with scrambled pancakes, but tastes different.

During extensive bike or hiking tours this dish is a real life saver, because it brings you a lot of carbohydrates and tastes very yummy. I had emailed the recipe to Kirstin from the Brush Mountain Lodge some months prior to the race with a request for preparing it upon my arrival. She agreed on the condition that she may not be able to get all the ingredients. Prior to the race in Banff, and during the race, I told other riders about 'The Emperor's Rubbish at the Lodge'. So I didn't ride some 1,400 miles to pull the plug just 90 miles before the prospect for a 'Kaiserschmarrn'.

For all riders, Rawlins is a psychological milestone because it marks the half way point on the route. Once you get there, quitting the race is more difficult than ever. So I gave myself one additional day and relied on the fact that the further I would get on the route, the more difficult it would be to quit. That day my further participation in the race was dangling on a very thin string. The 'Emperor's Rubbish' was the crucial factor that kept me in the race.

Good news at the post office—my parcel had arrived! After I finished my full resupply at a supermarket and tackled the first climb on a very hot paved road out of Rawlins, I was just about to quit. I still struggled with the loss of my camera, my empty legs, my fully loaded bike and backpack that seemed heavier than all the days before. My mind cinema was in full swing and I was not able to switch it off. I did the climbs at walking pace. The pavement turned into gravel. The climbs that could be seen in the distance and the barren land didn't lift up my mood at all.

After countless hours I reached the Medicine Bow forest, the first trees after two days. The first Aspen trees I had seen in my life pulled me a little bit out of my gloomy mind. The famous Aspen Alley did the rest.

In the dusk I hit the state line of Colorado. Taking the mandatory photos of the sign 'Leaving Wyoming' was not possible. Just two seconds after I stopped at the sign I was taken over by hordes of mosquitoes. Only at a certain speed I was able to shake off the beasts.

The question was what to do now? The Lodge was only 13 mostly uphill miles ahead. By my calculations, I don't know why, it was more than 20 miles. Setting up a camp together with my little blood sucking friends was absolutely impossible, so the mosquitoes basically made the decision for me. I tried desperately switching my GPS to the new Colorado track while I was riding at the necessary pace to keep the bloody-minded mosquitoes at bay. As soon as I loaded the new track, the GPS completely crashed. This happened three times. Finally the fourth attempt locked the track without any shut down. Apparently I had a deal with bad luck today.

I switched on my flashlight. Riding in the dark seemed to be a habit. I learned from my night rides that mentally there is a huge advantage if you don't see the climbs. It was already completely dark when the light beam showed something large on the road ahead of me. As I came closer I identified an animal lying in the centre of the road. I slowed and when I was just 30 feet away I recognized a dead deer with a head bathed in blood. Nice!

I did this hop-on-and-off-the-bike-game. My legs went on strike. The miles went by as slowly as the other bad days previously. Someone heard my inner desire for a bed, food and an ice cold Coke. I turned a corner and suddenly the lodge loomed out of the dark. I was totally surprised and at once really happy, because I expected to get there at least ten miles later on the route.

It was close to 11:00 p.m. when I entered the lodge. Kirstin, who runs the lodge, and has a well deserved reputation as a trail angel, welcomed me. Due to its isolated location, the lodge is a very popular service point on the way to Steamboat Springs, and Kirstin does a fantastic job at this outpost. She also identified me as the guy with the recipe for the Emperor's Rubbish. Some other riders had already been asking for the dish. But unfortunately, she was not able to get all the ingredients. She was very sorry about that. Quite honestly, I wasn't really disappointed at all. During the entire race I was eating so much sweet stuff every day that I was sick and tired of it. I felt like eating something hearty. Kirstin served pizza! In the lodge everybody already knew about the loss of my camera. Obviously my post at the forum was partly successful.

Day 22: Cuba

At an unearthly hour the rude alarm clock tore us away from sleep. Grants was Thomas' and my goal for today's ride. Having entered New Mexico, an early start was mandatory for me. The advantages: (i) no headwind until midday; (ii) no thunderstorms until early afternoon; and, (iii) riding in the chill of the morning until the heat came in.

The way to Grants was an almost 200 miles of paved roads on relatively flat terrain. Also the first fire reroute to Cuba was scheduled for today. We got an email from Matthew Lee about the two fire reroutes several days before together with a route description. There was no GPS track available for it but I read the email more than twice but not today or yesterday. A fatal mistake!

After our standard early start super breakfast, we rode out of Abiquiu at 3:30 a.m. Surprisingly, my legs were in very good shape and we made good time. After just a few miles, Thomas had to do his 'bigger business'. I decided to continue on. That was my second big mistake. I was riding and riding and riding with a really good pace on Route 84. Even climbing was easy today. With this pace I would be in Cuba for a second breakfast at about 10:00 a.m.

At 5:30 a.m. I switched off my flashlight and was wondering about Thomas. Where had he got to? Usually he was always faster than me and able to catch up in a short time. But even on that excellent road no trace of him. I said to myself that even Thomas could have a bad day and I was having a really good one.

The road had the typical long stretches of climbs and downhills. After a while I saw a billboard with an advertisement about tourist regions in Colorado. Very strange! Why on the way to Cuba an advertisement about Colorado? After some further miles I realized that I was totally lost.

I finally checked my direction on my GPS. The arrow indicating the travelling direction always pointed to the north when I should have been heading west. I got a queasy feeling. I scrolled down the screen to check where the reroute hit the original track again. Oh my goodness!

I immediately checked the email from Matthew Lee and painfully saw my own bloody stupidity. I got tears in my eyes, but they were tears of anger. Yes, so much stupidity at once really is saddening.

For a time I stood there in shock. It took a while until I was able to gather my thoughts again. I calculated my options. Getting to Grants today and finishing in less than 25 days was now out of sight. Spending a night ride until Grants was not possible, because I also needed a night ride for the second fire reroute two days later. Two night rides, and the second one with more than 250 miles overall, would definitely exceed all my optimism and faith in my own endurance skills. There was no option other than backtracking to the junction of Route 96 which would mean about 40 miles. Overall, the whole unintended excursion cost me 80 miles and some 6,500 feet of climbing.

That's the Tour Divide—recognize your own mistake, correct it, and live with it.

During the ride back it welled up inside me like a volcano wanting to bubble over. And of course I was just about to scrap the whole thing again. It was little comfort as I saw these gorgeous colorized rock formations I had passed earlier in the dark. This is a real drawback of riding in the dark, missing the landscape.

It was past noon as I reached the junction to Route 96. Eighty miles just dust in the wind and my legs felt like lead. The sun was burning hot and a light headwind came up. Except for Abiquiu Lake, which I should already have passed in the early morning, the boring landscape did little to pull me out of my dark mood. I couldn't calm myself down at all. What a bummer! I tried to kill the time with ranting and raving.

I passed the dreary dump of Coyote and stopped at a small grocery store right next to the road. After a quick resupply I took a seat on the bench in front of the store and tried to drown my frustration with some cans of Coke (not really the right stuff for that). The store was located across from the post office. So, why not! I stepped into the office and the female staff gave me the biggest box she had. I planned to ship the parcel to a post office in Vegas. While she filled out the address label, I went out to pack the box. I unpacked most of my bags. I put in the most of my warm clothes, my tent (stupid mistake), my bear spray and my dog dazer (stupid mistake too), as well as my rain pants and shoe covers. In total over 6 lbs (2.5 kg).

Back on the road again J.D. Pauls caught me up and passed me by. With such stupid mistakes I was an easy prey for the pack behind me. In Cuba I checked into the Frontier Motel and did a full resupply at the gas station right across the street. The self service laundry next to the motel took care of my stinky bike clothes.

As I checked my emails I got another shock from Matthew. The second fire reroute was closed now due to flooding and the Gila was open again. For a moment I didn't fully appreciate the consequences. With my excursion today I had definitely lost one day. With the Gila back in the game I needed an additional day. But to tackle the Gila in two days I needed my tent which was now on the way to Vegas. Without a tent, and even with a night ride, I would not be able to finish the race in a decent time without missing my flight back to Germany. Postponing my flight was not an option at all. I twisted and turned all options but the result was always the same. I had to quit the race. So close to the finish and then an email like this.

As I came back from dinner, Hamish McKee from New Zealand was standing in front of the motel. As I told him about the Gila he was not very amused. But he gave me the tip to ask Matthew if the Gila is a MUST and if the fire reroute would be still an option. Apparently in my clouded mind I forgot the simplest things. Of course, why not! I sent an email to Matthew and got an answer within the next hour. The Gila wasn't a must.

That day some other riders passed the fire reroute but with a delay. I hadn't got a clue what 'with delay' meant, but I would learn it well by myself two days later. Okay, I was back in the race and felt very much relieved.

Day 23: Grants

I left the motel at 4:00 a.m. for the 124 mile ride on paved roads to Grants. Today it's going be a double dog day! I heard the beasts at the junction to the Chaco alternate very close after the city limit of Cuba. I turned my head and in the light beam of my flashlight I looked in several pairs of glowing eyes. Actually, not funny at all! How nice that my bear spray and the dog dazer were on the way to Vegas! As the pack started their chase I was very glad for the smooth descending road. I switched to higher gears and sped up my bike as fast as someone with 22 days Tour Divide in his legs was able to do. After just one minute I was completely exhausted. Fortunately the barking faded away, a sign to me that my escape was successful. I slowed down to catch my breath again. I sent a prayer, please no more sprints today!

140

The wasteland I was riding through was a Navajo area. If I saw any houses I always kept my eyes wide open for dogs. The second attack came just a few miles before Pueblo Pintado. The dude in front of the house didn't give a damn about his dog that was slipping through the fence and right onto the road. Luck was on my side again. The road was descending, but the beast was pretty fast. He abandoned his chase once he noticed that I was faster. I deeply regretted that my bear spray was on the way to Nevada. What sort of dog infested area I was getting into?

I don't know if I first saw the flock of sheep or heard the barking dogs, but they were already heading towards me. This time I was a little bit more relaxed, because there was at least 1,500 feet between me and the dogs, and the road descended for the third time. So I did not have to speed up like one possessed, but I slowly increased my speed to about 30 mph. No chance for the mutts. Obviously, my flawless features, tired eyes, outfit like a beat-up bum, and my fantastic body after 23 days on the trail with curves in all right places made me irresistible. But just for dogs, unfortunately.

Miles later I was wondering about this bumpy road. With every turn of the wheel I got a bump. As I inspected the road I couldn't see any reason for the bumps. The road was just fine. But as I cast an eye at my rear tire I saw the problem: a bulge the size of an egg was decorating my tire. What the hell was that? I immediately got off my bike and analyzed the problem. First I thought the sealant was dissolving my tubeless tire, but it hadn't. The profile was so worn out that the inside pressure pressed the thin tire to the outside. What a bummer! No chance to go on with this egg. I don't like to think what might have happened if the tire burst during one of my dog getaways. A big mistake to rely on the paved sections in New Mexico and not to change at least the rear tire in Salida.

What to do now? Maybe if I installed a tube it would take away the pressure from the weak spot and I could slowly go on. The other option was pushing the bike under the hot sun until Milan or Grants which would take hours. I deflated the tire, lined in a tube, took my pump and ... nothing! Am I on 'Candid Camera'? The heat and the sleep deprivation made my mind work slowly, so it took some seconds before I realized that my pump (always worked before) was really done. Obviously someone was kidding me. I tried to figure out where the problem with the pump was. I disassembled and assembled the pump several times without any success. Unbelievable! Since New Mexico I was certainly attracting misery in a special way. I must be in a bad road movie, because in the nearby rock formation I heard the coyotes yowling and mocking me. For someone whose mental defences were completely lying on the ground, such small details could tip the scales.

As I pushed my bike towards Grants, again I considered quitting the race because neither Milan nor Grants had any bike services. Leaving the race for a good reason. To finish the race without missing my flight back I needed a tire. Today!

Totally exhausted from the heat I hit the main street of Milan. An older man on his bike asked me if I needed a pump. Yes I did! He handed over a pump and I pumped up the tire. But the egg still remained even with an inner tube. So a pump wouldn't have provided a solution to the problem. Carefully I tried to ride the five miles until Grants. The egg slowly disappeared. I rode up and down the main street to find any possibility for a tire replacement. Nothing! I phoned my wife to tell her about quitting the race. I really wasn't sad and I was just fine with it. No regrets. Nothing! After the call I gave myself a last chance and stopped at a shop for car tires and asked where I could find a mountain bike tire. He sent me to Wal-Mart.

Of course, my lock was in the parcel to Vegas too. I parked my bike behind three older ladies who were collecting money for a charity organization. In the sport section of this really big market I scanned the racks for tires. I saw bikes, but no tires. First I discovered the pumps, but without a tire a pump wasn't needed. I was just about abandoning all my hopes as I saw some small boxes in one corner of a rack. Tires! Now the question: 29er or just 26er? And in fact they had 29er tires. Okay, the profile was like a compactor and heavy like a downhill version, but a 2.35er 29er tire. I also got a pump where I understood the corresponding adapter for the presta valve was inside.

The old ladies did a great job. I took my bike and changed my tire in front of the supermarket. In the motel I took a bath, did my laundry one last time, and phoned my wife with the news I was back in the race. Because I didn't know anything about the resupply possibilities on the second fire reroute, I stocked up my groceries. Denny's restaurant gave me the chance for some pasta! Over the spaghetti I didn't know if I was happy or sad about the new tire. I had absolutely no emotions.

Day 24: Silver City

I woke up before dawn and was terrified of the next 48 hours. I was shaking like a leaf and not because of the air conditioning. Don't lose your nerves now—I thought to myself. There were so many doubts. 260 miles in one single push after 23 days, almost no information about the reroute (resupply possibilities, dogs, how much climbing), riding the whole night in a remote area and so on. I was paralyzed and couldn't get out of my bed. But quitting the race, because I am a pussy, was no solution. This would certainly be the toughest day of my life. Still in the dark I took the second paved alternative route towards Pie Town. The new rear tire (hereinafter called 'the compactor') together with the inner tube seemed to have a rolling resistance far beyond evil. The noise sounded like the tire would plow the pavement. In the dawn I reached El Malpais National Monument with some really nice rock formations that the rising sun dipped into a beautiful orange. I took all the time I could taking pictures and reading information panels. I did everything just to switch my mind to other thoughts.

I stopped at a small gravel covered parking lot with some trash cans to dump my trash. As I hit the pavement again my front tire suddenly slipped sideways. When will these miseries end, actually? There was a lot of broken glass around the trash cans. Obviously I got some into my tire. My sealant needed some time to fix the hole. Unfortunately the new pump had no adapter for presta valves inside and the combination of pump, my own adapter and tubeless valve didn't want to harmonize together. After almost an hour in the hot sun I was finally able to fix the problem and the tire kept the air. Just a short time after the puncture I left the pavement and with it the alternative route. The road was extremely dusty and dry and the ground was alternating from gravel to sand. It was a very exhausting section that further reduced my pace. The landscape wasn't boring at all. In the distance were mountain ranges, and some cattle ranches next to the road.

For a little bit more motivation I cramped my Smartphone under my front harness for some music. I opened the zipper of my jersey and the music pushed me onward, away from the noises from my new compactor.

As I rode over a washboard section, out of the corner of my eye I saw my Smartphone slip through the strap of the harness. I tried to grab it and just got the cable from the ear plugs between my fingers. The falling phone touched the ground right ahead of the tire. You guessed it, I ran over the phone! I didn't know whether I should laugh or cry. I did the first one. Unbelievable!

Of course the glass of my phone couldn't resist my compactor and I was not able to unlock the phone anymore. If the crap of the last few days had happened two weeks ago, I would definitely have pulled the plug by now. This was the point where I didn't believe in a combination of unfortunate circumstances anymore. This was a test, a mental endurance test. How much misfortune is someone able to bear within a short time? The problem that I now faced was that all the ACA maps, the cue sheets, my own excel list with all the distances and service points, and the email from Matthew about the fire reroute were on the now useless phone. I had to balance very carefully if I wanted be able to go on without this information. Fortunately, I also had service locations as POI's (Points of Interest) in my GPS. On the fire reroute all this information (except the email from Matthew) are useless anyway, and for the last jump from Silver City to the border not absolutely necessary. In contrast to the email for the first reroute, I had the description for the second one already stored firmly in my mind.

At Pie Town Café I met J.D. Pauls again who was struggling with a cracked frame. I was reassured that I was not the only one dogged by bad luck.

After two slices of pie I was absolutely convinced that Pie Town did its reputation more than justice.

I had to inform my wife about my damaged Smartphone. But without a Smartphone? I asked for a telephone call to Germany. The owner gave me her laptop so I was able to write an email and five minutes later my wife phoned me in the café. We discussed the options and I told her that I would go on. No way was I quitting the race so close to the finish. Now she had only to rely on the Spot messenger. No more emails or phone calls from my side.

I stocked up all my water resources and at 2:00 p.m. I left Pie Town, the last outpost, before I hit a lot of nothing. Seventy miles to the junction of Route 28 (Bursum road) and I hoped to get there before dark.

After I left the mountain ranges behind me, the landscape became increasingly boring. I reached a vast plain with ranch land. Who is running a ranch in this wasteland? The cattle I saw wouldn't even be enough for one burger.

The road at the edge of this huge nothing got muddier so I had to avoid the muddiest parts by zigzagging from one side to another. The mud slowed me down and in the meantime I hit the 120 mile marker. My legs were only pedalling because they had to. It was predictable that I wouldn't reach the junction to Bursum road before dusk. I switched my flashlight on and it was completely dark as I hit the junction. Left, the Gila with its original route and right the re-route: a leap in the dark, literally.

Fortunately, I had the entire Bursum road well marked at my OSM map on my GPS. If the map was correct I couldn't get lost even in the darkness. Slightly disconcerting was the fact that my wife told me some other riders needed more than 13 hours for this section. 13 hours for just 50 miles? Both Google Maps and my GPS stated this section is paved, but obviously it wasn't! My legs were totally done and I had not the faintest idea how much climbing was still ahead of me. Riding on a gravel road in the dark without any company was not a smart idea at all.

I took a seat on the ground right in front of a road sign, switched off my flashlight and leant my tired head on the pole for just a short break with some food. I saw the lightning in the distance and parts of the starry sky. This was maybe the weirdest situation of the whole TD, sitting tired in the back of beyond after 140 miles at 9:45 p.m., in complete darkness at a road sign without any idea how the next few hours would pan out, and having a snack.

This kind of gravel was new on the Tour Divide. More rough than smooth. No worn out track to follow. Together with my compactor and the ascending road I was done just after ten minutes. On most of the following uphills with this very inconvenient gravel I was pushing my bike.

Two hours later I became so tired that I began to search for a spot where I could place my sleeping pad together with my sleeping bag (my tent was on the way to Vegas). As far as I could see it in the beam of the light I was on a plateau with some huge pine trees and a lot of cattle dump. But with my Therm-a-Rest NeoAir pad I had to be careful. One sharp item on the ground and the pad was done. I was looking for a suitable spot but I couldn't find one. A sign pointed out nine miles until Willow creek. Willow creek could be everything, really just a creek, or some houses with an outhouse. I decided to wait until Willow creek with my nap. Also it would mark the halfway of the 50 miles.

I don't know how long I rode or pushed up and down this plateau, but at least the gravel became better. Matthew Lee had spoken of some significant turns in his email. Now I was standing directly in front of one. I rode on this wide gravel road and the GPS sent me with a right turn over a cattle gate onto a narrow track. I was quite sure I had not seen a single sign. What are those guys doing who are navigating without a GPS? Never in my life would I have made this turn, but instead stayed on the wider gravel road.

The track became more and more bumpy. Moments later I was struggling with a steep challenging downhill. I was wide awake. At the very last moment I saw the big hole in the road. Parts of the road had simply slipped away. This was a very close thing! For sure I was approaching the flooded area and finally reached the end of the downhill. At the right side there was something like a streambed. The road looked like the room of a three year old after the battle of the Lego warriors. Big boulders, all kinds of trees and heaps of wood were laying all over in a mess. The former waterline of the flood was several feet above me. Unbelievable! Now I knew what 'with a delay' would mean.

For what felt like an eternity, I pushed and climbed over trees and big rocks attended by some really freaky noises from animals, and these were not just birds. Normally I am not very scared, but I was happy when I hit a wider forest road again. That didn't change the situation at all, but that gave me a little bit more security than in this messy and confusing terrain.

Willow creek was really just a creek and nothing else. No outhouse or anything else where I could take a nap. But with all these strange noises around me I was not tired anymore. My GPS told me the road would go up to the plateau again. It was only a moderate climb, but I wasn't able to ride anymore. I pushed my bike.

Back on the plateau I looked into several pairs of eyes glowing in the beam of my flashlight. The eyes belonged to some kind of deer, perhaps Wapiti. They kept some distance but didn't run away. The right and the left sides of the road were crowded with them. When I saw the information panel I was thinking about my bear spray and my whistle in my parcel. I tried not to think about the fact that I was in bear country. The most important sentence on the panel was very encouraging to me: "Hike during daylight hours and in groups when possible!" A-ha! Now I was a little bit scared. Of course this was one of the spookiest nights of my life where all these childhood nightmares came up.

After I passed a "Road Closed" sign it was a steady up and down again on a twisting and turning road. Finally I reached a parking area with an outhouse. I was completely done. I parked my bike at the wall of the outhouse and took a seat in the entry, leant my head on the wall and within five seconds I fell asleep. With the dawn I woke up some 80 minutes later, shivering and stiff like a block of ice.

The road was leading a second time down to the creek. I compared the downhill more to a free fall. I didn't need a whistle anymore, because my brakes were making noises for three whistles. As I reached the end of the downhill the view was similar to the one earlier: the creek and to the right and left a mess. Apparently some workers had already started to clean up. The road was still bumpy and rugged from the water. I entered a narrow gulch with some very old and historical houses. It was a ghost town. The road turned from gravel to pavement and climbed steep out of the gulch, crested a hill and then a steep descent on a narrow winding mountain road down to the highway. Nine hours (without my nap) for 50 miles. What a delay!

After just after four miles I reached Glenwood. One more jerkwater town, but at least with a Trading Post and a café! The café was a real lifesaver. I ordered pancakes and some other stuff. A visit in the Trading Post for a resupply and some Coke was mandatory. It didn't bother me as I saw the thick dust layer on most of the packed groceries. What a weird store.

Just 64 miles until Silver City. Twenty eight hours and 190 miles were behind me. My legs were still done. Climbing on that hot road was torture. In Buckhorn I stopped for an ice cream and packed two cans of liquid gold into my back pack. But apparently I am not able to ride with two full cans of Coke longer than one hour without emptying them.

Dark clouds over the Gila were announcing the next thunderstorm. Today's air was extremely muggy. I compared the daily thunderstorms to playing battleship. During the whole TD I had been relatively spared from thunderstorms, but today the ship should be sinking. It started with a very pleasant light rain shower. The rain passed away and came back every few minutes, but the sun was still shining. I heard the thunder roaring and the alternating rain became heavier. Totally out of the blue all hell broke loose.

Within seconds the sky was covered with dark clouds and the wind was lashing the rain horizontally against me, pressing me towards the middle of the lane. I wasn't able to ride anymore. I got off my bike and pushed against the stormy rain. For the surrounding landscape I just saw silhouettes. Two minutes later I was soaked and after one further minute the inside of my shoes became a lake.

If that not was not bad enough, in five seconds distant lightning followed close by thunder was surrounding me. The rain was so heavy that the cars had to stop. I was totally pissed off. The final push to the border today—I could forget it now. This was not a usual thunderstorm. It seemed it was standing still and not moving. As the thunderstorm was raging above me I thought to myself that walking while the lightning is straight around me is not very clever and potentially a death trap. Unfortunately I was in a section with no cover at all. It was raining as if God had broken off the shower head. The soil left and right beside the road became flooded. The only chance was to hunker down right there on the road. In this moment a van stopped right next to me and the window wound down. "Do you wanna live?" I looked into the eyes of a younger guy. "Yes", I shouted against the roaring thunder. "Then come in". Wow! This is America, from a nightmare to a dream in just a few seconds.

Totally soaked I took a seat in the front of the van. Four guys and a dog were introducing themselves. We had a lot of time for some conversations until the thunderstorm passed by. Of course, I had to tell my Tour Divide story again. When I left the car I was still totally impressed by their kindness.

The whole way into Silver City it was raining. Though it was warm, I was shivering like leaves. I needed a hotel room as soon as possible. Even so, I visited Gila Hike & Bike and changed both tires just in case and arranged my pick up from the border tomorrow with Barin Beard, who by chance was in the shop. I checked in at the Murray Hotel and dried out my gear, even my money. The evening was filled with getting all the things in order that I needed for the final push to the border.

After I did my shopping at a gas station I passed the neighbouring hotel and saw Ed and James Hodges. It was a warm welcome. We talked for a while before I left the hotel. I was restless, assured they would catch me before the border.

Day 25: Antelope Wells

I was not fully convinced of getting to the border without any obstacles. I was really excited about what was in store for me today. After my last-self made breakfast I left the hotel at 3:45 a.m. If all went according to plan I would get to the border between 1:00 and 2:00 p.m. The new tires (Maxxis Crossmark) were a blast. What a difference! Not comparable to my compactor. It was more like floating or sliding over a new asphalt surface that was as soft as a baby's bottom.

When I switched the display of my GPS on for about the 20th time the track was gone. I scrolled down and saw I missed the turn toward Separ. It was just in time so I only had to cycle back 20 minutes, causing a short moment of shock to the people at home who were following me. The way back was all downhill and I hit the gravel road at dawn. It was an amazing ride. Sunrise in the desert. I didn't care about anyone who could catch me, even though I knew Ed and James were close behind me. With the rising sun I got the photos I had been looking for during the whole Tour Divide. And who cared if I would make it to place 54 or 56? During the whole Tour Divide my ranking was far from my mind. Just finishing—somehow! I never felt myself being in a competition with other riders. For me they all were good fellows in suffering. And even after 25 days nothing had changed: I WAS SLOW (but happy)!

A very charming landscape embraced me. Mountains in the background, and all around me cactuses sprouting up the dry ground. I made very good time on this dusty road. In the distance I could already see the trucks on Interstate 10, and a short time later I crossed the rail tracks just in front of the southernmost Interstate. At the 'Continental Divide' Trading Post I got a bucket of Coke to flush down the dust. I followed the Interstate on the gravelled frontage road. As I saw a sign for "Antelope Wells" I lost completely my poise. I cried my eyes out. The relief from the intensity of the last few weeks and the joy about accomplishing something incomprehensible all came out. Once I was able to see something again I took a photo.

The second time I cried was when I got to the actual Antelope Wells exit. Better now than later at the border where everyone can see you, I thought to myself. I hoped that I would not cry buckets at every sign (and there were a number).

The last 65 miles of the more than 2,700 were mainly flat, but not easy because the road was switching on its barbecue. Ed and James rushed up from behind, passed me by and disappeared over the horizon within the next 15 minutes. No chance to follow them at this pace. That would kill me just within the first miles Hachita, with no services, was the last sign of civilization before the border. Another jerkwater town looking like a ghost. Scrapped houses were the only witnesses of a former better life. Just 45 miles now, and these damn mile markers were mocking me. Every few miles I was looking for an excuse to stop. But due to the heat, stopping wasn't a good idea either.

The miles were slowly counting down.

At mile 17 a black truck came towards me and stopped. Somebody got out of the car. Maybe my eyes were still fogged from the crying session a short while ago, but I didn't recognize right off who it was. I had to look twice. Thomas was smiling like a cat that got the cream. It was a nice welcome. I was totally surprised to see him here because I thought he had already finished yesterday. Everybody was telling a very short version of the last few days before we went our separate ways again. This casual meeting gave me the necessary motivation for the last 17 miles, but when I saw this giant column of smoke toward the border station I was really concerned. With my 'fortune' of the last days the station most certainly had blown up and I could forget the finisher photo.

The border station came in sight and I hit the one mile marker. Just one fu..... mile out of more than 2,800. I suspect that besides the finisher photo, this last mile marker is one of the most popular photos around. Unbelievable. I had made it to the southern terminus of the Great Divide Mountain Bike Route! A dream or maybe a nightmare had become true. I was really not quite sure at this moment how I should evaluate this race. But as we would say in Germany: the candy was sucked! The synonym in English, I guess: the goose was cooked!

Ed came across me as I reached the station. He welcomed and warmly congratulated me. Immediately I recognized the officer from the movie. He congratulated me as well and handed over a finisher ice cream! Ed was waiting for his family who did a 14 hour drive from Colorado to pick him up. He was taking the MUST photos at the border sign for me. I stormed the vending machine inside the office for a cold Coke and a second and a third! What a shame! What I really missed was a big finisher party with all riders. After the finish the riders were dispersing in all directions. But I also knew that this was just a dream! My shuttle arrived. Barin, my driver handed me a really good Mexican beer and we touched the cans. I said goodbye and after we had puzzled my bike into the car we left the border.

Driving back all these precious hard-earned miles in a car really hurt (as well later on as I was flying over Wyoming and Montana in just a little bit more than one hour). Bringing me to Tucson airport where I could rent a car was not an issue for Barin. We talked mainly about bikes, the Tour Divide, and Matthew Lee who was shuttled by Barin a few times.

He dropped me off at the airport in Tucson and would only be paid for the gas. No way! I gave him almost the rest of my money and said goodbye without knowing that the rest of my money would have been very welcome later on in Vegas and my run of bad luck wasn't over at all, but that is another story!

2013 Result: 56th Place - 25:06:34

Conclusion

There was not a day when I was not ready to pull the plug. Focusing each day on hitting the 100 mile marker was a mental overkill. I had some very dark days! New Mexico obviously didn't want to see me in Antelope Wells, and due to my missing turns I unnecessarily did an extra 100 miles and more than 7,000 ft. of climbing.

After Rawlins the race was not a race anymore, but became rather something like a pilgrimage. Every day the same doubts, the thoughts about quitting the race, getting more and more fed up with all these climbs, and dealing with done legs. Each day I slowed down more and more. I was asking myself several times how much longer could I keep this up?

If I met other riders, most of them were riding together in groups. 90% of the race I was riding alone. Riding alone produced more dark days. But I wouldn't trade with them for anything, because the Tour Divide experience is much more intensive if you are alone on the trail.

Some people asked me if my expectations of the race were fulfilled and if I would do it again. Yes and no! Getting out of the daily rat race is simply just a lie. You get out of your daily obligations but enter into another, more simple rat race, often more stressful than the daily business at home. Much more 'Yes' was the matter of the landscape. This helped to keep me in the race. Even after some time has passed, I will never come back!

Why I didn't quit in the end? There is more than just one reason. You don't trash four years of preparation and spending a lot of money. All the tons of stuff I read during this time, the reports from former racers, all the four editions of the Cordillera, let me know that there were people on the trail who were sharing similar stories to mine.

I did it for all those riders who were not able to go on due to medical issues. I saw the huge disappointment in their faces, because they were not able to ride their bikes anymore. In contrast, I was blessed. A few hotspots at both feet and in the beginning of the race, some smaller saddle sore issues were it, even though I was riding with a 17 lbs (8 kg) backpack. That was it. Not a single day did I feel nauseous, no colds, no headaches or other issues. Nothing. This was a real miracle to me. Physically there was absolutely no reason to quit. Weather wise it was one of the best racing years ever.

Of course I did it for my family, because, not just in the year of the race, I left them alone very often either for long training rides or sitting at the desk. Last, but not least, as many other riders reported: all the countless human beings along the route. I am very happy that I was able to experience it on my own. I have never in my life had other people give me so much encouragement and affection. What a lot of 'so called' friends at home were obviously not able to provide, these people did.

What I've learned the hard way is that the Tour Divide is not a Pilgrimage, nor a sightseeing trip, nor just a getaway to work something out. It is, and shall remain, a race!

I would like to thank God that he protected me the whole time and held off all these little ailments, and sorry to my family for some sleepless nights.

Whether finisher or not, what we must all never forget, and for which we have to be very grateful, it's a huge privilege that we're healthy and have the financial resources for being part of something unique in the world like riding the Tour Divide.

Now go and enjoy The Emperor's Rubbish!

Kaiserschmarrn (The Emperor's Rubbish)

There are many different legends from whence comes the Kaiserschmarrn! Here the most popular version. In 1854, the Vienna court pastry cook created for the wedding of Emperor Franz Josef the first and Elisabeth of Bavaria (Sissi) a pastry. But Elizabeth was very careful to keep her slim figure and spurned this sweet pastry. Jokingly, the emperor took Sissi's plate and smiled and said. "Well then give me the rubbish". Emperor Franz Josef decided this sweet dish was so excellent that it was named Kaiserschmarrn.

> 100g (3.5oz) raisins
> 5 tb rum or cognac or water
> 6 egg yolks
> 1 Pck. (1 tb) vanilla sugar
> 1 tb sugar
> 1 pinch Salt
> 250g (9oz) flour
> 400ml (13.5oz) milk
> 50g (1.8oz) butter, melted
> 6 egg whites
> 4 tsp powdered sugar
> Time: 20 minutes

Place the raisins in 5 tablespoons of either rum, cognac or water

Beat the egg yolks with the vanilla sugar, a pinch of salt and 1 heaped tablespoon sugar with an electric mixer until it's fluffy. Gradually stir in alternating a spoonful of flour and a good splash of milk until everything is used up. Then stir in the melted butter. Whisk the six egg whites until the mixture becomes stiff and fold the beaten egg whites slowly into the dough. Then stir in the raisins without the rum.

In a pan, melt the butter and pour the dough about 1/2 inch high. Reduce the heat slightly and let it get golden-brown. From time to time look under it. Quarter the half baked dough and turn it around, and let it bake on again. Divide (scramble) the pieces into bite-sized pieces. Dredge with 2 tablespoons sugar and caramelize briefly.

Serve on plates and dredge with powdered sugar and any kind of jam or apple butter.

Traditionally, the Kaiserschmarrn is served with apple puree or cranberry compote (sauce). But any kind of jam is also very welcome.

Normally a recipe for four to six people. I have tested it and in my opinion enough for three people or one very hungry Tour Divide rider.

Profile:

Married – one child. Working in the development department of a supplier for the automotive industry as system engineer.

Starting with mountain biking in 1999. His favourite bike spots are the Dolomite Alps (the most beautiful mountains in the world) in northern Italy. The most challenging events during his bike career were joining the Transalp Challenge, an eight days supported race across the Alps, in 2006, the Transgermany, a four days supported race in southern Germany and Austria, in 2011 and of course the Grenzsteintrophy a 800 mile self supported race along the former border to East Germany in 2012.

Blog: http://mgtd2013.blogspot.de

Email: TourDivide2013@go4more.de

Riding Buddies

Mike Komp

My story begins on a rainy morning in Helena Montana.

Beard-o and I sat in Starbucks drinking our first coffee and talking about our pain. Beard-o had seat issues and I had knee issues. The longer we talked the more I thought he was trying to convince himself of dropping. I remember thinking he looked for me to assure him that it would be okay. Well, I had no part of that. I just kept reassuring him of the opposite.

Rain never helps bring about positive change when you are in the dumps like we were that morning. I cannot remember what lay ahead for us, but it certainly entailed serious climbs and my knees were killing me and his ass was killing him. Well we finished our cup and left slightly more determined and started our day.

As we headed out of town we ran into Hal Russell from Missouri, and Dustin, the young postal worker from Iowa. I thought "Cool! Some new people and maybe Beard-o would not feel guilty about dropping now." Well, about 15 minutes out of town on our mellow climb, he said that he was going back to town. Hal had just lost his riding buddy, who dropped out, and I thought the same was happening. Beard-o said he was going to wait for the bike shop to open to get a new saddle. I thought that was probably it for him. He quickly turned and rode away. Now Hal, Dustin and I were a new team.

Hal could climb like no other, and when he told me he was in his 60's, was I impressed! Dustin had Achilles issues and was going on about that for awhile; he kept the conversation rolling that's for sure. He was a great person to help get your mind off anything it was stuck on. You know when a record skips, like your mind zoning on something; well Dustin was the kind of guy to snap you out of it.

We rode together. I can't remember what happened exactly from there but Hal and I stuck together and Dustin slipped away. As several others and I would later experience with Dustin, he would just appear from nowhere, ride with us for a day and then just disappear, only to reappear a day of two later. So we all got used to that. Plus, Dustin always seemed to get free stuff; I mean hotels and food on several occasions. His timing was perfect. Hal and I really started a good bond and stuck together.

I think we complimented each other pretty well. I needed time to get rolling every morning because of my knees, requiring frequent breaks and he had no problem taking those as needed. I learned much about Hal over the next week or so. Found out he was a Vietnam vet and why he was riding the Tour Divide. A man with a giving heart, who put others before himself. How often do you see that these days? I also learned some of the things he used to do back home, and much to my amazement, I learned so much about cows.

Hal was a farmer/cattle guy back in the day and man he knew a lot about cows. As we rode past them he would have something to say. I of course had a bunch of questions too. Well, we finished Montana together, Idaho, and Wyoming. We rode into Colorado, stopped at Brush Mountain lodge, ate and drank very well as we all know, then pressed on and on. Hal was a heck of a survivalist. We both tested our skills on more than one occasion.

Once, when we had not resupplied properly we ran out of water and food. Hal was more confident than me which helped a lot. We bonked that day, so we took a long afternoon nap under a tree. We figured with the headwind, no food and water, that we would probably get blown backwards. Better to sleep. Man, did that ever help. We had agreed that we would ride to the border together. We also had the enjoyment of occasionally riding with a very young guy named Drew. He, as I later learned, had just turned 20 years old. At the time he rode mostly solo. I thought, wow I am riding with possibly the oldest and youngest riders to ever complete the Tour Divide and if we finish together that would be cool.

Drew was fast. I later realized that unless my knees healed, I would not be able to keep up with him. Hal and I however seemed to ride longer and earlier that him and we crossed paths throughout the race so finishing together was possible.

Well, in Colorado things changed, not for the better unfortunately. After leaving Steamboat behind we reached the dam and took a short break. Hal and I then pressed onward and up…again. After about an hour Hal, who was a little behind me yelled "shit!" I looked back and he said that he left his backpack at the dam. It had everything important in it. This also was the one time that he did not ask me if everything was zipped on his backpack. Man what a serious bummer.

I thought about going back with him but we were getting to the point where I had to think about the finish and my ride home (my daughters). It also was going to be about two hours by the time we got there and if it was not there Hal could not continue anyway. I made the decision to not go back with him. I felt terrible. Hal headed back and I continued on. It was lonely. I prayed for him that it would be there or some note saying who to call for it. The more I prayed and thought about it, the more convinced I became that it would work out.

I decided to wait each morning an extra hour for a couple of days in the hope he would catch up. Also I knew Drew was back there and they would be together so at least he had someone to ride with. When I finally was able to check trackleaders.com for him, I saw that he was a couple of days behind which meant it did not turn out so well. I later learned that the backpack was not there and he had to completely resupply from home: money, ID, and more.

Drew stuck with him until he was ready to go again. Instead of quitting, which is what most people would have done, Hal stuck with it. He resupplied and got back on his bike. I never saw them again or spoke to them. I healed and got faster and faster so I pressed on to finish and meet my ride. I was able to take off 2+ days the last short week of the race.

Hal and Drew finished together and I am very happy for them. The Tour Divide is more that a long race. It is a time to build relationships, have great experiences, and see things that happen to only those who ride it. Hal and all the guys I rode with will be indelibly burned into my mind to the end. I can't wait to do it again.

2013 Result: 66th Place - 28:08:24

A Typical Day on the Tour Divide

Mirko Haecker

It is day five of the Tour Divide. Less than a mile before Ovando, Montana I found myself in the eye of a hail storm. After being hit by some hailstones my speedometer was reset to zero but it still worked. My legs had just received a free but painful 'massage'. The Tour Divide has a reputation for broken gear and broken bodies. Earlier that day I had passed infamous Richmond Peak. Unlike the years before the conditions weren't intimidating at all. Crossing the peak I had clear blue skies and not an inch of snow on the pass. After crossing Huckleberry Pass I reached Lincoln and checked in at the first motel where the owner welcomed me with my personal name. I was a little bit surprised but he had spotted me and Thomas Borst. I was riding with the track leaders. I would experience this friendliness and great enthusiasm again along the route.

The next morning—my sixth day of the Tour Divide—I got up at around 5:30 a.m., packed my gear, and started the day with some sandwiches, having ordered more to go. The plan was to get to Basin or even Butte. An important lesson I had learned earlier was to bring along enough real food for the day. I can't live on energy and candy bars alone. The change in the weather from the day before seemed to persist. It started raining on and off and was definitely getting colder.

Because my speedometer had given me difficulties the previous day and didn't show some information it was supposed to, I had reset it in the morning. Shortly after Helena, just out of curiosity and to check if it was properly working, I glanced at my speedometer and was truly surprised. It showed a total of exactly 1,000 km ridden since Banff.

This was almost one quarter of the total. What a blast, I thought and took a picture. I was so involved in the daily routine—following the motto eat, sleep, ride—that the overall goal had somehow slipped my mind. With lots of positive

energy, I climbed the next two Continental Divide crossings. Before the ascent to Priest Pass we crossed a railway track which was a little adventure in itself as we had to climb and carry our bikes over a parked train. I thought of my 4-year old son who is a real railway enthusiast and took some pictures I hoped I could e-mail him later that day.

Meanwhile it was getting warmer and the sun was coming out so I could take off the rain gear. These were great conditions for the descent on the way to Helena. The last miles were paved, easy and mostly downhill along the highway to the largest city since the start in Banff. A few moments later I entered the first supermarket. Many other riders were coming and going and I really had to focus myself only to buy stuff I really needed (and no more). But it was a great chance to get some fresh fruit, which I could hardly wait to eat. Next door there was a drugstore where I bought some tape and bandages for my aching knees. Yes, I was starting to have some serious knee issues. I can't remember exactly when it started. It must have been around day two or three. Initially it was only the right knee, which really surprised me as my left side actually is my weaker one. Perhaps it was due to an accident and a twisted left knee I had on a training ride just a month before the Tour Divide. So this could be the result of a functional unbalance. I don't know. At least I had brought some kinesio tape from home, which I applied on day three during a lunch break. The taping job looked pretty good but it didn't last long as I had underestimated the thickness of dirt and dust on my legs. So I was quite optimistic having more tape and bandages. Unfortunately, as it turned out later, this wouldn't solve the problem. At this point I was convinced that after a few more days I would recover. It didn't even cross my mind that the pain in my knees could be a showstopper at a certain point.

Before pushing on over the next passes after Helena, I decided to have lunch at the burger joint next door to the supermarket. I ordered a plain hamburger with no fries and a side-order of salad instead to avoid any indigestion. Stocked up with food and water I hit the road again towards Basin. Clouds were darkening the sky. I had just reached the city limits when all hell broke loose. It was great luck that I decided to seek shelter in an open barn right next to the road where two other Tour Divide riders were already waiting. The hailstorm only lasted about 15 minutes but it was pretty severe so it was a great pleasure not to get another 'massage' like the day before.

Now that it was already afternoon, the plan was to get to Basin and stay at the B&B mentioned on the map. My personal cue sheets stated it was less than 70 km from Helena to Basin, which should be four to five hours. When starting the climb to another nameless pass, I felt weak and breathless like never before on the Tour Divide. I was surprised because I had eaten enough in Helena. So I blamed it on the burger. It felt like my stomach was extracting all the energy from the rest of my body. Thomas was riding faster so I decided to let him go. It was actually quite a nice stretch, but it started raining again and was getting pretty cold so I couldn't really enjoy it. Usually I like climbing and don't mind long ascents, but not today. What a difference compared to the day before when a few other guys and I were having fun racing up Huckleberry Pass. Some other bikers were passing me, I felt weaker and weaker and the long ascent to Lava Mountain was just beginning. I was getting pretty frustrated. This way I would never make it to Basin.

Most people had made plans ahead of the Tour Divide for what they would do in certain situations and so had I. If I got caught by the mental drain or in case of physical problems I always had the plan to keep on going and if necessary to push my bike until it's over. Just keep on moving. I was there. Pushing my bike up the pass gave me time to play with my GPS and calculate the distance and vertical climb ahead of me. This made things even worse. I realized it was another 2,000 feet upwards. I could hardly believe it and I was hoping the information on my GPS was wrong or I was temporarily suffering from dyscalculia. The vertical profile sometimes displayed wrong information if the speed was too slow. But this time it wasn't. So I kept on pushing my bike and started evaluating options as it was already getting dark. Should I set up my camp and get some rest? It was turning freezing cold and still raining, so it was not the best idea to sleep in the mountains. I would probably have wet gear until New Mexico and get up the next morning completely soaked.

While evaluating my options I was really surprised to meet up with Thomas again. He seemed to come out of nowhere. I was sure he had been way ahead of me. He also seemed a little irritated about the long way to Basin but wanted to get there badly. I told him about my calculations but I had the feeling he wouldn't believe me. But we promised to get over this pass. Before going on it was Tour Divide teatime. Drinking one of my little '5-hour-energy' bottles, eating a Power Bar and some gummy bears should give me the necessary push. Approximately five minutes later I felt like Popeye after eating spinach and we rode on. I still don't know what's in these bottles you can buy at every gas station. It was a good idea to have grabbed some on Day 2 for emergencies. If you get caught after drinking one of those on the Tour de France you'd probably be taken off the race due to violating the doping rules. I didn't care, and it helped.

Of course, on our way to Lava Mountain we missed a turn (for the first time) but realized our mistake after a mile when we reached a little lake, a wild campground and some fireplaces. The map says we had reached Park Lake as I found out later. It had finally stopped raining but the temperature had dropped to 35° F. Nevertheless, when I looked at the lake, the surrounding mountains and the fireplaces I thought this would be an awesome place to camp and spend the evening in front of a campfire. But this is a race and you are not supposed to rest where it's nice. Looking back it would have been better to have stayed there and enjoyed the adventure for a little while. The place where I actually ended up that night couldn't have been more different.

Back on track the fun began. The cue sheets stated "next 2 miles steep and rough". This was a huge understatement (most other descriptions had thus far been quite appropriate). The Lava Mountain Trail wasn't rideable for three or four miles, at least not with a fully loaded bike. It felt like it never ended but the scenery was truly amazing although it was getting dark. I had to stop to change my glasses and ate more gummy bears. If I had been in the Alps with my full suspension bike I'd have tried to ride this trail and probably would have had some fun, but not this day. Although I was now in combat mode and seriously wanted to get to Basin, I hadn't realized how exhausted I actually was. It didn't come to my mind until I started searching for my glasses. I was already getting paranoid because I am literally blind without them. A minute later—which felt like an hour—after searching for my glasses in my bags and starting to dig in the mud I finally realized I was holding them in my mouth so as not to lose them in the dark. Obviously, the subconscious mind still seemed to be in order but the rest of me wasn't. I was warned and now alert, so decided to slow down on the upcoming descent. This probably saved my life. It was only ten miles to Basin, mostly downhill.

It wouldn't have been a typical Tour Divide day if the story ended there. It was around 9:30 p.m. and already completely dark. No more rain. It started snowing! I wasn't sure at the beginning, but it really started snowing on top of Lava Mountain. I was truly happy about my 1100 lumen power LED light I had brought with me on this trip. It was worth every Euro I had spent on it. Otherwise, I might have seen the tree lying right across the forest road five seconds too late going downhill doing at least 25 mph, soaked, freezing and tired. I literally stopped one metre before this tree in the middle of the road.

A few more turns and around 10:30 p.m., after 170 km, 3,500 meters of vertical climbing and over 15 hours in the saddle, Thomas and I reached Basin and entered the only little bar that was still open. We met a few other Tour Divide riders who even wanted to continue on to Butte that night. I was deeply impressed but this definitely was no option for us. Someone called the B&B to check if they had a room but it was already closed. I didn't care anymore and just wanted to lie down and sleep. Allegedly there was a campsite in Basin, which we didn't find in the middle of the night, of course. So we decided to find a place where we wouldn't bother anyone else and that's not the backyard of one of the few houses in Basin. We finally ended up between I-15 and a trash container. Compared to Park Lake it couldn't be worse but I fell asleep within minutes despite all the trucks roaring down the interstate and literally over my head.

Postscript

I believe the day on the Tour Divide described above is very representative in many respects. It was not the longest day (measured in miles), nor was it my hardest, although it was quite tough. So what is it that makes it so typical? It was a little bit of everything, all packed into one day; getting proper food, physical and mental challenges, navigation, severely changing weather conditions, great scenery, the support of other riders, and lots of surprises. Riding the Tour Divide everyone will be able to tell many stories, maybe some comparable to mine.

My major goal was to reach New Mexico, my favourite state in the US and to which I have a very special relationship. I didn't get the chance this time. After ten days and one third of the total distance I was forced to drop out of the race as my knee issues worsened. I had to walk the last mile into Lima after a rest day in Polaris where I tried to nurse my knees. It was a tough decision and a very emotional moment but unavoidable as I couldn't get enough power on the pedals any more. Not quite a perfect prerequisite to ride another 1,800 miles on a fully loaded bike. Before the race I worried about severe technical issues, wild animals and my own fitness level. Besides a flat tire, I had no technical issues. I have not even seen a bear and most of the time I ranked much better than I had hoped for. Everything seemed to be just fine. In the end it was my knees. This had never entered my mind because I had never suffered from this type of knee pain before. I learned a lot on this trip but most important was that you will face challenges you haven't experienced yet and you least expect.

Riding the Tour Divide was an unprecedented experience. Many months of preparation and training and looking forward to an adventure of a lifetime were definitely worth it. It would not have been possible without the support of my wife and two little kids. I was blessed to experience what is known as 'trail magic', and to meet wonderful people, both participants of the race and people along the road. Finally all this happened on the backdrop of incredibly amazing scenery.

At the Start: Thomas Borst, Mirko Haecker, Michael Gruenert

Mirko Haecker, Germany

Rookie - Not finished

mirko.haecker@gmail.com

http://tourdivide2013.blogspot.de (here some information on my gear can be found)

I am 42 years and a proud father of two children (4 and 6 years). Mountain biking has been my passion for over 15 years. Usually I ride in the Alps, also multi-day trips. Besides a few 24h races, this was my first ultra endurance race. From the beginning I looked at it a lot more from the adventure side than from the race aspect, as I was realistic enough to know I wouldn't have anything to do with the outcome of the race. For me the Tour Divide also served as a door-opener to bikepacking which is quite unknown in Germany and Europe because you don't need to carry sleeping gear due to the very dense population, even in more remote areas. When not biking or spending time with my family I work as a financial consultant for my own company.

Special thanks to my friend Michael Wallace for proofreading the draft of this article. He also would have picked me up in Antelope Wells but I didn't get the chance to meet him. Hopefully next time.

Breaking Bread on the Tour Divide

Nick Legan

Eating on the Tour Divide is something for which every racer prepares. We make lists, spreadsheets, research online and make phone calls to ensure a given spot is still open for business. It's simple: without fuel we can't continue our long-distance quest. And while the food that passes our lips keeps us pedalling, the company we share with other racers at meals can do even more to keep us moving forward.

During my time on Tour Divide, I learned that a day full of struggle and frustration, aches and wrong turns could be completely reversed by a meal among new friends. It's amazing what a cup of coffee on a chilly morning, or several icy Cokes on a hot afternoon, can do for morale, especially when combined with the company of a fellow traveller. The fraternity of hungry, tired men (sorry ladies, I wasn't lucky enough to meet either of you this year) is hard to beat.

Several examples come to mind. After sweating my way along the dusty road to Holland Lake Lodge in Montana, I found myself in Paradise. The reception I and the other Tour Divide racers received was wonderful. We cleaned up, laid wet camping gear out to dry in the sun-drenched lawn and went inside to fill our bellies. Ordering my meal seemed to take several minutes. After requesting something in the neighbourhood of 10,000 calories, I looked to a fellow racer, Brett Simpson, and his reply was, "Are you sure that's all you need?" We laughed our heads off. Both the massive orders and the laughter became routine.

A particularly wonderful dinner came in Ovando, Montana. I had struggled all afternoon over the undulating gravel roads that lead to Ovando. When I rolled into town with Jason Gaikowski, Nathan Mawkes and Mike Johnson, we discovered that the apparent resupply spots were closed for the day. I had planned poorly and found myself very low on food. I wandered the porch of a café hopelessly, saying to my companions, "I need to sit down. I'm about to enter a dark place."

Looking back on that statement, it sounds comical, but I was serious at the time. The real mystery of this situation was that we saw the bikes of Brett Simpson and Scott McConnell parked outside the Blackfoot Commercial Co./Ovando Inn. I had heard that you can stay the night in Ovando in one of six rooms that the store's owners rent to hunters, fishermen, tourists and weary Tour Divide cyclists. Nathan had mentioned that they also have a covered wagon and some Divide racers had slept there in years past. My calorie-depraved mind deduced that Scott and Brett had stopped for the night (never mind the early hour or apparent lackadaisical security measures Brett and Scott had taken).

Fortunately, Mike Johnson kept searching while I sat down to gather myself. He saw a local and asked for help. The man pointed to the general store that we had assumed was closed. Mike knocked and we found that the friendly shopkeeper, Peggy, had stayed open for us. She had been tracking our dots on Trackleaders. Brett and Scott had been inside shopping during my moments of despair (and had not haphazardly parked their bikes as my poorly functioning mind had thought). Peggy invited us in and we eagerly bought supplies. I was dragging and therefore the last to get to the counter to pay.

I asked how long the friendly shopkeeper had been in Ovando. She said she moved there over 20 years ago and loved it. The winters weren't as bad as you'd think and she gets to see lots of outdoorsmen and certainly cyclists. She remembered John Stamstad passing through during his first time Great Divide ITT ride. National Geographic journalists were in tow, making sure that he didn't receive outside assistance. She'd been hooked ever since. (It sure is nice to meet locals on the route that appreciate the adventure of the Tour Divide and efforts of the racers.)

With my spirits buoyed, she pointed us towards Trixi's Antler Saloon, a bar just up the road that was sure to be open. Laden with food, water and other necessities we rolled up the hill to Trixi's. There we found many other Tour Divide racers. Aussie Aaron (badass single speeder in a tight race with Scott McDonnell) was finishing up his meal and the Swiss duo we had seen over the past few days were setting up camp in the yard next to the restaurant (they seemed to excel using the "early to bed, early to rise" approach).

Inside, the five of us sat down and the long food orders began. We took turns heading to the bathroom to clean up and the stories from the road and elsewhere began to bring smiles to the entire group. As food arrived it was quickly devoured. With Cokes downed and food arriving all the time, we were high, on calories and camaraderie. The food was tasty and the buxom waitress that served us added "flavour" to our Trixi's experience. She even delivered aluminium foil to help us wrap up our to-go orders.

As we rolled out of town, my moment of despair seemed like a distant memory. In fact, though I was only a mile down the road, there were several thousand calories and many laughs between my happy, pedalling self and the shadow of a human I had been an hour before.

The hospitality of every restaurant, bar and lodge that I visited was phenomenal. Maybe I was lucky, but I prefer to think that people are, for the most part, happy to help a tired stranger. And there's something very vulnerable about a cyclist, carrying only what he or she needs, that makes us approachable.

While few would ever consider the food I ate on the Tour Divide gourmet, it got the job done. Along the way, I became an aficionado of both chicken strips and tater tots (they keep much better than French fries, in case you were wondering). And while I learned a lot about the food that works well for me when choices are limited, the bigger lesson was that fellow adventurers really lifted me out of dark places. I only hope that I was able to return the favour on an occasion or two.

2013 was Nick Legan's first attempt at the Tour Divide. While he didn't finish he plans to return to the event to experience more of what the route and its travellers have to offer. In the meantime, he spends his days freelance writing, working media relations for several cycling industry companies, and plotting new adventures.

A Father and Son

Peter D Kraft Sr.

Where to begin?

I guess it all started in June of 2011 when Peter, my then 18-year-old son, came to me and asked if I would watch a movie called 'Ride the Divide' He said it was a documentary about a mountain bike race starting in Banff, Canada and finishing at the Mexican border. The distance was a mere 2,745 miles while climbing 200,000 feet in elevation along the way. Peter wanted to compete in the race, and he wanted me to do it with him. After watching the movie, like everyone else that has seen it, I was hooked. The million dollar question was could we realistically handle something of this magnitude? For years we have ridden motocross (dirt bikes—that is, two wheels with a motor) having only gotten involved in mountain biking about six months prior to seeing the documentary. We did have a few major issues to overcome; at that point in time neither of us had ever ridden longer than two hours in the saddle, we lived in Florida where there is almost no elevation to speak of and neither of us had ever heard of the term 'bikepacking'.

Before we got too excited about the whole thing we decided to look at the 2011 finish list and find someone who had completed the race that was reasonably close to us geographically. We would then drive/fly to see them and spend a day with them getting answers to the hundreds of questions we had already compiled. Two particular questions, and the answers to them, would determine if we were really going to attempt this epic adventure: how long would it take to get in Tour Divide shape, and could we race this event safely with very little mountain biking and no backcountry experience? We hit the lottery when we found Derek Bentley, from Gainesville Florida. Derek raced in the 2011 Tour Divide finishing in 21 days. Ironically, he lives about six miles from my home. What are the chances of that! Derek became our mentor, although I am not sure he knew what he was in for when he first agreed to meet with me and let me pick his brain. For two years and countless phone calls, meetings and texts he spent hours and hours of his time answering our never-ending stream of questions and sharing the wealth of knowledge he accumulated during his divide race and the many years of his 'outdoors' lifestyle. Based on me having my own business to look after, a family with a child still at home and my son being a Bio-Medical Engineering Major (not the easiest major) in college, Derek's opinion was that it would be wise to put it off an extra year and make our attempt in 2013. This would allow for more time to train, test equipment and experience bike-packing. So with the blessing of my wife, our adventure began. A chance of a lifetime: to spend a month with my son crossing the country unsupported on a mountain bike, seeing and being with Mother Nature up close. There was a lot of learning and training to be done. For two years we read a lot, trained a lot (did some bikepacking), and tested numerous pieces of equipment.

Goals

We had three of them. The first was to gain the experience of a lifetime seeing the country in slow-motion and doing it together—basically, we wanted to have a great time with each other. The second was to finish the race at the border of Mexico. Our third goal was to complete it in 27 days—which, at the time, was defined as competitive for the Grand Depart. We were successful with the first two but the last one was wiped out in the Gila National Forest, in New Mexico (more on that later).

Tour Divide 2013

Wow! 134 determined souls at the Grand Depart headed south from Banff, and nine more headed north from Antelope Wells, New Mexico. This was the largest group ever to take on this epic challenge. All of us SoBo's (south bounders) met at the traditional gathering spot, the Banff YMCA, and took care of the annual group picture with Crazy Larry running around like a kid on Christmas day. This guy just loves the Tour Divide. Other than a few pictures, there was not really much going on except some conversation about a last minute email from Matthew Lee advising of a detour because of bear activity near Boulton-Creek (some 60 miles from the start). There was however, that obvious 'nervous energy' that almost every rider seemed to exhibit—the ridiculous amount of time, energy and money that each and every person in that select group had put forth in the previous weeks, months and even years (in our case) was coming to fruition in the next few minutes, and it showed.

We left the YMCA in group formation and headed to the start at the trail head behind the Banff Springs Hotel. Oddly, I was very calm once we were at the starting line. Peter and I lined up towards the back unsure as to what was about to unfold in front of us over the next few weeks of our lives.

And then it started…..

For the first ten minutes we were in a massive pack of +100 riders with the fast guys already off the front. My son Peter was hell bent on moving forward to get out of the masses and pushed the pace. Just as we seemed to clear the pack and find 'space' I had my first mechanical, well, sort of a mechanical. As we descended a rather steep grade, at speed, both of my fork-mounted water

bottles ejected. One landed in the middle of the trail which was promptly run over by the some 75 or so riders we had just passed, and the second bottle went over the side of the mountain. After retrieving the bottles I bent the cages in a little tighter in hopes of firmly securing my wandering bottles. I said this was sort of a mechanical because it was a constant issue throughout the race. I chased a lot of water bottles! No matter what I did, if it was a fast and bumpy descent then I was eventually 'chasing my bottles'. Although I broke and replaced three bottle cages during the race, this was my only bike/equipment failure.

After securing my bottles I again started pedalling toward Mexico. An hour or so later I caught up to Peter at the top of the hill coming onto the wide gravel Smith-Dorrien Spray road—he was waiting for me. When I saw him there, the lyrics "I will wait, I will wait for you" by Mumford and Sons came to mind. It wouldn't be the last time I heard that song.

Riding Together

I knew from the start that our pace would differ and that we would not ride 'side-by-side'. Keep in mind that we did not train together. He is a college student living away at school. For two years we each did our own 'thing' preparing/training in ways that we thought suited us best individually. The first day of the race I found out rather quickly that I could ride with Peter on the flats and the typical '"up and downs', but when it came to the climbs, he was gone…

For the first week or so we would start each day packing up our sleeping gear, eating and then riding together for an hour or so until I slowed or a climb was at hand, at which point he would separate rather suddenly. Two, three or four hours later, depending on the climb, there was Peter at the top of the pass waiting for me (Mumford and Sons coming to mind again). This would happen periodically throughout the day and we would end the day at an agreed upon place to camp. We would set up camp, take care of our bike and body maintenance. We would then eat, talk about the day, read maps and make our plans for the following day. As the weeks progressed our riding relationship evolved into a second stage—we would start the day riding together for an hour or so until I slowed or until that first climb of the day was staring us in the face and we would not see each other again until the next supply stop or the agreed upon camping spot at end of the day. Occasionally, I would catch Peter during the day when he would stop to eat or filter water (I usually ate on the go and don't drink much). We would always resupply, eat in towns and camp- together. This riding relationship allowed the two of us to ride within the spirit of the rules and truly experience being 'alone' for probably 90% of the route and at the same time allowing us to have a father/son experience that was shared together and forever bonding.

Our race was progressing absolutely perfect—insignificant mechanical issues, minimal physical issues, good daily mileage average. We had fallen in love with the Tour Divide and we were on target for a 26 day finish. Life was grand as we lived this exciting new simple yet demanding lifestyle for 24 days. Then, 2.5 days from the finish, we entered the Gila National Forest, and it all changed.

A long week in the Gila

301.6 miles from the finish—only 2.5 more days… It must have been about 12:30 p.m. Monday afternoon when we left Pie Town after eating lunch (and having pie of course) at the Daily Pie Café. I remember the slight uphill riding out of Pie Town and seeing Peter pull away into the distance. The weather was sunny and hot! The next thing I remember is riding up to Peter, in the rain (with full rain gear on), at the church in Horse Springs about 40 miles out of Pie Town. Fortunately for me, due to the remoteness of this part of the route, we had agreed at lunch to meet there for a mandatory water refill. The next available water was at the Beaverhead work station nearly 100 miles from Pie Town. It was about 6:00 p.m. when I arrived and Peter had been concerned because I was an hour or so later than expected. He later said a brutal storm hit right when he reached the church and that he thought maybe the road turned to 'soup' and that I was probably 'pushing' through the mud. He was worried and contemplated going back up the mountain to search for me.

I was confused when I saw him and remember saying "I hurt myself". I really have no idea what happened to me but I know where it happened. In the last video that I took before the accident, I mention that I was at Continental Divide Crossing #23—10 miles before the church. Based on the amount of damaged to my body I know I crashed on a fast descent. The only real fast downhill between that video and the church was the Mangas Mountain descent some six miles before the church. I have since gone and looked at my GPS logged track in that area and I went from 29 mph to zero descending Mangas. It appears that I was motionless for one minute and 43 seconds then my track shows me walking the bike around in circles randomly for twenty minutes. I then move on for a few hundred feet, and stopped for another twenty minutes or so, possibly putting my rain gear on.

I probably fell asleep coming down the mountain or possibly hit a large rock and crashed. The back of my jersey was shredded but my rain gear was in perfect shape, no tears, no mud, no nothing. So obviously I crashed in good weather and then later put on my rain gear: Jacket, pants, socks, hood, gloves and 'over-mitts'—but I remember none of it. I don't remember being unconscious, I don't remember waking up, riding or anything—just leaving Pie Town then riding toward Peter at the church. The weirdest part is that 5 ½ hours of my life evaporated and I have three videos and 14 pictures I took along the way, but when I look at them I don't remember taking them. Also at the church were Fred Arden and Mike Arenberg, two great guys who we had seen earlier at the Daily Pie Café. They had left Pie Town before we did and Peter had passed them during the day and they met up with him at the church. I want to thank both of them for their positive support while we waited for help.

Unbeknownst to me, I was bleeding from everywhere. At first glance I looked fine because I had on all of my rain gear. Peter told me he figured out I was in trouble when I removed my helmet and rain hood from my head. I had landed hard on my face/head (cracked my helmet outer and inner shells) making hamburger (as the doctor would later described it) out of my forehead and splitting my head open over my right eye. The back of my left ear had a large 'flap' cut out of it, exposing my ear cartilage. My head was quite swollen and oddly shaped. Fred went around back and kind of found an open door to the church (another story for another day), and we were able to seek shelter inside. As I removed my rain gear I learned that both elbows and my right knee were in pretty bad shape. All three had been split open and were very jagged, deep and full of pieces of rock. I had also peeled about 50% of the skin off my back.

Peter was absolutely calm and logical, asked if I was okay and if I needed him to do anything. I told him I was fine and that I was going to stop the bleeding and clean up a bit in the bathroom. I was carrying on with some brilliant idea about super gluing my wounds closed and that I was going to be fine to ride. He knew I needed to get to a hospital and told me he was going to go stand by the road (this was a little country road in front of the church) and try to flag down some help.

Now you have to remember, we are in the middle of no-where at this point. Peter stood out in the rain, at first by himself, and then a few minutes later thought enough to go and get his bike so that if someone did drive by they would think he had a bike problem and hopefully stop. 45 minutes later, the first car and the only car (actually a truck) that he had seen, stopped. He explained to the stranger what we were doing and what had happened to me. This man was a trail angel like none ever.

He introduced himself as Jay Platt and told us he would help us in any way that he could. First, he had to make a call and cancel a work obligation he had with someone that was waiting on him. Jay then called his wife and told her he was bringing two strangers in need of help to their home. Peter and Jay loaded the bikes into the truck and we were off. It was at Jay's home that we met Kimberly, his wife, and their three small children (one of which was an infant). These unbelievable people welcomed two complete strangers (and I looked horrendous) into their home. His wife made us dinner and arranged for a volunteer ambulance service to come from a town called Dactyl (I think) 40 minutes away to pick us up. Peter and Jay put the bikes in their small barn while we waited for the ambulance. It must have been 9 p.m. when we left in the ambulance headed for Socorro, New Mexico.

Jay said he would pick us up in Socorro but he had to get to his earlier obligation. Kimberly then proceeded to tell us that if we needed a ride back from Socorro to just call her and she would drive the hour and a half and pick us up. Now, this is a mother of three small children. "I'll just load up the kids and come get you guys" she told me. I thanked her profusely in disbelief that there were really people like this in today's world. The ambulance drove us an hour and a half to the hospital in Socorro. While riding in the ambulance it occurred to me that I had hurt my back and neck. I figured the concussion and stitches were manageable and certainly would not prohibit me from continuing to race, but the back issue seemed, at the time, to be a show stopper. Having had disc issues in my back before, I was fearful that I was done. I was suddenly discouraged in a big way—it was a long ride to the hospital. Peter was asleep in the front of the ambulance, mentally drained from the ordeal.

After getting all of the wounds flushed out, stitched up, and a drain tube inserted into my left elbow, we waited on the results of the MRI on my head and neck. I purposely didn't tell the doctor about my back. While waiting on the MRI results, which would determine if I was cleared to go, Peter and I discussed him finishing. I asked him if he would be continuing if I could not, or if was he done. His response was an immediate—"We are two days from the end, obviously I'm going to finish". I smiled.

During our hospital stay, Joe, one of the nurses took an interest in our story and told us he or his dad would give us a ride back to our bikes at the Platt's barn in Horse Springs. Joe was a 30 something year old guy, and was as genuine as the Platt family, another trail angel! I was relieved when the doctor said that I had a bad concussion, but with a little rest could continue on to Mexico. I was discharged and Joe gave us a ride to a little motel– it was now 3:30 a.m. The phone rang at 8 a.m., it was Kimberly Platt and she was worried about us and wanted to know if we needed a ride. I shook my head again, amazed by these selfless people and I told her we had a ride later that afternoon and would be by to get the bikes around 5 p.m.

On time, Joe's dad (another unbelievably nice person) dropped us off at the Platt's barn. Kimberly, who had washed all of our clothes while we were gone, insisted on driving us back to the church with the bikes in the back of her truck. She dropped us off and we hugged goodbye. It occurred to me at that moment that these people I had met in the last 24 hours had changed me as a person, made me a better soul and helped me better understand what is important in life. I thought it peculiar that although they had such an impact on me, I would probably never see them again.

From the time we left the church the previous day it was literally 24 hours before we arrived back at the church. Somehow, a lot happened in that 24 hour period to get us back there so quickly. On a side note, I have since looked at our path from the church to the hospital and back. At no time did we move forward on the route—we were always off route. Onward to Mexico!!! My back was still a huge concern and was really bothering me. Strangely, when I got on the bike, the bent forward angle actually gave me some pain relief.

A few hours into the ride that evening, the Gila struck out again with a monsoon that eventually rendered the bikes useless. We slogged through the mud stopping every 100 feet to use sticks to clear the wheels and drivetrain of mud. We rode the bikes, slid them, pulled them and pushed them. It was tiring and awful on the mind. The rain never stopped. We did this until about 11 p.m. and then camped; wet, cold and muddy.

We were up early and hoping to reach the brutal CDT by dark. After a long day we ate and resupplied off-route in Lake Roberts, then rode back up to the Sapillo campground where the CDT trail head is located. This was originally a mandatory alternate for the main route. However, early on in the race the Gila was closed due to fires which required a less demanding detour. I had emailed Matthew Lee just before Pie Town asking for clarification on what was the proper route. He advised us that either option was acceptable but, in his words "Gila main route is TUFF...but rewarding". So we opted for more pain and went the way of the main route and the brutal CDT. After all, reading between the lines of Matthew Lee's message, we understood his message, "you get out of it what you put into it".

It was Wednesday evening and was getting dark when we reached the trail head. We decided to knock out the CDT in the dark (I don't recommend this) and then camp on the other side. In the morning we would then ride 140 miles to the finish. The plan was good, but the Gila wasn't done with us just yet. We started up the CDT just as it was getting dark. It was hell...very dark, bumpy and hard to navigate. There was quite a bit of hike a bike on the way up to the top. After 'some time' it occurred to me that the trail seemed to have narrowed but it didn't feel like it was as 'tight' as it had been. I manually turned my light to the left off of the trail, and got that feeling you get when looking off a tall building or bridge: my breath kind of went away. It was steep and it was scary. Steep on the left and steep on the right. I shouted up to Peter (who strangely wasn't way out in front of me like usual) to stop!!! I told him to get off the bike and push because it was too dark and much too steep and if we had an accident here there would be no trip to the hospital, it would be permanent. Peter responded like a son that I did not know. He was pissed and responded in a lousy manner that he was camping if he wasn't riding, so we camped. I would later find out that he had been feeling really sick and it was easier for him to ride than walk.

We pitched our tarp tents sometime around 11:30 p.m. and not ten minutes later he started throwing up. This went on and on and in no time at all he was in really bad shape. I knew we needed to go back down to the trail head in hopes of finding someone in the campground area. I also knew he needed to rest and we would have to wait for the sun to come up before we could safely go back. Peter was sick all night long, literally all night. Knowing he was in trouble he tried to stay hydrated utilizing his water carefully. He would later tell me that he stopped drinking water in the middle of the night when he got down to a half of a water bottle because he knew he would need it in the morning. I lay in my tarp tent all night asking him if he was alright from time to time, until the morning finally came.

When the sun came up he was a disaster. Zero energy, completely dehydrated and still sick; he looked terrible. The previous night it had taken us two hours to ride/walk up and in the morning it took us 3 hours plus to walk down. He could not ride, had to push and absolutely refused my water. He had a complete suffer-fest all the way down. I was scared, fearful of how bad he really was—he kept making this weird/disturbing groaning noise. Thankfully there was one family camping in the camp ground. I explained to the man (another selfless awesome trail angel) our predicament and he said he knew of the Mimbres Forest station about 20 minutes away. He and I loaded the bikes and drove to the forest station. When we got there I ran to the building and they were having a meeting with all of the forest service people. I interrupted, and the guy leading the meeting came out to check Peter. He checked his vitals, and then got a very serious and concerned look on his face that made me panic inside. He instructed one of his rangers to call an ambulance. "Tell them to hurry" he said. He told me Peter's vitals were really bad. This would be the second ambulance ride in my lifetime, only three days after the first one.

Before the ambulance arrived a young guy named Eric told me he would keep an eye on our bikes and store them at the ranger station. He said to call him if we needed a ride back from the hospital and he would find someone to come get us. Again, I cannot begin to describe these people; they were so genuinely nice and very concerned for us and our situation. The ambulance took us to the hospital in Silver City of all places(again, never moving forward on the route), where the doctors filled Peter with five litres of saline to get him hydrated, and ran tests to try and find out what was wrong with him. They came back telling us that his calcium was low and he was Done! Out! No More Riding! They didn't know what caused it, but they were worried that there was an underlying issue causing this calcium deficiency which could lead to some pretty bad results. Peter told me that he didn't care what they thought: he was finishing what he started. I told him no, let's just call it a day and head home. We had accomplished the most important goal: #1—to have the experience of a lifetime seeing the country in slow-motion and doing it together—basically, having a great time with each other.

So, at this point I was in a quandary; I had the doctors saying no, my wife on the phone saying no and a 20 year old determined on finishing. I have been an athlete of one sort or another most of my life and I could relate to where Peter was coming from. That said, he and I were in no position to put his life in danger. I explained Peter's stance to the doctors and asked if there was anything else they could do to figure out what, if anything, was causing the calcium problem. A new doctor suggested that it was simply an electrolyte imbalance due to the massive dehydration. He went on to say that an electrolyte imbalance can cause low calcium and since they had rehydrated him they would wait a few hours and let his electrolytes settle out and then retest. We did just that and when the test came back his calcium was much closer to 'acceptable' and the doctor released him to ride in 48 hours as long as he was eating and drinking without getting sick. They were still not sure what made him sick in the first place, but they suspected giardia. We explained that we filtered all of our water and they concluded it was probably from 'bottle splash' and could confirm with more tests over the next couple of days, but we had more important things to do.

Silver City does not have taxis so the local Police came to the hospital to give us a ride to a nearby hotel. For the next 36 hours I hitchhiked back and forth from the hotel to the local Wal-Mart for supplies. I was beat to hell, tired, bandages all over me and a wool hat on my head to hide the damage to my face. I literally looked the part of a homeless person yet people still gave me rides. I remember standing in the Wal-Mart parking lot, hands full with food/drinks. I was tired and trying to figure out how I was going to walk the ¾ miles to the hotel with all of these supplies. I asked a guy and his wife, trying to explain my story to them, if they could give me a ride, 'just down the street to the hotel'. He basically ignored me and said no because he was going the other way. I said I understood and remember being angry because he would not go ¾ of a mile out of his way. But I said to myself "you would have done the same thing".

Then as I was walking through the parking lot the same guy pulls up to me and says, "Hop in" and he gave me a ride to the hotel. He said he was sorry for ignoring me earlier but that my appearance had startled him and his wife, but they realized I was in need of some help. The people along this journey just continued to amaze me. Peter had gotten sick on a Wednesday night late; we arrived at the hospital around 10 a.m. Thursday morning and were released around 6 p.m. that same Thursday. Sitting in the hotel I figured, at best, we would restart Saturday evening (the doctors said 48 hours rest) again attempting the CDT in the dark. Realistically though, we would camp at the trail head and set off on Sunday morning.

After 36 hours of forcing very little food and drinking water, Peter insisted he was ready to go. He was still in the bathroom more than he was out but kept telling me all the time, "I'm fine", but I knew better. Saturday, late morning, we got a ride (again never moving forward on the route) back to the Sapillo camping area (more great people helping us get there), picking up our bikes from the ranger station along the way. It was around 1 p.m. and we sat in the dirt near the trailhead for a few minutes putting on our bike shoes, sun block and getting ready to ride. We both looked like hell and felt terrible. Peter was obviously still sick and I was mentally shot from being in 'dad mode' over the last two days, worrying about my son. Not to mention my back and neck seemed to be getting worse. So we started moving forward. We walked and walked and walked. Peter was too weak to ride the CDT alternate. He just put his head on his aero bars and leaned on the bike for just about the whole section. It typically takes someone 2.5 – 3 hours to get through it; five hours later we emerged from the CDT and the struggle finally eased, somewhat. We had gotten through the CDT and now had 15 miles to, ironically, Silver City. We had ridden (walked) only 27 miles that Saturday and rolled into Silver City in shambles.

Our plan was to leave early in the morning and finish that same day. We got on the bikes the next morning and had ridden only a minute or two when Peter said he had no energy, felt sick and needed to stop. It was now six days since I had crashed in the Gila and we had moved forward a mere 135 miles. The Gila had punished us and had put a huge damper on our 750 mile weekly average. The old saying 'so close, yet so far' was constantly in my thoughts.

We waited another day and finally rolled out on Monday morning to make the long haul to the finish at Antelope Wells, 123.9 more miles. This normally takes 6-10 hours depending on the winds. Peter, still sick and fatigued, thought it would take 13 hours. We headed out at 8 a.m. and the ride to Separ was long, hot and slow. After an hour and a half rest/resupply we left Separ at 2:15 p.m. for the final 75 miles to Antelope Wells. It was really hot at this point and as the day wore on Peter was getting worse. He was hoping for rain, to cool him down. Be careful what you wish for! 37 miles from the finish, a monsoon of monsoons let loose and it was ugly. This was the storm that the local news channel was reporting on the television the night before as I sat in the hotel room. They spoke of flash flood warnings from Silver City to Antelope Wells.

As the miles trickled by the rain and headwinds were relentless, probably the worst we experienced the whole race. Peter moved at a snail's pace and had to resort to getting out of the saddle and doing what I termed the 'pedal, pedal , pedal , stand and coast' method of keeping forward progress. He was just too tired to sit and grind it out. For every mile we rode south the water from the roads edge crept slowly to the other side threatening to breech the road and stop us dead in our tracks.

We made it to the finish without incident at 9:07 p.m. (13 hours almost to the minute as Peter had predicted) in the black of night and pouring rain. About 300 feet from the boarder Peter stopped. I was probably 100 feet behind him and had been all day, respecting, as we had the whole race, the no drafting rule. We had not spoken since we left Separ some seven hours earlier. I rolled to a stop next to him and asked "what's wrong". He simply replied, "I want to finish together". So we rode side-by-side to the finish. It was dark, and difficult to see where exactly the boarder was. That last 300 feet happened in slow-motion as my emotions started quietly pouring out of me. I was having a good 'dad' moment. One of those moments that is forever etched in your mind. I thought back... I had cried a few times during the past four weeks while riding out on the trail, alone in the middle of no-where, thinking about this moment at the finish, thinking about what my son and I were doing together, the unbelievable memories that we were making, the laughter we shared, thinking about him in front of me these past four weeks navigating and making major decisions on his own, thinking about him dealing with adversity at thresh-hold levels and doing it calmly, thinking of him taking care of his own physical ailments, and mostly thinking how proud I was of him. Peter has always been a great kid; 2,859 miles later I had learned that he was an even more incredible man.

We finished in 31 days. Due to my accident and Peter's illness we gained 4.5 days in our race. Yes, I said 'gained' and not 'lost'. As weird as it sounds, it was a blessing that I was hurt and Peter got sick. Not because the last 260 miles were pure mental torture and physical misery, but because of the people that we met during those trying times. It's hard to express in this write-up the empathy, kindness, selflessness and just plain old being nice that we experienced from complete strangers not only during the race on a day to day basis, but especially when the 'chips were down', in the Gila. These special people popped up everywhere and it happened all the way to the very end when Roger Payne was there at the border to pick us up. He was there waiting and had actually been watching and waiting for 4.5 days (at his home), watching our 'blue dots' trip and fall in the Gila.

I had called him from Pie Town a week earlier and had arranged for him to pick us up at the finish in 2.5 days. I then called him a second time the night of my accident and told him it would be an extra day to which he replied, don't worry about me, I will watch your blue dots and pick you up whenever you get there. Just keep pedalling south he said. A week later, there he was, waiting for us at the finish, with sandwiches and drinks in hand. He was an unbelievable sight for sore eyes! He drove us out of Antelope Wells (in his massive diesel truck) through the flash floods that had formed over the road just behind us as we rode our bikes in. He drove us three hours to El Paso that night. He had arranged to drop us off at a hotel that was two blocks from a bike shop and three blocks from the airport. He made it so easy for us. He was kind, helpful, and nice—there's that word again, nice. Yet another unbelievable person on the Tour Divide. He dropped us off at 12:30 a.m., we said our goodbyes and he was gone. I laid in bed later thinking that he probably wouldn't get home until nearly 4:00 a.m. This man didn't pick us up for the modest fee he charges to transport Tour Divide riders, hell, that barely pays for his gas. He does it because he is a good and genuine person and enjoys being helpful. These people that I met along the way on this journey were just incredible. The world that I lived in for those 31 days was unlike anything I had ever experienced or ever will again.

And then it was over.

The Secret

So many people have asked me what it was it like to have such an adventure and to be able to do it with my son. Every time I am asked I keep coming back to the same answer… it is a secret! It is a secret that is unable to be told. I want to tell you about it but I just don't know how to tell you! I am incapable of putting into words what Peter and I shared, it is something that we will have for the rest of our lives, something that cannot be taken away from us, it is a secret that only a few hundred people know about.

Only those few souls that have reached Antelope Wells truly know the meaning of it. And the strange thing is that this secret is different for each and every person that learns about it. It is what they make of it. I can give you a hint in the hope that those of you reading this will go and live what we lived, and experience what we experienced. The secret contains: beauty, the grind, landscapes, pain, laughter, tears, smiles, an argument or two, chasing food, mountains, chasing water, sunshine-rain-sleet–snow, worry, fear, confidence, the dark side, dogs, failure, clouds, thought, deep thought, self-discovery, joy, self-discussion, mental breakdown, deserts, cold-warm-hot, mechanical breakdown, new friends, broken body parts, candy, bears, success, stars, down-hills, walking, camping, pushing, moose, rivers, compassionate strangers, sleeping, eating and riding—and after all of that you will fall asleep wondering what the next 24 hours on the Tour Divide will bring you.

2013 Result: 76th and 77th Places - 31:13:08

Father/Son—is that self-supportive and solo?

Some have written or expressed that this father/son adventure is not within the spirit or the rules of what the Tour Divide was meant to be and I say to that …. nonsense! Quite frankly, we rode alone for most of the race while riding with other competitors on only a few occasions for a few hours here and there. The following is from the Tour Divide web page under rules: "#3. Spirit: Above all, attempts are intended to be solo / self-supported, self-timed, and observed as one stage, the challenge is complete upon arrival to the opposite GDMBR terminus from start". Peter and I probably rode alone more than most riders.

Our riding relationship was as much in the spirit of the rules as was Ollie Whalley's riding relationship with Craig Stapler during his record setting run in 2012. The following are quotes from an interview Ollie did with twentynineinches.com: "Craig Stapler and I separated from the other leaders and we rode together a lot of the way … it was great to have a rider so similar in pace for moral support" "During the climb we post-holed up to our knees in some places. Craig and I swapped duties breaking trail" "When we got down to Eureka we stopped to get some food in town and Craig says, 'Do you want to keep pushing on or stop and get a room and warm up' ". The same can be said about Matthew Lee's riding relationship with Reuben Kline in the movie 'Ride the Divide'.

For the most part these riding relationships are constantly forming, changing, and in some cases maintained throughout the Tour Divide from the leaders in the front to the back of the pack. As long as your effort is solo and self-supported, I say there really is no argument.

Peter had a food debacle that illustrates just how solo we were; we left Platoro on the long stretch to Abiquiu with the only services just after Horca (or so we thought). The services near Horca were not there and Peter was out of food (he ate his emergency pack the night before thinking he had supplies in the morning near Horca). Now there were no services for 100 miles until El Rito just before Abiquiu. I had plenty of food (as I said earlier I really don't eat or drink too much) but we had to go off route to Chama New Mexico some 17 miles away with a large loss of elevation for Peter to resupply his food. Including a brief breakfast, it wound up being a six hour 'off-route' trip, but we remained within the rules maintaining a solo/self-supported status by not sharing food. In my opinion the Tour Divide has evolved into two different types of racing that have two different sets of characteristics. The ITT is mentally more difficult, it has to be a 'one-man-show' simply because there are no other riders out there, while the Grand Depart brings so many more variables to the race that the relationships created amongst all of the riders are inevitable. The Grand Depart is more physically difficult because unlike the ITT you do not get to choose the best time for weather and winds, you go on the second Friday of June regardless. Enough said!!!

I miss it every day.

Will you do it again? Well, this is an interesting question. Peter Jr. is definitely going to do it again. Probably in 2014 if he can fit it in between summer internships. He wants to go faster and finish in 22-23 days. For me, for at least two weeks after the race, my answer was no. In fact, not a chance! Experiencing the Tour Divide was incredible and I wouldn't change any of it. However, it was so unbelievably difficult. It was insanely hard. So hard that I said I would never attempt it again, ever! Then a funny thing happened a few weeks after I settled back into the 'real world'. I began to miss it. Then I started thinking about it when I would lie down at night, reliving my way through the days on the Tour Divide—from town to town, mountain pass to mountain pass then falling asleep somewhere along the route. I still do this every night. I literally miss it every day and that probably sounds idiotic to most people, but I am willing to bet that nearly everyone that has completed all or even some of the race has that 'need' to be out there, on the Tour Divide.

Yes, sooner or later, I'll do it again.

Dave Blumenthal

Unfortunately for me I never met Dave, but I wish I had. I have read a lot about him and the amazing person, father and husband that he was. I thought about him from time to time while I was riding the Tour Divide and, being the emotional soul that I am, it brought tears to my eyes on more than one occasion. I felt so lucky to be out there riding the Tour Divide with my son, doing something that Dave probably would have done with his daughter later on when she was a young adult. Thinking of Dave made me appreciate every minute of every day, good or bad, that my son and I shared together. It is cliché, but it can all be gone in an instant, we never know when or why, it just happens. So live life… every minute… every day.

Dave would want it that way.

An Interview with Peter Maindonald

TC: Tell us a little about yourself

I am a radio engineer. I build and maintain broadcast and telecommunications equipment in Rotorua, New Zealand.

TC: How did you first hear about the Tour Divide and what made you want to race?

Back in 2008 I listened to a radio interview with fellow kiwi Simon Kennett, who had just completed the GDR. During the interview Simon suggested a similar shorter event could work here in New Zealand. Two years later Simon organized the first Kiwi Brevet. I lined up on the start line not really knowing what to expect. I set off riding up a very steep learning curve. I had way too much equipment, including full camping kit and too many spare parts. I completed the course but failed to make the cut off time. I really enjoyed the riding and decided to learn more about 'bikepacking' and ultra racing. Two years later I lined up at the second Kiwi Brevet with much less equipment and a new ethos. I completed the course in five days, almost at the 'pointy end' of the field and was noted as the most improved rider.

TC: What experience did you have with long distance racing before the Tour Divide?

Like fellow kiwis, I have completed various Brevet style races here in New Zealand over the last three years ranging in length from 300 km to 1,100 km. I have also completed several 12 hour solo mountain bike races and 24 hour team races.

TC: How did you train for the race?

The New Zealand government has recently funded a series of mainly off road cycle trails, so a lot of my training has been linking up these trails by various back roads, creating multi day rides along with the brevet style races mentioned above. Most of my day-to-day riding on the local Rotorua trails is on single speed building strength.

TC: Tell us a bit about your rig and gear

Niner SIR 9 steel frame, Niner carbon fork, Shimano XT 2 x 10, Easton Haven wheels with tubeless Maxxis UST Crossmarks [without sealant], aero bars, Revelate Designs saddle, frame and bar bags, Z Pack tent, Thermarest neo air mat, Garmin 62s GPS, A couple of Fenix LD22 lights. All clothing NZ made Ground Effect, merino base layers, this stuff just works.

TC: Tell us about some of the highlights of your ride

People. The kindness of strangers and also the comrade-ship of fellow riders.

TC: How did you handle the nutrition and hydration challenges on the ride?

One of the big challenges was the supermarkets. Very time consuming trying to locate stuff. By the second week I just went to gas stations and grabbed what I could find. I used restaurants and fast food when available for hot food. I would hate to think how many litres of chocolate milk I consumed over 22 days.

TC: Did you have any major mechanical problems during the race and, if you did, how did you deal with them?

No major problems, a creaking bottom bracket for the first couple of days until I worked out the Niner bio-Centric BB bolt had been over torqued, small tweak and silence. I changed the chain at Steamboat Springs as a precaution and minor drive chain problems with mud and crud.

TC: All riders eventually hit a rock bottom, a new low during their race. Could you tell us about your darkest hour during the race?

Day 4, between Ferndale and Holland Lake. I lost focus, misread map detail, ran out of food, hot, dehydrated, unable to find rhythm and then my nose starts bleeding badly.

TC: What advice would you give to future Tour Dividers

Race your own race. Try not to let others influence your decisions.

TC: Will we see you again on the Tour Divide or are you going after other challenges?

I would like to return to the Tour Divide at some stage, but I am also keen on trying a fat bike on the snow and ice. However, as the weeks pass my mind still returns to the Tour Divide.

2013 Result: 34th Place - 22:08:45

peter.maindonald@gmail.com

We Do Things Not Because They Are Easy But Because They Are Hard

Scott Thigpen

"Hey, you're that Rohloff guy" I said as I caught up with someone just a few miles before Elkford. "Huh? Oh, yes yes." The Rohloff is a hub with internal gears that switch in and out. Many Tour Divide riders have them. I have always coveted one, but with a $1,200 sticker price? No thank you.

"I'm Scott" I said and he nodded and quietly said "I'm Ty" and we kept riding in silence. I would wager that like me, many of Tour Divide riders are rather introverted, I mean you have to be to take on such a tumultuous race that you're forced to ride solo. We exchanged a few words and then rode through the rain, cold and bitterness before popping out onto a road which led to houses and a country store littered with Tour Divide bikes all around it.

"Dude, I'm just not gonna stop eating" a racer said as I came in. He was tall, wiry, with blonde hair, and had attempted the Tour Divide last year but due to a knee issue, he had to drop out. His name was Eric and unlike most people was definitely not an introvert. "Dude I remember last year being here, like all the racers were here. I got out before most of them so I could get a jump start to the next town. Dude you pushing on?" I was still processing everything he was saying, so I just nodded to most things. "Dude you're going to love this race. Dude, I'm going to finish it and be up at the front as long as my knee stays together." "That's great man." I said and then wandered into the restaurant portion of the country store. In there were Prentiss, Ty and the kids Taylor and Kristen. I sat down next to them freezing and took off most of my now dripping wet layers. We all sat and talked about the day so far and what lay ahead.

"Sparwood is up ahead" said Prentiss, we can camp there. Ah camping, the thing I'd been looking forward to the most. I'd purchased a bivy sack (a tent/sleeping bag) with tent poles that made for a nice little cocoon I could slip into. While I wasn't really excited about sleeping out in grizzly bear country, a Tour Divide Racer has got to do what a Tour Divide Racer has to do. Or something like that.

As everyone warmed up and magically the rain had ebbed, we all left the restaurant and started to pedal away. With a full belly and miles to go, this wasn't smart for me because immediately we hit a huge climb that seemed to go on forever. My legs felt unnaturally strong and I was climbing fine for a while when WOOSH a semi truck passed me which felt like he was going 100 miles per hour. I don't do well riding on the road with cars zooming up next to me; I certainly don't do well when my belly is full and my legs aren't warmed up causing me to lean left and right on the road. WOOSH, another truck zoomed up by me. Then slowly Kristen came up next to me. "It always takes me a bit to warm up to climbs" she said, but as she continued to hammer she got faster and faster and faster. Then all of the sudden zooming by both of us was Taylor. I was also riding a single speed and I marveled at his climbing prowess with only one gear. He seemed to not even be fazed by the steep climb and disappeared around a corner. Kristen went on up ahead of me, and I went from a slow climb to finally off my bike and walking.

I felt sorry for myself and down on my luck because I couldn't climb like them. I popped on my iPod and started to listen to some music. I don't know why, but John F. Kennedy's "We go to the moon" speech came on, so I listened to that. The words Kennedy uttered instantly changed my mood and thoughts when he said:

"But why, some say, the moon? Why choose this as our goal? And they may well ask why climb the highest mountain? Why, 35 years ago, fly the Atlantic? Why does Rice play Texas?

We choose to go to the moon. We choose to go to the moon in this decade and do the other things, not because they are easy, but because they are hard."

Immediately I was set on fire. I got on my bike, told my legs to shut up, and climbed the rest of the mountain. When I got to the top I was immediately met with a pleasant downhill and zoomed down turning off onto a dirt road. The sun was setting and I started to get fearful of bears. Why? I don't know, I just had it in my mind that bears wait until dark to pounce on their prey. I kept my eyes peeled, especially when I whipped around corners. The road turned into rocks and then the rocks turned into something unrideable. I tenderly crossed over a series of giant loose rocks paying special attention to not slip as the potential for error was great, and it was pretty far down to the river below.

The terrain went down, which I was happy about as my legs were very spent by now. As the last bit of the sun peeked through the woods, it made for nice memorable scenery. I sort of zoned out and would periodically check my GPS to make sure I was on the right track. I looked down once and then flicked my eyes back up. When I did, I saw a large black animal coming straight at me. In horror I slammed on my brakes with my bike skidding to one side causing me to almost lose my balance. "OH SHIT!" I screamed thinking I was about to collide with a bear.

I'd heard a few years back that a Tour Divide rider came across a bear and fell off a cliff (he didn't die). I didn't want this to be my same fate, especially on Day 1. When I collected myself and looked up, I realized it wasn't a bear but a cow aimlessly standing in the road. It sat there and stared at me with blankly chewing its crud. "SCREW YOU COW!" I screamed with my adrenaline surging. "GET THE HELL OUTTA THE WAY! GO ON! MOVE! MOOOOOVE!" It wouldn't move. It just stood there. So I took my bike and pushed around it and on back to the dirt road. I kept riding, the sun started setting. However, it being June, and being somewhere in Canada, it never really got dark for a long time so I was able to go for a long time without turning on my lights.

I would go by fields that had elk prancing around, but fortunately no bears. The fields turned to houses and then the houses turned into a town. It was late into the evening now, around 10 p.m. or so. I knew I was in Sparwood however I didn't know where everyone was camping. "I'll just keep looking" I said to myself. I saw a hotel sign "NO!" I said out loud "NO HOTELS" I said to myself. I kept pedaling and saw a sign for camping. "Finally" I said to myself and started going that way through the little town of Sparwood. "SCOTT!" I heard someone yell. "YO SCOTT HEY!" I looked over and there was Scott McConnell, Ryan and Kevin. "HEY!" I yelled back and rode over to them. They were standing in front of some burger joint that was closing. Ryan said "Hey man, so we got here about 20 minutes ago and they were closed, but then they felt bad for us and gave us all these burgers!" I looked into the sack and there were tons of burgers in there. "You want some!?" He said "I can't eat anymore" and I dove into the bag immediately. I felt like I ate one burger in two bites and grabbed another.

Scott McConnell said "hey man, we're thinking about getting a hotel for the night and skipping the camping, we're all nasty and wringing wet, we want showers." I caved and didn't even think again about camping ... I wanted a shower too. I love showers, they are my favorite thing in the world. I agreed and we all pile into a hotel room which seemingly was hosting several other racers as well. We all took turns showering then I went and called into MTBCast.com leaving my message that we'd made it to Sparwood on day one.

Then I called Kate who was just beside herself. "Baby you are just flying! You are so far ahead of everyone else! Great job!" I smiled and told her it was a tough, but epic day. We said I love you to each other and then I went back into the room. There were two beds and four guys. Kevin and Ryan were in one bed and Scott McConnell was in the other. So I slid in the bed with him and right before I fell asleep Scott said "Hey, I need to warn you about something my wife tells me I do in my sleep, I kick."

He definitely kicks in his sleep.

2013 Result: 40th Place - 23:07:46

Less Risk, More Fun!

(How I couldn't escape my job on the Tour Divide and loved it!)

Thomas Borst

Dear reader, if you expect another account of hair raising situations and almost-tragedies; this story is not for you. This story is for all the guys who dream about racing the Tour Divide some day and want ideas on how to increase the chance of touching the famous border stone in Antelope Wells.

Still here? Okay, let's go:

When I was dreaming of riding the Tour Divide I was, of course, looking for adventure. I was fascinated by stories of people who were able to deal with breathtaking situations like Eric Foster who dislocated his knee in the 2012 and managed to still ride on for a few days before inconceivable pain caused him to quit. Or how about Georg Deck who broke his frame in the climb to Marshall Pass the same year and had to hitch-hike back to Salida to get a new bike to finish the Tour Divide successfully.

When I was a blue dot junkie I followed these guys on the Trackleader's page. They gave me sleepless nights and I admired them for the way they dealt with their crises.

But when I was planning to race it myself, and especially when it got closer and closer to the Grand Depart, I came to the conclusion that I do not need this type of thrill to make the Tour Divide a real adventure. I had the chance to visit Georg earlier this year and to talk to him about his experience. He was able to solve his problem in a very superior manner, but it became clear to me that situations like this consume valuable mental and physical resources which you might need further down the track.

At this point some kind of an 'occupational disease' got hold of me. I am a project manager and risk management is one of my daily survival strategies in this job. So I tried to deal with as many perceived risks as possible beforehand, and tried to work out strategies simple enough to recall when things got tough. This means avoiding risks whenever possible and dealing with them when they occur. Just like Georg developed a strategy to deal with the risk of a broken frame when it occurred, and was able to execute this strategy in the middle of the night after endless hours of riding. From this point on risk management was part of my preparation and it was with me until the last mile of the Tour Divide. Sometimes I was aware of it, sometimes not, but I was always glad it was there. I want to share a few examples of when it worked for me and when it did not.

Pre-Race Paranoia

When I started my preparation in the summer of 2012 I already was aware of one major risk from following the Tour Divide in previous years. My impression was that most people have to quit because their ankles and tendons cannot handle the load of this ride. In response to this, I modified my training plan spreadsheet. I added a column that indicated the extra load that I carry with me on my bike during my training rides. As a rule of thumb I increased the extra load slowly but continuously up to about half of my Tour Divide load on my intense training rides, and full load at the long base layer units. From August 2012 I did not do a single training ride without an extra load.

In order to close the motivational gap that I always face in the dark and cold winter months I bought a Surly Moonlander and registered for the Rovaniemi 150 Arctic Winter Race. That helped me to keep moving in bikepacking mode throughout the winter, and had a few unexpected spin offs: I could test some of my material in really cold conditions which might prove helpful for the colder nights on the Tour Divide. Secondly, it gave me lots of opportunity to ride a bike in snowy conditions and to prepare for excessive post-holing in hike-a-bike-sections. The latter turned out to be complete risk management overkill. During the Rovaniemi 150 race I pushed my bike in a single night for at least ten times the distance that I had to push it on the entire Tour Divide. But better this way than vice-versa.

By the way, in my preparation I also did not change my training routes much compared to the previous years. They cover terrain that is much more technical than what awaited me on the Tour Divide. By the end of my preparation I felt quite confident with my fully loaded bike on technical single-track so I was pretty sure that bike handling would not be a problem on the Tour Divide.

Like everyone else I did a few overnight rides in my training. With no previous bikepacking experience it was essential for me to sort out the material and work out a system that I could handle in the worst of conditions. But it also was necessary to develop a race tactic for the Tour Divide. It took me quite a few overnighters to figure out the balance between longest possible saddle-time and shortest possible regeneration breaks. It turned out that 16 hours in the saddle is sustainable for me. Whenever I exceeded this significantly it became hard for me to deliver regular performance the next day. It helped me a lot on the Tour Divide to know my personal limits in this area, and I strongly suggest that everyone finds their limits before they head for the start line.

For logistical reasons I did most of my overnight training rides in the Taunus hill range in Germany which is close to my hometown. Compared to the real thing the Taunus hills are ridiculously small. From any point in the Taunus I can ride back home within a maximum five hours. This bore another risk that compromised my preparation efforts: you tend to stay inside your comfort zone. Sometimes it happened to me that I planned to sleep outside but did not because conditions were bad. So I preferred to return home through the wind and rain and sleep inside. This resulted in some 20-plus hour brute force efforts that made me feel like I had a good Tour Divide-training ride when I finished them. But the next day I always had the feeling I'd missed a chance to refine my system in really bad conditions.

This is why I decided to do a final test ride that put me far outside of this comfort zone. Starting from my front door this four day ride took me about 600 km one-way through Germany. Looking back this ride was as close to real life on the Tour Divide as it could be. It gave me confidence in most of my material, but also led me to change a few things that I thought worked perfectly before this ride.

In-Race Tension

The first day on the Tour Divide was a complete failure of every risk management plan that I prepared beforehand. I made every rookie mistake you can imagine! Determined to reach Sparwood that day, I was completely stoked and taken by the euphoria of the day I started to ride much too fast.

Unfortunately I didn't take the time to eat and drink enough, and also didn't take the time to protect against the rain and the cold that crept in over the day. Soon I developed signs of dehydration, bonking and hypothermia. Mirko Häcker—my riding companion on the first days of the Tour Divide—and I arrived in Elkford at about 6:45 p.m. which was not too late to carry on to Sparwood. While we were having our dinner at the Elkford Motor Inn, almost all of the guys who arrived after us left for Sparwood that same evening. It was frustrating to see them leave and tempting to follow them. But at least one of the rules that the risk manager inside me had prepared before the Tour Divide worked on that day: when your body is at its limit there is no use in keeping up with your pre-set goals. You would pay a much too high price for that on the following days.

Eat, drink and sleep as much as you can to recover and carry on the next day. At that moment I recalled the personal limits that I plumbed during the overnight training rides in my Tour Divide preparation. And I knew I was far beyond these limits that day in Elkford. I am sure that Mirko would have been able to push on but he stayed and I am glad about that because the next day we pushed each other to what I believe to be the best performance we had on the Tour Divide. We made it to Eureka, Montana, that day and on our way we met quite a few guys who had carried on to Sparwood the day before.

We arrived in Eureka late in the evening and had to camp in some kind of a recreation park downtown because all the motels were full. But we still had this positive feeling that a strong day on the Tour Divide can give you and that pushes you through the days ahead.

After day two this particular risk management strategy was part of my plot for the rest of the Tour and I applied it quite a few times. Some guys who followed my blue dot found it hard to understand why I sometimes built a camp only a few miles away from the next oasis on the Tour Divide. Here is one more example: after my push through the Great Basin I arrived in Rawlins before noon and carried on with a vague chance to reach Brush Mountain Lodge the same day. But the heat was unbearable that day and I completely underestimated the challenges. I ran out of water in Medicine Bow National Forest and out of power exactly at Aspen Alley. I decided that it was more efficient to build a camp in a beautiful place near Aspen Alley than to push on to Brush Mountain Lodge.

I purified some water from a nearby stream, composed some kind of a dinner from what was left in my stock, and slept for almost eight hours. Quite a few riders passed me later that evening and pushed on to the Lodge. I met most of them in Steamboat Springs the next day.

At this point it became clear to me that I needed some kind of a rhythm of 'Eat Sleep Ride' on the Tour Divide, and that regeneration was paramount for my successful finish.

I was just riding in the mid-pack of this race but even there I faced guys who rode through nights, sometimes for 48 hours in a row or longer. I admire them for their power of will to do this, and they will no doubt report in their own contribution to this Cordillera volume how it paid off for them. Of course, sometimes I rode in the dark too if I couldn't avoid it, like the final push to Eureka or the descent from Lava Mountain to Basin. I also started my final push to Antelope Wells between Silver City and Separ shortly after midnight because I knew it was the last day. But my internal risk manager tried to avoid night rides, because even with the best lights you are more prone to accidents in the dark. Furthermore, I consider it inefficient because you move slower in the dark and you pay a high price from trading off regeneration against progress.

For me it was also relevant that you can't enjoy the landscape on a night ride. Again, this is the point of view of a guy from the mid-pack and every prospective rider has to find out his own strategy. If you want to finish among the Top 20, extreme sleep deprivation is the price you pay. I finished in 53rd place and I doubt if less sleep would have helped me to finish 52nd or better.

One typical example is the Great Divide Basin. Some riders arrive in Banff already with plans to ride the Basin at night and stick to this plan by any means. When I arrived in Atlantic City at about noon it was a hot and sunny day but I decided to push on immediately because we had a perfect tailwind and the heat decreased in the afternoon. I rode further into the Basin on that day than I expected and spent an almost magical night and next morning that became one of my personal highlights of the Tour Divide. Glad I didn't miss this view of the Basin on a night ride.

There are some risks that the project manager in me loved, because I could work out redundant strategies for them beforehand. The best example is the risk of getting lost on the Tour Divide. It took me quite a few multi-day bikepacking training rides before I came up with a foolproof solution with some probability to not stand in the middle of nowhere with no clue where to go.

The easiest way to navigate on the Tour Divide is by GPS. But my unit consumes lots of electrical power and I couldn't count on being able to recharge it every day. It was only two weeks before the Grand Depart when I came up with a solution of hub dynamo and USB-power-converter that worked. But based on my bad experiences on the rides before, my internal risk manager asked me to take a few backups with me: cue cards printed on waterproof paper and wrapped in a waterproof map-case, and a bike computer with adjustable mileage, original ACA maps, cue cards scanned on my smart phone, and a battery USB-charger for my GPS. Sounds paranoid? It probably is but it completely eliminated one of the biggest worries I had beforehand. Funnily enough I ended up with the low-tech version of navigating by cues and odometer most of the time, and just confirming with the GPS when the cues left me in doubt. The GPS is pretty useless when reroutes come into effect with short notice. I was glad to carry my good old paper map with me on the fire reroute from Abiquiu to Cuba.

On the other end of the spectrum are the risks that the project manager hates: dangers that you cannot eliminate no matter how hard you try. They come upon you in different shapes: breaking frames, illness, bear attacks and thunderstorms, just to mention a few.

Obviously you cannot prevent them but you can prepare some risk minimization strategies that help when you get struck by them. For risks like this I prepared rules to apply when they occur. I have been inspired by emergency cue cards that leaders of commercial mountaineering expeditions hand out to their clients. These cards give clear but easy rules to decide when a client has to abandon his push to the summit and when it is okay to carry on. I found it helpful to memorize a few rules of behaviour for my ride that were on the same basic intellectual level.

One example, that I fortunately didn't have to apply on the Tour Divide, are rules for bear encounters. I was recommended Stephen Herrero's book 'Bear Attacks—Their Cause and Avoidance'. While reading it I wrote some rules on cue cards and memorized them. But in doing so I restricted myself to a few basic rules that were simple enough so I had a chance to recall them if it got serious. Herrero offers a complete codex of behaviour in case of all imaginable circumstances in which you encounter a bear. Most of them are not really practicable for a biker who suddenly gets confronted with one. So I felt comfortable to apply some Pareto-like 80:20 principle in this case.

On the Tour Divide one type of risk struck me in the form of a few thunderstorms that caught me exposed.

My first serious encounter with this species happened on my way from Hartsel to Salida. Thunderstorms were already brewing when I left Hartsel and were closing in when I was on a flat high plain a few miles after Hartsel. At that time I was riding into a strong headwind and thus had a close look at the clouds and lightning ahead, when I suddenly realized that a heavy thunder cell was catching up from behind, moving significantly faster than I was. I felt uneasy when I realized that I was the highest point around. Fortunately, I recalled some basic rules for dealing with thunderstorms that I learned before the Tour Divide and looked for the next depression where I hunkered down a few yards away from my bike until the worst was over.

Even worse were the thunderstorms awaiting me after Silver City in the middle of the night. The bad thing about thunderstorms at night is that you can't see how the clouds move. After Silver City you cross some hill tops which might be prone to lightning strikes. So again I recalled the basics and, from time to time, sat by the side of the road and watched exactly where the lightning struck to find out if the next miles were safe. Sounds trivial? To be honest it does so for me now that I write these lines but it definitely wasn't when I was out there. Applying these rules had a very calming effect on me beyond what my limbic system suggested.

Multiple Risks Striking at Once

Before I left for the Tour Divide I had heard of guys who quit the race for as simple a reason as a flat tyre and I couldn't believe it. But if you take a closer look, you find that the flat tyre was the straw that broke the camel's back. I had a similar situation on the Tour Divide although in that moment I didn't think about quitting the race but rather to go off-route and have my bike repaired. But this was enough to understand why people quit for such reasons.

On Day 20 I had an early start from Del Norte and felt good when I crossed Indiana and Stunner Passes. I ate lunch at the Skyline Lodge in Platoro, the typical burger and fries that you get along the way. A few days before a 'bison burger' with fries had helped me to push over Ute Pass to Silverthorne on a late afternoon. But on this particular day in Platoro it didn't work at all.

The road from Platoro to Horca is mostly downhill but I was feeling weaker by the minute. I felt like I was bonking although I had just consumed a few thousand calories. The subsequent climb to La Manga Pass felt like a wall to me. In addition, I had realized already on the climb to Indiana Pass that something was wrong with my rear wheel. It felt very shaky and the chain gave strange noises. During the climb to La Manga Pass I finally decided to have a look at my rear wheel and found that its bearings had excessive play. The combination of mechanical and physical conditions was enough to stop on this climb a few times in order to check and re-check my bike. I was somehow glad for these breaks because I found it hard to carry on with the climb due to my weakness and suddenly some kind of a downward spiral started. At one point I turned my bike around to descend to Horca in order to leave the route to have it repaired.

At that point I recalled another risk management strategy: break down multiple risks striking at the same time into their components and handle them separately. This strategy is aptly named 'Divide and Conquer'. In this case I sat down by the roadside, put in some calories and caffeine and drank some water to improve my physical state. After a while I started to evaluate my choices for bike repair on the map and came to the conclusion that my bike had to survive until Abiquiu where I could reconsider my options. By the time I arrived in Abiquiu I had almost forgotten this matter. When I returned home it turned out that the bearings were worn out completely but this is absolutely not a show-stopper on the Tour Divide. Looking back now I have a glimpse on why somebody would quit because of something as simple as a flat tyre. The worst thing about this particular case is that the frequent stops on the climb ruined all my chances to win Cjell Money's La Manga Challenge ;-)

Post-Race Wisdom

I encourage everyone to explore their individual risks and strategies to deal with them before they take on the endeavour of the Tour Divide. Strategies that work for me might not work for anybody else. Everyone has to test and retest their strategies before they start their ride, depending on their risk affinity. In my case it helped. The risk manager inside of me is as happy as he can be. My strategies worked most of the time and where they didn't work one thing came to my help that is absolutely essential for everyone: luck!

Purists might think that my risk averse approach to the Tour Divide is not according to the true spirit of the race. In some ways they are right. I didn't race all out, and looking back I might have been able to save maybe two days with a more risk affine approach and thus better meet the spirit of 'truly' racing the Tour Divide. But at what price? I knew before that if I failed I would have to come back again and again until I finished it. For a guy from Germany this is a logistical project that gets harder every time you face it. I would never trade one single minute I spent on the Tour Divide for a better finish time. Not one of the photo stops in breathtaking landscapes. Not one of the beautiful moments of talking to the trail angels I met. Not one of the precious moments of joining forces out there with other guys who shared this ride with me. The top priority of my first Tour Divide was to enjoy it and to finish it. To avoid turning a passion into an obsession.

Others might think that worrying about risks all the time and working out strategies on how to handle them takes the fun out of the whole thing. No risk, no fun! This brings me back to the subject of my story. Everyone who takes this endeavour is on a risk management project even if he or she doesn't want to be. On one end of the spectrum are the really experienced guys who have developed some kind of a sixth sense and don't need the kind of risk management that I suggest. On the other end are guys like me. Not being able to find your place in between these extremes might spoil the whole experience of a ride that you probably take only once in your lifetime. For me, I have found my place and I am perfectly comfortable with it because I was able to enjoy the ride as it happened almost every minute. That's why I titled this story 'Less risk, More fun!'

Antelope Wells, 9th July, 10:56 a.m.

I finished the Tour Divide 2013 after 25 days and 3 hours in 53rd place. Now that I have done it I feel some kind of freedom and room for improvement for another ride on the Tour Divide. Race it even faster or enjoy it even more? Time will tell...

2013 Result: 53rd Place - 25:02:52

Thomas Borst (Flörsheim, Germany)

tborst@ac-itg.com.

Blue Dot Junkies

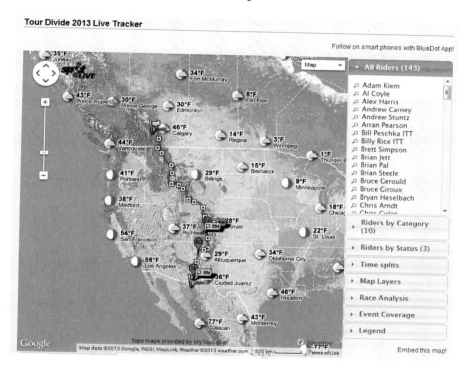

A Proposed General Classification for the Blue Dot Watcher

James Gilles

I'm a fettler, as I suspect are so many other blue dot watchers. But I've not always been. I blame this affliction firmly on my academic training and long distance cycling. The former taught me to analyse the world, to develop hypotheses and models to explain it. The latter has seen me spend hours thinking about different ways to attach route instructions to my bars, pondering the effects of tyre pressure on saddle sores, and the calorific and nutritional content of petrol station food. Both require an attention to detail, the ability to problem solve, to reflect at length, to fettle with ideas and things, to classify approaches and solutions.

The hours of attention that blue dot watching requires means that, like other areas of my life, it's also become the subject of a classification.

By reflecting on my own experience and that of others, I propose a general classification of the blue dot watcher for consideration. I have to caveat my reflections by acknowledging that 'us' blue dot watchers are a breed apart from the general public. What turns us from a normal person into someone that eagerly awaits that few weeks in June when we watch a series of blue, pink and maybe other colour dots travel along a red line marked on a Google map, is not discussed in this musing.

I see that there are four basic groupings that a blue dot watcher can fall into.

Group One—The Fan. Up until this year I myself have fallen into this category. We are the avid fans of the Tour Divide (other blue dot events do exist). We don't know anyone personally that is doing or has done the ride. We have not ourselves completed the event, but many of us would probably like to. We watch the dots, listen to MTBCast, and read the forum trying to imagine the people and stories behind the dots. We develop our own theoretical race plan for when we get to be a blue dot ourselves. Maybe we look for a connection to some of the dots to better allow us to imagine what it's like to be out there. I always look out for the Brits, but also follow the single speeders. Our emotional attachment to the race is that of an avid fan so on the whole we are looking at the big picture, the general flow of the race, have a real interest on the front runners along with our selected riders.

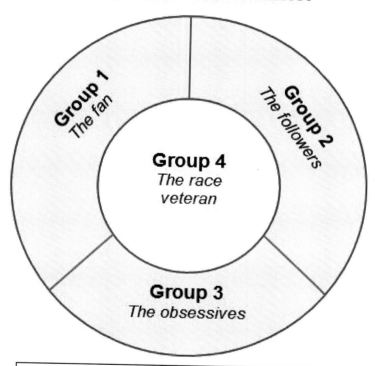

Notes

Blue dot watchers display common characteristics, which allow for a general classification. While all groups form part of the Tour Divide audience, it is the riders, the veterans that bind them. Without the riders there are no watchers.

Group Two—The Followers. This year I fell into this category. We too have not competed in the Tour Divide, but would like to. However, we know a person behind one of the dots, perhaps not very well, but we know them. Maybe as with me, you trained with, and had your arse kicked by them, during a few cold winter months. They are not close friends or family but you know their smile, know how they talk, and maybe know what it looks like to watch them disappear up a hill in front of you. This means that you have an idea of the story behind one of those blue dots and, as such, their dot becomes the most important one in the race. You're still interested in the 'Big Picture', what's happening at the front, maybe even still look out for fellow countrymen, but you now have a reason to focus in on some detail. The Tour Divide suddenly takes on a new level of interest, you update more frequently, you use the blue dot phone app, you use satellite view to look at the towns, roads and landscape they travel through. Anything that allows you to also be there.

Group Three—The Obsessives. In many ways I feel sorry for this group. I've heard their struggles on the forums and been told first hand why they would rather not be blue dot watchers again. This is the group that have close family and friends in the Tour Divide. I was a blue dot in the Highland Trail 400 this year and my wife became an obsessive member of this group. I can only imagine what it would be like for her if I actually went to Banff and became a dot for several weeks.

This group have a level of obsession that goes far beyond that of the previous two. They will stay up until the very early hours to make sure their loved one has bedded down in a good spot for the night. They will shout at the computer if their dot goes the wrong way, or if another dot is catching up. They will worry like hell if the dot stops without explanation or communication for hours on end. They know the story behind the dot, but at times they would rather not. They don't care that much about the big picture, they might look at the front of the race but are more concerned with the dots immediately in front of, and behind, their loved one. This group is also unique in that before their son, daughter, husband, wife, etc. became a blue dot, they themselves were not blue dot watchers. It is also unlikely that they will watch another blue dot again once it's all finished. They do not necessarily come equipped with the background Tour Divide knowledge to make sense of the events as they unfold. As a result, you will find them on the forums being advised by members of groups one, two and four.

Group Four—The Race Veteran. This categorisation is reserved for the small but ever growing pool of Tour Divide veterans. They have been out there. They know what it's like to plan the ride and finally roll down the trail from Banff, what it takes to keep the Spot tracker signal going for the folks back home so they have a blue dot to watch. On the forums they tend to be the calmest of posters, the ones with the wisest words for those in group three. Maybe with all the build up to doing the Tour Divide, they themselves once having been in group one, possibly group two, having put their close friends and family through group three, they then back off from the event. It becomes less romantic to them.

That's my four groups explained in brief. There may be other groupings or you may consider my proposals to be wide of the mark. This is to be expected. I wish to start a discussion. Regardless of our grouping, we can be sure that ours is a strange sport to spectate, unique even, given its grassroots amateur nature. The ITT rules all but exclude us from watching in person and there is no corporate interest. Despite this, the race directors and others have used technology, through MTBCast phone-ins, forums and satellite technology to create a truly unique event to spectate. In the process they have created a blue dot following which itself needs to be increasingly managed. Like it or not we have become as much part of the Tour Divide experience as the riders themselves.

I wish to thank Mike Hall for putting me in group two during the 2013 Tour Divide. It was riveting!

James lives in Birmingham, UK and will be a group two blue dot watcher again during the 2014 Tour Divide.

http://everydaystories.wordpress.com/

So Near Yet So Far

Dennis Carlsson

I felt like one of those scientists at Mission Control, Houston when I first entered the website to follow the 2013 Tour Divide. Like many others I became a little obsessed, scrutinizing and registering a distant landscape for signs of activity and progress. Day and night I followed the little blue balloons heading south across the Rocky Mountains like a procession of Chinese lanterns. Each balloon contained riders' initials like an identifying DNA code.......

"I am JC, LC...come on this journey with me. Know that I am well; know that in the night my light shines bright. The darkness is parted and I slip through. Although you are so far away I know you are watching and I am not alone. Invisible strings connect us and we will be together till the end. Share my wilderness, my triumphs, my exhaustion. My victory is also your victory and you and I will be forever changed when it is over."

And so we who watch are there. We internalize the effort, the cold that strikes like a hammer. Now a climb, now a headwind; will this strain ever ease? The struggle is interminable. Suddenly the balloon freezes and we panic. With all our mental powers we will it to move. Something supernatural possesses us and we become transfixed. What catastrophe has occurred? The minutes drag on like hours. Eight minutes ago, twenty minutes ago and eyes stare like a surgeon's waiting for some sign of life. It is impossible to leave the screen until we know what is happening as disaster after disaster knifes through us. The severity of the panic is matched only by the relief experienced when the balloon suddenly jumps several miles. We breathe deeply and prepare for the next section.

"We the riders feel the earth beneath us as it tries to defeat us, but we keep pushing it away. All we know is we are here; the road and the mountains draw us on. Like the conquistadors on their horses we are at one with our bikes. To the wild things out there watching, we are one strange being. Our energy feeds the wheels and hidden eyes make their primeval assessment. The little screen before us documents and directs and we too become mesmerized by numbers and lines. We feel connected to you at home by memory and signals in space and know our details are getting through. You ride with us but we must be alone for now. We must keep going. We will survive, we will conquer. The words speak back to us and become our mantra."

We who watch become astronomers. We zoom in on the alien terrain. What life forms exist among the rocks and trees? Where is the water to renew parched throats? Each new stretch offers new challenges. We worry. And now it is hot and the miles ahead are many, too many. We calculate; at least six hours before any promise of water, but we might be mistaken. A headwind can alter the situation dramatically as when a community has a forest fire turn on them. We find ourselves praying for a tailwind and when the bike suddenly picks up speed we smile like sailors watching the sails fill.

"We who are riders cannot think of you now for we are hungry, thirsty, exhausted and tired. We wonder how much our young bodies suddenly grown old can take. But we have no choice. We have to keep going. We must survive and if we do survive we must finish. The darkness consumes us and we must sleep with the wild animals. Our exhaustion takes our fear and we sleep, just one more of God's creatures, taking our chances. Well before the sun rises a primeval sense stirs us and we know it is time to move on. The crisp night air fills our lungs and miraculously we feel restored and once more the journey begins."

Back home we become geographers. We examine the contours, calculate climbs and descents, follow valleys and match bike speed with what we find. We take fright at how long some of the climbs are, as the bike speed slows to a walk. Time is stretched and progress is agonizingly slow. We feel every push of the pedals and grunt in sympathy. And now a blessed relief as the bike picks up speed. We have a sensation of flying and breathing becomes easier. If only the descent would continue but it never does. We tell ourselves we will stay with our screen until speed is sustained. Ironically time passes swiftly as another ascent challenges. Finally another descent and you enter a town. Now we can rest for you are safe for a little while.

"We the riders feel our bodies and minds changing, conditioned by the elements and the will to survive. We become wiry and ravenous like wild animals consuming what we can, when we can. Our legs are like pistons and need energy like never before. We have become creatures of the elements casting our fate to storms, blizzards and hot desert winds. We play chess with the devil and win but there are scars. We enter strange towns which are now more alien to us than the tracks through the mountains. We look to either side assessing, calculating. Where can we eat and drink? Which strangers will welcome us? When should we depart as we know we must because urgency bites at our heels?"

At home we see you stop and take rest knowing a haven has been reached. We work out the distance to the next town and possible rest places. We research the history of these places and find we know it already: Yellowstone and Rockefeller, the pioneers heading west along the Oregon Trail, clashes with the local tribes, Civil War armies spawning new settlements, songs of the Rocky Mountains and Woody Guthrie, the lawless Wild West. It seems that you travel though time and space and much of what we know about America returns to us. Pictures and music mingle in our minds and we wonder if you have time to know this.

"We the riders do not know rest. Our bodies take in whatever fuel and water we can and, when sleep claims us, a little sentry is on standby in our minds, hovering above ready to waken us at the earliest possible time. Time is of the essence. It is as though as soon as we sleep we wake and something magical has happened. Like a spring releasing, we rise and, guided by routine, we are quickly away passing the snoring houses and silent streets. But we are not outlaws and we say goodbye to the kind and gentle folks who took such pleasure in knowing us and helping us onward."

We at home see at last, the border within reach. Antelope Wells conjures up images of animals and fresh water. We look more closely and realize it is a remote customs post with little passing traffic. No welcoming crowds or anything to indicate a finish. It seems like the anticlimax of all anticlimaxes. Furthermore the temperatures are extreme and the weather becomes the last obstacle. You began in picturesque snow-capped mountains and now enter Dante's Inferno. It all seems so cruel. The joy of seeing a finish is tempered by an image of riders stranded with no alternative but to ride back to the nearest town so many hours away.

"We the riders enter an oven but nothing can stop us now. Hot winds from the desert mock us but we and the memories of what we have survived urge us on. We must drink, but water now is a very critical calculation; we feel like we are running on empty. Knowing the finish is near makes time stretch in our minds, but time and distance are eventually conquered. Yes, we are jubilant but strangely melancholic. It seems like a life has finished and nothing will be quite the same again."

When we at home see the balloon stop at Antelope Wells elation claims us. We are emotionally drained because we have been riding too. But what will happen now? We wait and wait. When we return to trackleaders.com we see the balloon moving at sixty miles per hour in a northerly direction. Then realization hits.

God bless Roger and Lloyd

The Tour Divide Race—a Small Town's Perspective

Kathy Schoendoerfer

Organizer of Frivolous Affairs,

Ovando, Montana 59854

In 2011 several riders doing the Tour Divide Race came through Ovando, Montana en route to the next waypoint of Lincoln. Some spent the night. Some ate at the local cafes. All were interesting to talk to and the entire population of 50 residents came to enjoy their quick ride through.

The next year brought in almost 100 of the riders, despite horrendous winter-like weather. The town businesses rallied to help them out, warm them up, and occasionally drive them to the nearest airport. That year, 2012, we discovered the addiction of Blue Dot Following, and the entertainment that ensues with people of outrageous stamina and courage. However, when we got the title of 'Trail Angel' from a woman who was near the end of her rope, and met her with food, lodging, warmth and care; we found our calling. We wanted to help these riders succeed!

In 2013 the town of Ovando prepared for 'The Riders'. With encouragement and advisement from Adventure Cycling, we got a shower tent, another enclosed lodging facility, the Old 1860's Hooscow [jail] to join the teepee and Sheppard's wagon allowing cyclists to sleep in comfort. We had signs posted where to find help, maps of the trail, sign-in boards, and one shop was able to stock emergency tires, tubes, and other items from a bike shop not on the route. The habit of watching Race Tracker went into full addiction.

The first two riders, Craig Stappler and Mike Hall were met with cameras, applause and mouths agape, after all they had travelled here in under 48 hours! And so began the long procession of riders for the next three months, some from the south; most from the north.

Although names may not have been exchanged, the memories still linger of a majority of them. Billy Rice coming through, TWICE, to be the first official Tour Divide Yo-Yo and always with the biggest darnest smile! James Hodges arriving with a spent tire and astonished to find his exact replacement in town. The group of Thigpen, Halloway and Stroot and the first 'Full Gear Wheelie' competition.

The town tried to greet each rider we saw by name and take their photos which were then posted on the Divide Forum. That allowed forum participants to contact us for updates or, as with Cjell Money, to pass along a message from Mom to "be sure to wear that helmet!" Greeting Mark Proia, the self-proclaimed oldest rider on the circuit, with a light for his perennial stogie; cheering on the 'caboose' Yukon Krauss; offering a portable heater to the 20-something year old rookies who feared hypothermia, while we reminded them Montana's cold would seem like heaven when they reached Colorado.

When we called out to a rider and yelled "Welcome to Ovando!" Eddie, or Dale, or Allison or Dustin, or Ty; their smiles were as wide as the Big Sky country. As one rider said; "During a long arduous trek like this, you don't know how good it felt to have your name called out. Like you had been expecting us. It was heartwarming."

Well folks, we were expecting you! We'd been watching your Blue Dot for days. We lived vicariously through your adventures and your stories. If we noticed a rider's Blue Dot delayed coming in; someone from the town of Ovando went out to search for them. Twice we found riders on the brink of dehydration and brought them into town; then watched them continue on the next day. I guess we liked the title of Trail Angel. For us it was heartwarming.

We are already preparing for next year. Hope to see some familiar faces!

Dot Watcher

Marion Esfandiari

Back in 2011 my partner, Kevin Cunniffe, achieved one of his long standing ambitions—to compete in the Tour Divide. I can't recall when he first spoke about his plans; I remember vague references to a big route in the USA that he wanted to do if he was able to take early retirement. My response was probably something along the lines of, "Really? That sounds nice; I bet there's some lovely scenery." Let's be clear here, I don't cycle—more chance of me being abducted by aliens than me getting on a bike, and I had no idea what the Tour Divide involved. I 'support' his cycling adventures because he loves cycling, and I love him. That support mainly consists of (sometimes reluctantly) agreeing that he can go off on his adventures, big ones and not so big.

I have been known to watch stages of the Tour de France (quite proud that I've seen it in three countries—France, England and Ireland), to be in the vague vicinity of single speed championships, and other events like orienteering on a bike (can't remember what the correct name is). I've sort of enjoyed watching some events, and I've sort of been quite bored at others.

So, he gets his early retirement in 2010 and this USA thing now includes some of Canada and he plans to do a bit of riding afterwards so he'll be away for two months. Okay... then bears are mentioned, mountain passes, hinterlands and badlands (what on earth is a badland?!), sleeping rough, snow and heat, mountain lions, but no need to worry. I can follow him on a Spot tracker, he'll be shown as a little blue dot with his initials on it and I'll know exactly where he is at all times, I'll even be able to see the course of the race on the map and other people's dots. Oh, that's okay then. WHEN I SEE THE BLUE DOT TRAVELLING ACROSS THE TOP OF A MOUNTAIN I'LL KNOW THE BEAR HAS NOT ONLY EATEN HIM IT'S EATEN THE TRACKER TOO!!!! And breathe.

Months passed and I become calmer.

This is his adventure, he's a grown up, he isn't going to take stupid risks; he'll be doing something amazing that he's wanted to do for a long time. He researched and prepared well and by the time he left the UK I felt very proud of him for attempting the challenge.

Two other people with connections to Derby Mercury RC (Derby, UK), which KC is a member of, were also taking part: Martin Wimpenny and Mike Hall (yes, that Mike Hall). I envisaged checking to see how they were getting on each day, maybe in the early evening so I would see their progress in the middle of the day (they would be about six hours behind me). I didn't know anything about the others so why would I be looking at their blue, pink and yellow dots? I have a full and busy life, places to go, people to see; no way would I be watching dots on a screen.

Kevin also gave me a link to 'bikepacking.net' because they had a thread about the Tour Divide that I might want to read if I wanted some more information. Hmm, thoughtful of him but unlikely. He mentioned MTBCast but he didn't think he'd call in as he wouldn't have a cell phone with him. We've always worked on the principle that no news is good news so I only expected to hear from him if there was a problem.

On 10th June 2011 I logged on to the bikepacking.net forum—just to see what it was all about. They seemed quite a pleasant lot. Feeling a bit lonely, I posted a question. Nobody told me I was stupid and knew nothing about the race. It was good to have some company whilst waiting for the start. I watched the Grand Depart of those blue and pink dots—okay so far. Oh... then someone posted some photographs... I found a video... better check Trackleaders again... discover Facebook comments... back to the forum... the first call-in's to MTBCast... where's KC now? What about MW and MH?... JV's wife posted on the forum... interesting back story... start following him too... what is JS up to... where are the women... what updates on Twitter... and someone is doing a blog... wow look at the leaders go. And on... and on... AND ON.

The next month of my life was a blur of dots, checking first thing in the morning (most of them sleeping but checking how they did the previous day), afternoon (everybody up and peddling and if not, why not?!) and most of the evening, leaving them to finish off the day ready for me to check in the morning. I discovered that the trackers don't always work. The fact the tracker hasn't moved doesn't always mean the rider hasn't moved.

The forum taught me about the route, the challenges facing the riders, the people and places that the riders value such as Kirsten at Brush Mountain Lodge and David at Como Depot. Dave Blumenthal's Spot appeared on the route; I learnt about his life through his blog and bought my own copy of The Cordillera. I cheered on JS as he made his way over the 'closed' sections and cried when he fell in the final stages. I zoomed in on KC's dot to see where he'd stopped, shouted at him when he was on his own in the middle of nowhere, worried when he seemed to be going round in circles, cheered when he was having a fast day, fretted when I saw the climbs he faced. He made it to Antelope Wells and I watched his finish at some stupid o'clock in the morning 'with' another friend via Trackleaders Facebook comments and telephone. We cheered and jumped up and down as though we were standing at the border. The first call I had from him was when he arrived back in Silver City, he'd had an amazing adventure, was overwhelmed by the kindness of the people he'd met along the way, and he'd left his cash card in the cash point, so could I send him some money!

I, on the other hand, had an addiction to deal with and I'm just coming to the end of my annual fix. A lot more riders this year so I started following those I know or know of—Mike Hall, (who provided me with an additional fix last year by organising (and winning) the Round the World Race). Craig Stappler, who Kevin had met in 2011 and who he said was a really nice guy, James Olsen, who Kevin had email conversations with before the race and James Hodges, who I had followed in 2011 and 2012. Right, I thought, I'll stick to them and not be drawn into following others along the way.

Photographs from 'Angler' in Ovando brought a lot of the dots to life and I was soon drifting from my initial short list of riders and consumed by the usual round of constant checking, Trackleaders, Bikepacking forum, MTBCast, Twitter, Facebook, blogs and REPEAT. Russ Kipp of Montana High Country Lodge provided more photographs and the updates from Kirsten and David and others along the way gave us blue dot watchers a real feel for the race. Forum posts from family and friends gave an insight to the personalities out there and the blue dot watchers. A very funny post by Mrs. NH about the trials of being a mum back at home and a photograph of JO's niece in her blue dot outfit brought welcome smiles to the forum.

I'm sure others will give a better description of the race than I can but my highlights and low times included MH's breathing difficulties providing a few tense days and an exciting time watching him catch up with CS. I was saddened by CS's withdrawal, but being a fickle blue dot watcher picked up on Jesse Carlsson who provided yet more race drama. Very disappointed at the re-route because of the fires but still cheering at MH's incredible time. Then I had the three amigos to follow—cheering for James Olsen along with Alex Harris and Liam Crowley. As the leaders made their way in, I found myself drawn to the back of the pack to watch the incredible tenacity of those who keep going long after the leaders have made their way back home. As a blue dot watcher I found these riders just as interesting and inspiring as the leaders. Special mention to Peter Kraft Sr and Peter Kraft Jr who's eventual arrival in Antelope Wells was greeted with relief, amazement and respect in this small flat in Camden Town, London.

I'll never ride the Tour Divide but I will live the Tour Divide, loving every minute of watching and wondering, of discovering who these incredible, and often brave, riders are, of reading blogs and stories on the Bikepacking forum, of listening to the funny, heartbreaking, joyous and weary call-ins on MTBCast.

What next for this blue dot watcher? We've started talking about a 'not the Tour Divide' journey, maybe next year, getting as close as possible to some of the route. I want to see some of the incredible scenery and meet those amazing people along the way. By car, no rough camping, regular showers and clean clothes, sacrilege I know, but the only way for a pure blue dot watcher to do it! Maybe we could organise a blue dot watchers rally, with trackers...

"Blue Dot Mania" aka "La Manie du Point Bleu"

Pat Olsen

"Our son is doing the Tour Divide...." we explained to French friends and neighbours in our village in southern France.

"Le Tour??!" they asked, obviously thinking of THE Tour—the Tour de France.

"Oh, no," we explained, and tried to convey the ethos of the incredible race that is the Tour Divide, but it was totally lost on them—if it wasn't THE Tour, a Gallic shrug was the total response!

We have to admit that our knowledge was not very detailed—James sent us links to websites, and talked about it over previous months when we saw him. Having experience of his interest in things like this before, I'm afraid I thought I would worry about it if/when it happened.

However, once his name was on the Starters List, and his flight booked, we realised this was really going to happen! He had trained and prepared rigorously over the past year, but despite other long distance mountain bike rides, never attempted anything like the Tour Divide, so we were all, including him, rather apprehensive.

A photo at the start said it all—"What on earth have I got myself into?" was written all over his face!

Once the race was underway, we soon got to grips with the Trackleaders website, and then we found the bikepacking.net forum. We were really getting into this, and the Tour Divide was becoming a huge part of our lives—hearing of the dreadful weather in Alberta and British Columbia, the mishaps of some of the riders, and, of course our own son's progress. We really felt we were part of it all, albeit in a very sedentary way. We were full of admiration for the sheer guts of those who had entered...

As the days went by, our Blue Dot addiction increased, and it was soon a topic of conversation with the same friends and neighbours who had not shown much initial interest. The distance travelled and the elevation climbed each day, began to register with them, and they asked about 'rest days', 'support vehicles' and 'TV coverage'. When we explained how the entrants are unsupported, and that for each one it is a personal challenge, not a media circus, they were amazed. Gradually, many of them became affected by the same addiction, our French neighbour across the road even giving a daily report to his work colleagues each morning!

We were also discovering the wonderful humour, information and support that came from the forum—it was like finding a new family around the world. We all had one thing in common—a friend, partner or relative facing huge personal challenges and coping as best they could. We made new contacts, we cheered on those who were experiencing particular difficulties, and commiserated with those who had made the brave, but sad, decision to pull out.

Our daughter in the UK had become similarly addicted, and we were Skyping daily to compare thoughts and interpretations of the blue dot positions, and to add to the fun, she made a Tour Divide T-shirt for James' ten month old niece, with a big JO 'blue dot' across her tummy. When their internet was disconnected temporarily, she did consider putting our grand-daughter on a large map of the USA to crawl round it, wearing her Blue Dot outfit, so that she could still get her fix!

By this time we were all registered Blue Dot junkies, and found it hard to leave the screen for a moment—how many time records could Mike Hall break? What had happened to Jesse Carlsson that night? When the tent sign showed, was James really sleeping, or was this a tactic? When a wrong turn was taken, the howls and shouts must have carried to Colorado, as well as the cheers when things were going well.

As our son was nearing the final leg of the race, it was thanks to the forum that we made contact with wonderful Lloyd Payne, who went out to Antelope Wells with cold Cokes for the 'Three Amigos' when they were on the finishing straight—James said it was like a mirage in the desert!

Finally, it was over for us, and we could celebrate his safe finish, and a challenge met with grit and determination. We, with our friends and neighbours, were delighted he had done so well. At the same time we came to learn so much about this race and its ethos, which is so different from the razzmatazz of the Tour de France.

The withdrawal from the Blue Dot addiction was severe, despite continuing to follow the rest of the field who were still battling along the route. However, the weekend after his return to the UK, we had the very best antidote—James here in person!

To all the entrants of the Tour Divide 2013, we thank you for the opportunity to follow your race, and to empathise with your successes, your trials and your tribulations. We salute you all for your courage and sportsmanship, and thank you for giving us the opportunity to educate some French people about cycling challenges other than their "Le Tour"!

Refresh, load... ... zoom, zoom, zoom... (repeat)

Ruth Olsen (Jame's sister)

As I am not a great one for screen media, my husband struggled to understand why I was suddenly glued to my laptop. We have a ten month old daughter, James's niece, so spare time is precious. But I found myself using all of it to refresh Trackleaders' website (having to zoom in again EVERY time) and the bikepacking.net forum to check for messages and information.

I had started out very interested, but unsure of what the Tour Divide was about. It sounded like a great adventure, but the forum gave me my first insights into what it might actually be like for the riders. Then two things dawned on me. Firstly, that it would require amazing luck, physical endurance and psychological resilience to even *finish* the race. Secondly, that just thinking about it and hearing the riders' MTBCasts was going to stretch my notions of what is possible in life. I was amazed to hear what they were going through and saddened to hear the out's.

It was a great relief to connect with other friends and family on the forum too, as it was a solitary experience checking that dot all the time. I was reassured to hear people were looking out for him and fascinated to hear local knowledge about the terrain, culture and weather, things that added colour to the otherwise pretty clinical process of hitting 'refresh'. As I absorbed all of this, my daughter's mealtimes became more and more focussed around the computer. Having been the centre of our attention for the past ten months, she was suddenly looking a little lost. She seemed to be carb-loading in sympathy and we had a 'broom wagon' come and tidy up what she left. She even got a blue dot 'JO' t-shirt in the hope that her Mum might pay more attention to her then!

We watched James's blue dot get into the top ten, something he had not anticipated at all. I began to look at his peer's details, trying to imagine what they were like—were James and Alex racing each other hard or riding together? Was Brian Pal just going to steam through them all? I remember the day when I opened my laptop and saw James in third position—I must admit I went straight to the forum to check this wasn't some mistake!! Having not competed since local races in his school days, I had no idea at all of how he would get on, which only added to the excitement and surprise. Knowing James, I was aware that the main thing for him would be (to quote a great American, Bill Hicks) "just enjoy the ride", so to see him in that top ten was strange—I wasn't cheering on his time, or position, but more his values or philosophy. It was great to see it get him so far.

Then from Silver City down to Antelope Wells... what a stretch. James had been off-dot for some hours and then he re-appeared. The dot moved so fast down the map I wondered if he'd got a lift. It looked like he was making a break for third. Then Alex and Liam appeared to give chase and they jostled all the way South. By the time they reached Antelope Wells I was beyond caring who came in where. The extraordinary accomplishment was complete for all three of them. I will never forget the sight of those blue dots jumping up and down as they finished– it seemed to represent the great feeling I had—so happy for someone to have achieved so much.

Embracing the Tour Divide

Tammy Pal

My son Brian was born for Adventure. With a capital "A".

If you tell him something can't be done, he will invariably reply, "Oh yeah?" He doesn't say it with hubris or even insolence; it's nonchalant. But you know he's turning over all the possibilities, like a poker player sizing up the hands at a table.

When he was very little we'd say, with a gleam in our eye, "You probably can't do that." And then he'd promptly prove us wrong.

A year and a half ago Brian ventured, "I'm thinking about doing a mountain bike race called the Tour Divide," and then proceeded to explain the course, the rules and the fact that some people try it out as a tourist first. Being faithful to all moms everywhere, I replied, "You'd do it that way, right? Tour it first?" That was received, in Brian Pal code, as: "You probably can't do that."

"Oh yeah?"

Brian grew up on Lopez Island, in the San Juan Islands of Washington State. He finished his last two years of high school at the local community college on San Juan Island, which is about a 20-minute boat ride from Lopez. We'd bought a 13-ft, solid-hull inflatable dinghy with a 50hp motor that he swiftly commandeered for his daily commute. There would be winter days where the wind would howl at 35 mph with 5+ft. waves churning like a washing machine. I would worry, pray and worry a bit more and soon my 15 year-old would return home, acting like nothing was out of the ordinary. "How did you do out on the water?" I'd ask, trying valiantly not to act like one of 'those' helicopter moms. "It was fun. I rode the wave crests the whole way there and back," was his casual reply.

Oh my goodness. I had so much to learn.

Next it was bungee jumping over a Canadian river. Skydiving. Backpacking all over Europe. Construction work in Mexico and Panama.

Then Brian moved to Colorado to attend the Colorado School of Mines. He bought a mountain bike and earned his novice patch on the trails of the Colorado Rockies. Soon he found out about Fourteeners. He would hike up those majestic 14,000+ ft peaks, sometimes with a friend, other times solo. I went to REI and bought him a fanny pack full of survival stuff, for Christmas. Isn't that what moms do? He merely smiled.

After graduation Brian got hired as a mechanical engineer with Honeywell Aerospace. It was 'the' job with—you guessed it—Adventure. He was guaranteed a world tour in the first year, visiting far-flung stations where huge satellite radar arrays awaited his input. His globetrotting took him to relatively normal places like London, Hawaii and Guam, and then to remote locations such as Diego Garcia and Greenland. Stopovers in Japan and Southeast Asia gave him more opportunities to explore. After the tour was over he shipped his mountain bike to New Hampshire and settled into a hotel with a normal nine-to-five schedule. Moms love nine-to-five.

I feel compelled to insert here that I'm no couch potato. My husband Tom and I have travelled every highway and byway in the Western US, from Alaska to Mexico, on our trusty Honda Goldwing motorcycle. I ride a Vulcan 800 on shorter trips. One time we powered the 13-ft. inflatable dinghy from Lopez Island to Desolation Sound—450 miles round-trip, over some big water. I love adventure! But it's a whole different ballgame when you watch your son doing things that you only see on TV, that involve real risk. I was secretly bracing myself for the announcement that he was going fishing in Alaska after watching 'America's Deadliest Catch'.

Meanwhile….the trail was still calling.

Brian and his friend Craig decided to circumnavigate Iceland on the famed Rim Road. It was the first time Brian confessed to the challenge of the 'mental game'. The headwinds were a ferocious contender. Brian and Craig won. "At least," I reasoned, "he had a companion."

For his next challenge Brian chose to conquer the trail between Melbourne and Sydney, Australia, solo. "It's only seven days," he said with assurance and I echoed that, feebly. It was a new continent, half a world away. I knew he could take care of himself, but the 'WHAT IFS' loomed large. They always do. It's the mom thing. We love our kids—our flesh—almost more than life itself. I've stared tragedy squarely in the eye before; I didn't want to go there again. Our history has a way of colouring our present.

Brian is a man of few words, so when we got the rare message from Australia it would be something like, "Doing okay" "Missed a turn" "Found my way eventually," just enough to let us know he was alive. Alive is good.

I'm a Jesus follower and so I did what comes naturally, I prayed. Once again, Brian won. He sent us a picture at the end—his girl Sarah had flown to meet him in Sydney. His grin was so worth it. I whispered, *Thank you*, to my heavenly Papa. A friend said "God has assigned extra angels to Brian". I believe it.

Last summer brought the news: the Andes. Brian and Craig were going to bikepack a high-elevation route in South America, from Lake Titicaca, Peru, to Quito, Ecuador. Two thousand miles in five weeks; 12,000 – 14,000 ft elevation would be the norm.

"How does a mom ever get used to this stuff?" I wondered. "Will I still be feeling this catch in my gut when he's 55?" I spent August praying against trail bandits, kidnappers, altitude sickness and every variety of venomous critters. The guys conquered. I exhaled.

After that trip Brian enrolled in a Master's program at the University of Washington. "AH," I thought to myself, "No money for dangerous adventures," thinking the Tour Divide would be shelved.

"Oh yeah?"

Did he hear that???

"Mom, once I graduate I'll have to get a job and then I'll have money but no time. Right now I have time but no money. I'm going to do what I can while I can."

How does one argue with such flawless logic?

June was here. Shoulder-deep in finals and pesky dentist appointments, Brian hardly had time to prepare for the Tour Divide.

"How do you train for this?" I enquired. "Aw, I'll just round-trip the trail from Seattle to Ellensburg and make sure my equipment works okay." That's 200 miles, round-trip. *That's all?*

Off he went to Banff. His airline/shuttle connections were down-to-the-wire tight so when we loaded the Trackleaders web page we didn't even know if he had made it there until 24 hours into the race. That's when we discovered that his Spot tracker wasn't working very well. Wonderful.

I'm convinced it was a mom that invented the Spot tracker. I don't care who tells me anything to the contrary—I know there was a dedicated woman behind that amazing little device. It was touch and go whether Brian would even carry one—"Aaah don't know if I need it." By now I know better than to argue—it will only make things worse on my end. His brother lent him his unit. Bingo!

When Brian's blue dot appeared, we all cheered. We sent the link to our friends so they could follow as well. That was a double-edged sword because when Brian's dot didn't move for long periods we got lots of emails and texts. I could see how just carrying a Spot changes the texture of the race. Observers start to become participants.

I got a text: "Eureka". Okay, he's alive. He tried pushing the 'OK' button on the Spot that's supposed to shoot us an email. Sometimes it worked, sometimes not. Scott Morris (who developed and maintains the Trackleaders webpage) contacted me to dissect the possible issues until we landed on the real suspect— a first generation unit that had a weak antenna. Okay, so be it. Scott was an angel… he didn't make me feel like an idiot or one of 'those' moms. *Thank you.*

As I familiarized myself with the trail, the discussion board and the amazing people in this small bikepacking community, it became obvious that the veterans were hard-core and nonplussed by 24+hour silences, even from the scorching New Mexico desert the north bounders were enduring. They'd been there, conquered, and reminded us to have faith in our rider's skills. It was good to be reminded. There were other times when I read their posts that I had to exert extreme self control. *"No, our family members aren't texting all day long. They're riding all day long. You know that, right?"* was my silent retort. There was a bit of tension on the discussion board, between the founder's vision of what the race should be and the reality that each rider created in his own experience and the role technology played in both.

Personally, I like diversity. I'm pretty sure other family members were with me.

I scrubbed the Internet, looking for blog posts, pictures, tweets, any information about what was going on. Brian would text a town name and when I queried his condition, his reply was always, "Doing good." Good is good.

After a couple of days we realized with a start—he's actually racing this thing! And he was doing well. We would follow his blue dot into the night and stay up until he stopped (which was difficult because we didn't really know if the last spot was the last spot.) By the time we got up in the morning, he'd already been on the trail for an hour or two. We were losing sleep and we couldn't even imagine him pushing his body this hard with so little rest.

Then came the text: "Bad diarrhoea. Think it's giardia." *OH NO*. I asked his medic brother what it could be. "Probably ischemic bowel disease. The big muscles are using all the blood that should be carrying lactic acid out of the bowel. Diarrhoea is the backup evacuation system." GREAT. "What's the worst case here?" I asked. "Kidney failure. But he'll piss red before that happens." Wonderful. Is he even watching his pee? Can his body do this? I went from concern about the external threats to the serious one that was happening internally. Is he pushing his body way beyond its limit? What if he collapses, alone, out in the middle of nowhere? *Please…*

That's when I realized that every single rider on that trail has a back-story. Pain, fatigue, drama at home, more pain… My kid was soldiering through something awful—how many more were dealing with even worse? Respect for these riders was increasing by the minute.

The next morning we expected him to be resting. Nope. He put in 18 hours that day. Unbelievable. Respect for my son was increasing exponentially.

After several days the skids stopped. Then there was a close encounter with a grizzly bear, followed by an almost-fatal lightning storm on Medicine Creek Road above Lima. "Whoever is behind us could get killed," Brian texted, as he and Leo Pershall bedded down early to rest. They had had to scrape mud off their tires nearly every revolution as they tried to escape the violence. Forest Baker and Thomas Lane were still on the mountain behind them. They won. *Thank you, God.*

Brian rode about half the trip with other racers. Leo and Forest were wonderful companions. Leo's wife Laurel and I started to correspond through the discussion board. It was comforting to have another woman to talk with who understood the nuances of being a family member of a Tour Divide racer. 'Nuances' is such an elegant word, isn't it? But it stands for something that isn't nearly as nice. Worry is ugly. I realized that about eight days into this. I didn't like it. During a sleepless night I read the verse in the Bible that says: "Don't worry about anything; instead, pray about everything. Tell God what you need, and thank Him for all He has done. Then you will experience God's peace, which exceeds anything we can understand. His peace will guard your hearts and minds as you live in Christ Jesus." I desperately wanted my heart to be protected by that peace.

Montana, Idaho, Wyoming flew by. Headwinds in the Great Basin were brutal for everyone. "I can't wait for Colorado," he texted. Brian loves to climb. He'd been climbing steadily in the rankings and by this time was in the top ten. He was chomping at the bit to get back into the mountains and trails where he'd learned to ride.

I'd had several sleepless nights. We had read the story about David Blumenthal's fatal accident. Jesse Carlsson had his skirmish with a lightning bolt. Brian had a dance with an end on a cattle guard at 27mph with, miraculously, no damage, to either him or his bike. These scenarios haunted me. I'd wake up in the inky darkness and my imagination flew to all sorts of murky places. If there was a 'What if?' I went there. I had to get up, turn on the lights, and tell myself, repeatedly, "Don't worry until there is a reason to worry." Recite the above verse. Pray more. Calm down. Go back to sleep. This was a real test of faith for me. *Please, Papa, please...*

When we got this most recent text, "I can't wait for Colorado," my heart melted. This kid of mine wasn't just enduring this race; he was embracing it and revelling in it. *<tears>*

It was then that I realized something transformative. I was allowing fear to rob me of the joy of watching my son do something truly amazing. I had to dig deeper to uncover the root of that fear and when I got there, it wasn't pretty. It wasn't just losing this precious son that gripped me with anxiety; I was terrified of going back to that place of gut-wrenching agony, of unbearable loss. Losing a child is upside down and it had taken a long time for my world to turn right-side-up again. I was allowing the fear of it happening again to rob me of vulnerability. Without vulnerability, I couldn't really enjoy this with him; I could only suffer it and that was robbing us both. God had stuck like a burr to me through the last storm; I was sure He wouldn't abandon me if it happened again. Taking a deep breath, I relaxed. And then I knew deep in my spirit that Brian was going to be okay. Releasing the fear liberated me. Joy flooded in. I was no longer confined to just enduring Brian's Adventure-with-a-capital-A; now I could embrace it as he had done.

I kept a record each day of Brian's mileage and bivy points as well as I could with that spotty Spot tracker. On Day 12 he left Forest behind and mashed for 186 miles. Day 13, 172 miles. That was in Colorado, on those huge mountains. He caught up with Liam, who was in fifth place, and rode with him for most of a day. Liam told Brian he was really glad to talk to another rider as he'd been racing most of the trip alone. At the next stop Brian texted: "Liam is an incredibly strong rider, I would not be well served to try to keep pace with him."

Oh yeah?

The Southwest was hit with a serious heat wave. I deplaned in Phoenix to 118° and it felt like a blast furnace. Friends were emailing and texting, asking how to pray. I replied, "Pray that the temps drop and the winds shift." There had been a strong and steady headwind from the south down at the finish and the temperature there was 104°. A couple of days later I picked up Tom and we headed to Antelope Wells.

When we reached the turn at Hachita we saw a Jeep with three bikes on a carrier. Knowing they were Tour Divide riders, we flagged them down to say hello. It was James, Alex and Kerrin. Liam had gotten another ride. They finished only hours ahead of Brian.

The afternoon temp had dropped to 85° and the wind had shifted to the east at 12 mph. *Thank you, Papa.*

At mile marker 22 we came over a rise and there he was, this solitary man who had been pedalling for almost three thousand miles, still going strong. We passed him and bawled.

He met us at the border; dirty and thin but smiling, glad to be done. For the rest of the evening he talked, ate, napped, talked, ate some more, and then slept luxuriously. I stayed up, just gazing at his peaceful face. He did it. Safely, wisely and true to himself. I'm a little slower on the uptake than he is, but I did it too.

Joyfully.

Afterword

Christopher Bennett

I wrote my Letter of Intent for the 2013 Tour Divide early February after the death of my father. It was a time for reflection and I ended with:

So I'll be riding in 2013. To hopefully finish the unfinished business from 2011 and 2012. But even if I don't finish, it doesn't really matter that much. For those of us who have the health and optimism to ride the divide, no matter what the outcome, we are truly blessed.

The same thoughts returned to me as my wife and I were working on this edition of the Cordillera. All of us who raced in 2013 were blessed. Not only because the conditions were as good as they will ever be, but because we were out there riding the Tour Divide. The friendships, the challenges, the good—and the bad—times are now but memories to be relished.

For those of us who have moved on to other challenges, the Tour Divide is now off our bucket list. But many of us will return, against our better judgement and prognostications after the race. Why? Because there really is no other experience quite like the Tour Divide.

Tour Divider's are a small community, and this book—and the proceeds—are dedicated to one of our own who didn't finish the race, and will never have the chance to ride again. My sincere appreciation goes out to all the contributors for your support for the Cordillera. We are truly blessed to be part of this community.

Annex 1: 2013 Tour Divide Finisher's List

The following was compiled from the Trackleaders.com web site. Any corrections or additions contact chris@lpcb.org.

The Cordillera V5

South-North-South - Billy Rice	22:18:41 NoBo	20:08:00 SoBo	43:02:41 Riding

Men's Record – Jay Petervary ITT 2012	15:16:14
Women's Record – Eszter Horanyi 2012	19:03:35
South-North-South Record – Billy Rice 2013	44:00:22

Place	Name	2013 Time
1	Mike Hall	14:11:55
2	Jesse Carlsson	15:12:08
3	Alex Harris	17:05:28
4	James Olsen	17:05:29
5	Liam Crowley	17:05:36
6	Brian Pal	17:09:28
7	Leo Pershall	18:01:45
8	Saemi Burkart	18:12:08
9	Reto Koller	18:12:10
10	Forest Baker	18:12:22
11	Markley Anderson	18:14:42
12	Ethan Stewart	20:11:56
13	Thomas Lane	20:20:34
14	Brett Simpson	20:21:05
15	Luke Ragan	20:21:07
16	Mike Johnson	20:21:07
17	Scott McConnell	20:21:07
18	Arran Pearson	20:23:32
19	Tim Van den Daele	20:23:42
20	Gunther Desmedt	20:23:43
21	Evan Deutsch	20:23:44
22	Robin Schwartz	21:04:50
23	Hugh Harvey	21:12:38
24	Nick Hutton	21:15:51
25	Nathan Mawkes	21:15:52
26	Chris Arndt	21:23:22
27	Christopher Bennett	22:01:26
28	Sean Putnam	22:04:06
29	Ryan Sigsbey	22:04:39
30	Bryan Heselbach	22:04:46
31	Chris Culos	22:06:59
32	Peter Haile	22:07:00
33	Ezra Mullen	22:07:29
34	Peter Maindonald	22:08:45
35	Kevin Campagna	22:10:17
36	Jean-Louis Doridot	22:16:43
37	Ron Babington	22:16:48

38	Sara Dallman	22:19:05
39	Rob Orr	23:07:41
40	Scott Thigpen	23:07:46
41	Kristen Arnold	23:12:02
42	Michael Partheymuller	23:12:04
43	Taylor Kruse	23:12:04
44	Eric Foster	23:12:06
45	Ty Hathaway	23:12:08
46	Joseph Holway	23:12:24
47	Greg Thompson	23:15:10
48	Jeff Mullen	23:17:11
49	Ian McNab	24:05:11
50	Drew McIntosh	24:08:06
51	Greg Strauser	24:08:42
52	Kent Davidson	24:09:23
53	Thomas Borst	25:02:52
54	Edward Turkaly	25:05:02
55	James Hodges	25:05:22
56	Michael Gruenert	25:06:34
57	J.D. Pauls	25:07:56
58	Hamish McKee	25:07:58
59	Dennis Loewen	~26 Days
60	Fred Arden	27:05:29
61	Michael Arenberg	27:05:38
62	Matt Bialowas	27:11:58
63	Matthew Liggett	27:11:58
64	Mauro Nappolini	27:15:20
65	Greg Andre-Barrett	28:04:05
66	Michael Komp	28:08:24
67	Martin Ortmann	28:10:37
68	Michael Mead	28:11:36
69	Dustin Hill	28:12:03
70	Velimir Letoja	29:05:13
71	Rick Ashton	30:08:45
72	Richard Costello	30:09:48
73	Brian Steele	30:12:04
74	Hal Russell	31:08:09
75	Andrew Stuntz	31:08:14
76	Peter Kraft Sr	31:13:08
77	Peter Kraft Jr	31:13:12
78	Mark Proia	33:03:18
79	Ralph Yukon Krauss	47:07:33

Annex 2: 2013 Tour Divide Gear Survey

Several readers and 2013 Tour Divide racers requested a gear survey. What follows reflects inputs from 56 of the riders who completed the online survey. No scientific accuracy is claimed—and the survey did evolve slightly as it was realized that there was not enough granularity to some of the questions.

The Cordillera V5

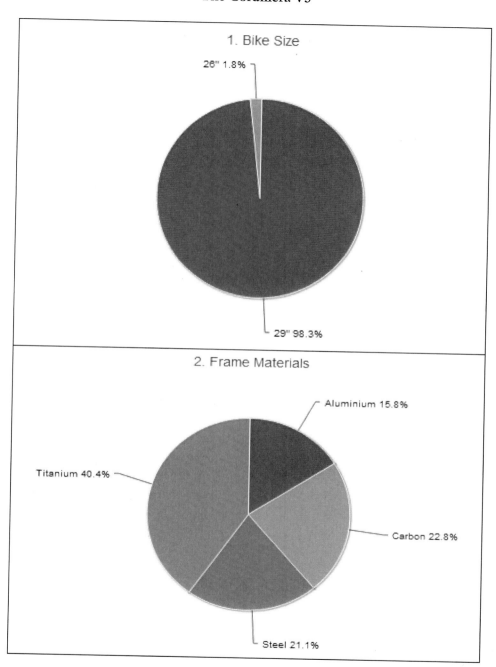

1. Bike Size

26" 1.8%

29" 98.3%

2. Frame Materials

Aluminium 15.8%

Titanium 40.4%

Carbon 22.8%

Steel 21.1%

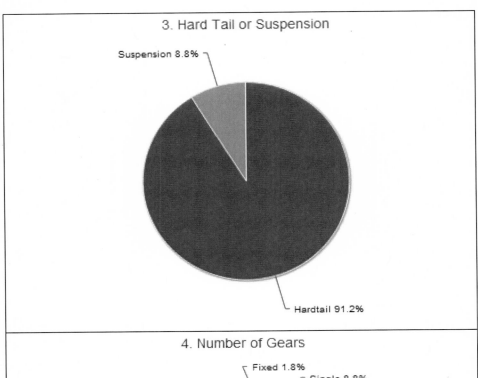

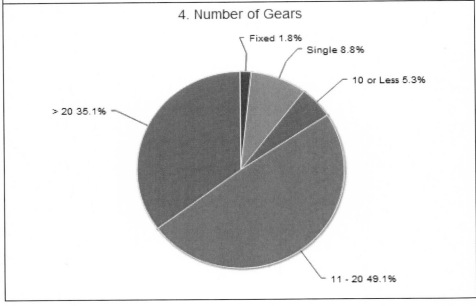

The Cordillera V5

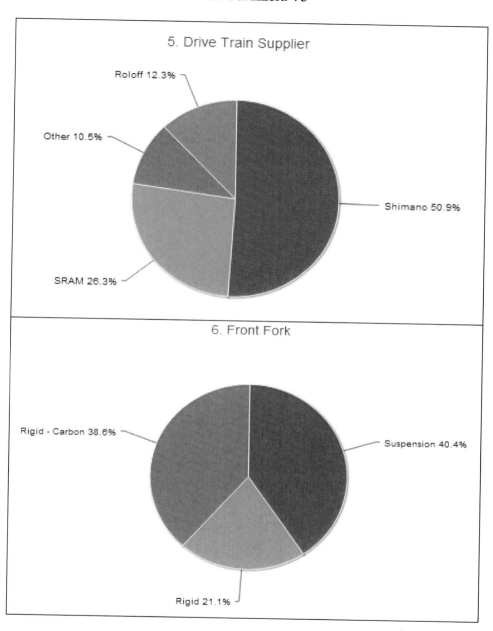

231

The Cordillera V5

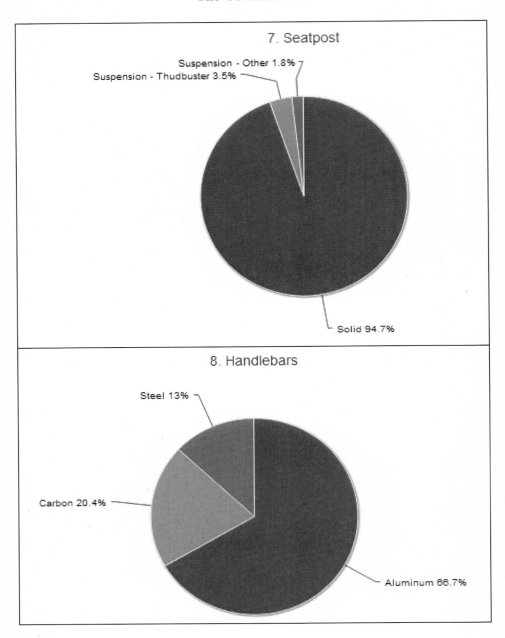

7. Seatpost

Suspension - Other 1.8%
Suspension - Thudbuster 3.5%

Solid 94.7%

8. Handlebars

Steel 13%

Carbon 20.4%

Aluminum 66.7%

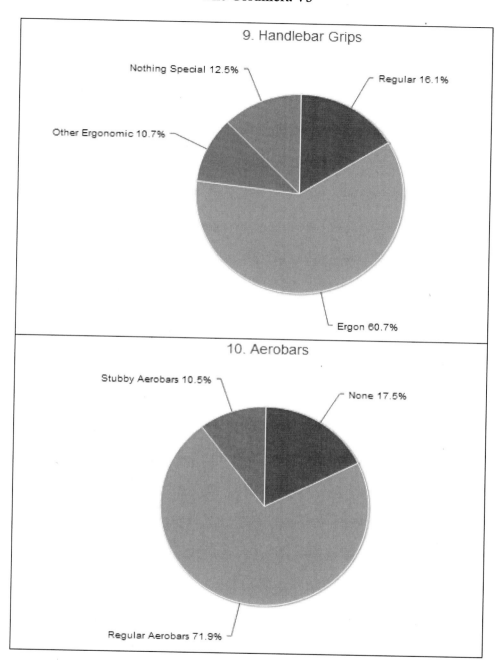

The Cordillera V5

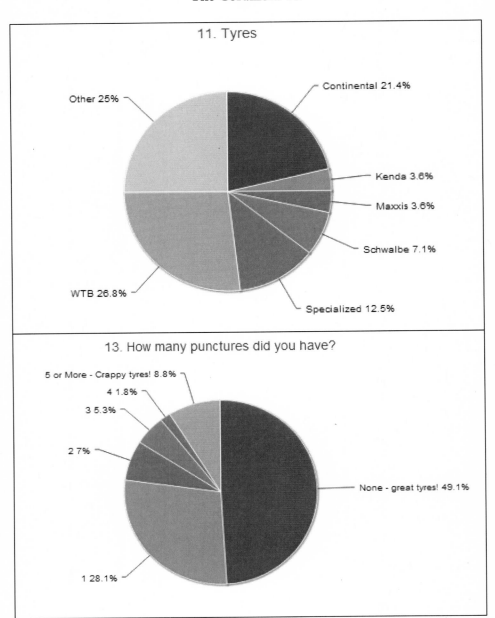

11. Tyres

Continental 21.4%

Kenda 3.6%

Maxxis 3.6%

Schwalbe 7.1%

Specialized 12.5%

WTB 26.8%

Other 25%

13. How many punctures did you have?

5 or More - Crappy tyres! 8.8%

4 1.8%

3 5.3%

2 7%

None - great tyres! 49.1%

1 28.1%

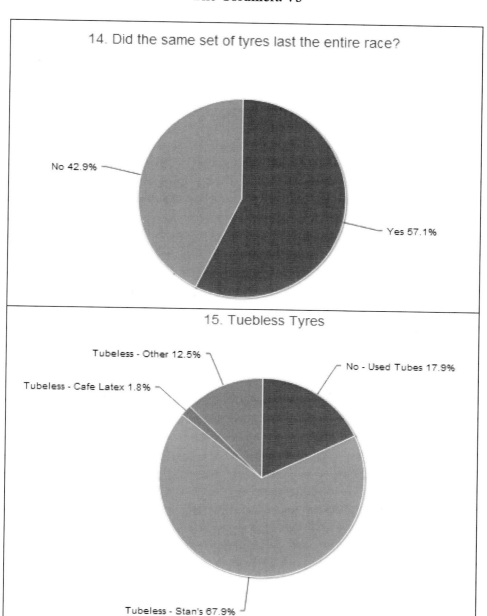

The Cordillera V5

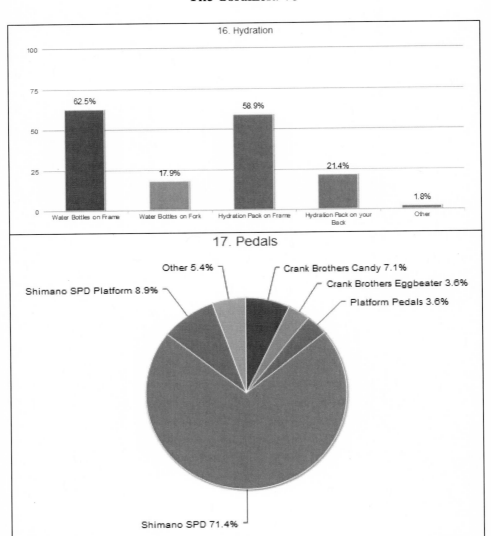

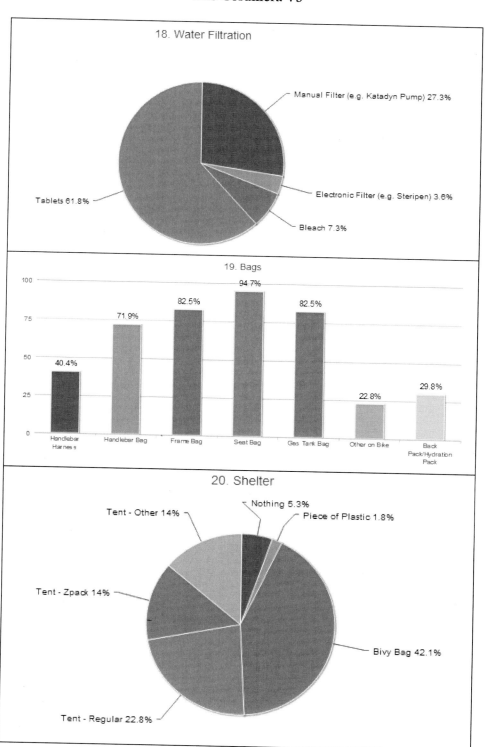

18. Water Filtration

- Manual Filter (e.g. Katadyn Pump) 27.3%
- Electronic Filter (e.g. Steripen) 3.6%
- Bleach 7.3%
- Tablets 61.8%

19. Bags

- Handlebar Harness 40.4%
- Handlebar Bag 71.9%
- Frame Bag 82.5%
- Seat Bag 94.7%
- Gas Tank Bag 82.5%
- Other on Bike 22.8%
- Back Pack/Hydration Pack 29.8%

20. Shelter

- Nothing 5.3%
- Piece of Plastic 1.8%
- Tent - Other 14%
- Tent - Zpack 14%
- Tent - Regular 22.8%
- Bivy Bag 42.1%

The Cordillera V5

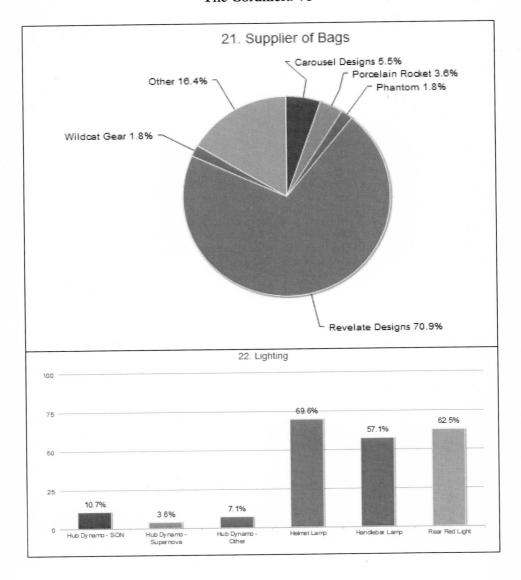

21. Supplier of Bags

- Carousel Designs 5.5%
- Porcelain Rocket 3.6%
- Phantom 1.8%
- Other 16.4%
- Wildcat Gear 1.8%
- Revelate Designs 70.9%

22. Lighting

Hub Dynamo - SON	10.7%
Hub Dynamo - Supernova	3.6%
Hub Dynamo - Other	7.1%
Helmet Lamp	69.6%
Handlebar Lamp	57.1%
Rear Red Light	62.5%

Tyre Models

9	Continental Race Kings
5	Nano Raptor
4	Geax Saguaro
2	Conti X-King Protection
2	Specialized Fast Track Control
2	Maxxis Crossmark

1	Bontrager Team Issue 29.3, as recommended for the Tour Divide by THE Mike Curiak.
1	Captain
1	Continental
1	Front: Schwalbe Rocket Ron Rear: Maxxis Crossmark
1	Geax
1	Kenda Small Block 8 John Tomac Signature Series
1	Maxxis
1	Maxxis Cross Mark UST LUST [No sealant]
1	Maxxis icons changed to Conti race kings in steamboat
1	Nano - Non UST
1	Nano 120tpi
1	Nano race
1	Nano tubeless 2.1
1	Racing Ralph 2.25 tubeless
1	Renegade 1.7" Control 1.8"
1	Rubena Scylla 2.3s
1	Schwalbe Marathon Racer
1	Small Block Eights
1	Surly Knard 29x3 120tpi
1	WTB nano TCS
1	Continental race king replaced one of my specialized fast track controls
1	nano but cut one early in the race and put on a kenda sm8 in butte
1	nano raptor. NEVER AGAIN!
1	Geax 2.2 Saguaro TNT - only made 1/2 of race due to injury. tires looked new at that point. currently listed at 780 grams per tire. mine were 740 each, new.
1	Started with WTB Nanos and finished with Continental X-King on front and Continental Race King on rear.
1	Started with Maxxis CrossMax and WTB nano raptor in front. Had to replace CrossMax with Nano Raptor and had big problems. Would not reccomend the Nano Raptor for this race
1	Geax Suguaro - lasted from start to finish and have been running it for 3 months still. Maxxis Ikon
1	I start with schwalbe but a soft models definitly bad choice (7 punctures) and finished with Continental (0 puncture..)
1	Ah! I ran three tires! One WTB nano raptor, one specialized something, and one continental tire.

Light Models

3	Exposure Revo
2	Exposure joystick

2	Black Diamond Icon
2	Fenix
2	Hope Vision
2	Stoots
2	Supernova
2	Supernova E3 triple
1	BUMM Luxos
1	Cygolight expillion
1	EOS
1	Exposure
1	Exposure Diablo
1	Exposure Diablo (front) Sigma HIRO (rear)
1	Exposure Revo dynamo headlight + Diablo helmet light.
1	Fenix and Princeton tex
1	Fenix BT10 350 Lumens
1	Fenix LD
1	Fenix LD-20
1	Fenix LD20 (helmet) Cateye TL-LD 610R (rear)
1	Fenix LD20 Rear: Blackburn FLEA
1	Fenix LD-22 Torch on the bars Princetontec EOS on the helmet
1	Finex LD22
1	Gloworm
1	KLARUS XT2C Cree XM-L T6 and Fenix LD20
1	Lezyne
1	Nite Rider
1	Petzel head lamp Knog rear
1	Petzl
1	Petzl Myo XP
1	Princeton Tec
1	Princeton Tec - EOS (2), Swerve and Corona.
1	Princeton Tec EOS Bike - front Princeton Tec Swerve - rear
1	Princeton Tec EOS Fenix LD20
1	Princeton Tec IOS, Fenix LD22, Blackburn Mars 4.0 rear
1	REVO Exposure
1	Serfas
1	Sigma LED EVO
1	Supernova S3 Dynamo Fenix LD22
1	Urban 400 - handlebar lamp EOS - Helmet lamp Wish I had gone with a Hub system

Other Advice

Bags are nuclear stichworks, love them. frame bags are sweet. keep it aero and light

Bausch & Müller E-Werk to load USB-devices from SON dynamo

Brooks Saddle!!!! if you have a brooks saddle you will finish!

Cooler weather clothing perhaps, cooler temp sleeping bag, additional helmet mount light and probably 2 brakes and a freewheel.

Don't get hung up on kit. Find what works for you and enjoy the cycling. Carry as little as possible.

Garmin 62s, Extra chunky ESI silicone grips.

Go with tested GPS device. Carry Lithium batteries - super light and no need to worry about recharging. 2x10 shimano drive train has gone 6100 km - still using it for mtn bike rides around Canmore

Gore rain gear (pants and jacket, X-Alps model)

GPS - Garmin eTrex20 - awesome, make sure you have a leash! It WILL pop off at some point! Most likely while ripping down the Gold Dust Trail!

High capacity battery

I ran mountain bike drop bars for comfort. Worked well. A Ti seatpost is great and offers some compliance for dampening the ride. Much better than a carbon or alum post.

I'd go for a Lupine Piko helmet light (or equivalent) instead of the Exposure Diablo for better battery life. I did the race singlespeed this year but would definitely run the SRAM XX1 drivetrain if I were to do it again. And for nav I recommend a primary approach of cues + cyclo with GPS as a backup. Keep it simple..

My bags had been a mix of Ortlieb, Porclain Rocket and Revelate

Pack light

Packable backpack for big days (extra food and drinks), cue sheet/map case holder was super handy.

Ride with the lights on rough trail and see if they work after days of abuse.

Sun sleeves

Taking a tent next time

Tent : bivy tarp terranova mattress : ferrino merino textile for top mountaineering jacket with large hood to include helmet.

Tiny map reading light affixed to helmet. Garmin 800. Lots of chamois cream. *theres this first aid cream called Brave Soldier--priceless.

Titanium handlebars were used sawyer squeeze water filter platypus hoser water reservoir Niner tapered carbon fork Rohloff

Water treatment drops as backup

Would skip the backpack next time. Or just go with a hydration pack (nothing else on back). Would skip tent in the future and go with a lightweight bivy sack. I used Aqua Mira drops for hydration (not one of the options above)

Wouldn't change a thing.